Y0-AQM-975

PAST AS PRELUDE

PAST AS PRELUDE

History in the Making of a New World Order

EDITED BY

Meredith Woo-Cumings

AND

Michael Loriaux

Northwestern University

Westview Press

BOULDER • SAN FRANCISCO • OXFORD

D
16.9
P27
1993

Published in 1993 in the United States of America by Westview Press, Inc., 5500 Central Avenue, Boulder, Colorado 80301-2877, and in the United Kingdom by Westview Press, 36 Lonsdale Road, Summertown, Oxford OX2 7EW

Library of Congress Cataloging-in-Publication Data
Past as prelude : history in the making of a new world order / edited
  by Meredith Woo-Cumings and Michael Loriaux.
    p.   cm.
  Includes bibliographical references and index.
  ISBN 0-8133-1622-7 (cloth).—ISBN 0-8133-1623-5 (pbk.)
  1. World politics—1989–   2. Cycles.   I. Woo-Cumings, Meredith.
II. Loriaux, Michael Maurice.
D16.9.P27   1993
909.82—dc20   92-25866
                                                                    CIP

Printed and bound in the United States of America.

   The paper used in this publication meets the requirements
        of the American National Standard for Permanence of Paper
        for Printed Library Materials Z39.48-1984.

10   9   8   7   6   5   4   3   2   1

For Ian, Sunyoung,
Alain, Paul, and Dominique

CONTENTS

ACKNOWLEDGMENTS

No one writing in 1988 could have foreseen the toppling of the Berlin Wall in 1989, nor could one have predicted the peaceful reunification of West Germany and East Germany in 1990 and the collapse of the Soviet Union in 1991. No one writing at the time of the European monetary crises of 1981–1983 could have suspected that European leaders would subscribe to the momentous commitments of Maastricht in 1992.

How does one explain these events? The editors of this volume are political scientists. Political science as a discipline, however, was overwhelmed by the events. There is simply no nomothetic theory in the discipline that provides a satisfactory *ante hoc* explanation of them. For this reason the editors solicited the reactions of scholars who, because of their area expertise and familiarity with history, could place the events of 1989–1992 within the context of a larger narrative and identify forces, constraints, evolutions, and opportunities that increase our understanding of what has happened.

A collective effort such as this is impossible without generous financial support. We express our gratitude to the International Studies Program, the Gordon Scott Fulcher Chair of Decisionmaking, the Edna Files Weber Fund, and the Alumnae of Northwestern University and specifically to Madeleine Bennett, Jonathan Casper, David William Cohen, John Godfrey, Marie Jones, John McLane, and Benjamin I. Page.

A special thanks goes to our colleagues Evelyne Huber, Benjamin I. Page, and John Stephens, whose pertinent and insightful comments are hidden in the folds of the revisions that these essays have undergone. We also thank Christine Margerum, who helped put editorial order into chaos, and Jennifer Knerr of Westview Press, who herded the manuscript through the editorial process with remarkable efficiency. Finally, we wish to thank our colleagues of the Departments of Political Science and History who provided much appreciated advice and support: Ibrahim Abu-Lughod, Lee F. Anderson, Peter Hayes, Herbert Jacob, Juergen Kohl, Jane Mansbridge, Harold Perkin, and Donald Strickland.

Any error in the book is entirely the responsibility of the other coeditor.

Meredith Woo-Cumings
Michael Loriaux

MEREDITH WOO-CUMINGS
MICHAEL LORIAUX

1

INTRODUCTION

The world as we knew it for nearly half a century has come to an end. The onrushing changes of the late 1980s and the early 1990s were neither violent nor cataclysmic, but they ushered in changes no less profound and fundamental than those built on the terrible ruins of the world's last two wars. This book assays these recent changes in world politics and suggests directions for the future. It is a study of political economy that is also historically informed. By summoning the past and by asking why certain ways of organizing politics, economics, and the military persisted over time and with what variations and repetitions, we hope both to explain our turbulent present and to suggest what the future may hold.

An initial problem is to decide which history we choose to remember. It will not be just any "past," but a past selected and illuminated by theory. Chapter 2 forces this issue on us by using world system analysis to compare the recentering of the world in 1989–1991 to that in 1919, calling the long interregnum the "seventy-years' crisis." In this choice of how to remember history, Bruce Cumings shows that the current restructuring can be understood as the settlement in Europe of World War II, which itself was part of a European civil war beginning in 1914 and ending only in 1990. What is left at the end of this long crisis? A 1990s world system in which three great capitalist poles function as the "custodians" of the world economy and in which one of them—the United States—deploys hegemonic power in that same system.

In another sense, though, this settlement was also the maturation of the political economy of containment, broadly conceived here as the American doctrine of containing both the enemy (communism) and the ally (mainly Japan and, through NATO, West Germany). The Cold War may have ended in Europe in 1990, but the costly American project of containing postwar Japan and Germany has not. Cumings argues that this outcome of the Cold War will yield only more problems for the United States and puts off the important project of an American *perestroika*, a domestic

1

revival that will enable the United States to compete with Japan and Germany.

The choice of the past is perhaps nowhere as self-conscious and deliberate as in Chapter 3. Whereas the first chapter presents an internationalist vision, James Kurth offers a regional perspective on Japan and Germany, as countries that are actively transforming and even hollowing out the meaning of the New World Order. The vision that illuminates this drama of interacting and intersecting architectonic logics is one of organized capitalism and the social market in Central Europe and East Asia, reinforced in Central Europe by the supersession of liberalism by Catholic democratic tradition and carried out in East Asia by placing much of the area in the vale of Japan's formidable political economy. This vision might be thought of as a Pax Bismarck and a Pax Ito (Hirobumi), a rehabilitation of the historical model of the 1870s to the 1920s.

In Chapter 4 Peter Katzenstein takes issue with this second coming of German history, however, using instead the recent past to underscore the importance of discontinuities rather than continuities in modern history. For him, Germany's gradual entanglement in the webs of its domestic political system and of interdependence in the international system has led to a lasting accretion of liberal norms and a German unification that seems unlikely to return Europe to the era of power competition and rivalry, that is, to the old Central Europe that Kurth calls *Mitteleuropa.*

The political structures and processes that evolved in West Germany locked powerful actors in the embrace of their domestic political opponents, obliging these actors and institutions to pursue incremental political goals. Similarly, the policy of Allied containment made West Germany more penetrated and interdependent than other large and middle-sized powers, particularly in comparison to the German Reich, the Weimar Republic, or the Third Reich. Since German reunification has been achieved basically through the introduction into the East of West Germany's political and economic institutions, norms, and processes, Katzenstein argues, there is little reason to suggest that such mechanisms will not continue or that liberalism will be superseded by something else. He thus concludes that the ending of the bipolar conflict and the launching of German unity have deepened, rather than transformed, the situation of Germany's embedded systems at home and abroad.

In Chapter 5 Michael Loriaux likewise views Germany and France as deeply attached to the European Community (EC) through anchors of economic interdependence and the evolution of new norms of European international behavior. But for him this liberal internationalism and the recent strong drive for European integration are unplanned and adaptive solutions to old problems of geography and, hence, geopolitics. He shows how the Rhine River's longitudinal gash across a continent contributed to

the development of a thriving urban commercial and industrial civilization and how Europe's nation-states converged upon each other along this
same axis. He examines French policy after 1919 amid the clash of national
claims to the Rhineland and shows how those conflicting claims could find
their solutions only within the framework of increasing liberalization of
the international market and binding supranational institutions. Loriaux
then provides a persuasive and parsimonious account of France's recent
role as the vanguard of internationalism and even free trade, quite in contrast to what presumed lessons of history might tell us about French national pride and insularity.

Michael Loriaux is more tentative than Peter Katzenstein, however, in
stating how much this recent past is likely to predict the future. Economic
liberalism has a weaker pulse in France than it does in Germany and the
smaller democratic-corporatist nations of Europe, and an economic down-
turn throughout the European Community that adversely affects France
could well revive habits of protectionism and sovereign prerogative over
the market. But a fundamental rupture would occur, he thinks, only if the
French confronted again their geopolitical nightmare: the return of the
wealth of the Ruhr to unconstrained German sovereignty.

Geopolitical forces provide a compelling explanation for yet another return of history in Russia, according to Valerie Bunce. Russia's absence of
natural borders and its location on the fringes of the West, she argues in
Chapter 6, has bred a distinct elite culture that compensated for insecurity
with despotism at home and expansionism abroad. A system-threatening
crisis (generated by rapid international changes, sudden military reversals, or the onset of an economic crisis) has often in the past spawned ex-
ceptional leaders capable of enacting fundamental reforms. Thus Alexander II (1855–1881) emerged from the torpid reign of Nicholas I (1825–
1855), and Mikhail Gorbachev emerged from the stagnation of the regime
of Leonid Brezhnev—the latter having proved that the Soviet Union was
unable to catch up with the West and had exhausted itself in trying.

Reforming Russia à la Alexander II and Mikhail Gorbachev had two
predictable consequences: redistribution of power at home and restructuring vis-à-vis the international system, yielding a better alignment of domestic capabilities with international realities (if only through contraction
of Russia's world sphere). Thus Gorbachev's "diplomacy of decline" created the basis for more cooperative interaction among states and established the necessary conditions for liberalization at home, albeit at the cost
of giving Germany new room for expanding its influence. Gorbachev's reforms, like those of Alexander II, fell short of the mark in terms of invigo-
rating the system and could not overcome the constraints of Russian geopolitics so much as accommodate them.

In Chapter 7 Meredith Woo-Cumings shifts the focus to East Asia. Although agreeing with James Kurth and Bruce Cumings that U.S.-Japan cooperation is likely to last, she argues that the relationship is increasingly afflicted not just by trade tensions but also by a cultural and rhetorical divide that increases friction at the same time that it obscures the continuing realities of the relationship. This divide, in turn, is due to asymmetries of power that derive from the past, especially from the political logic of single-market dependence—which has been a constant factor in U.S.–East Asian relations for decades.

Woo-Cumings argues that East Asian moves toward diversified markets—primarily with regard to Europe—signal a growing departure from the previous structure going back to the World War II settlement whereby the United States interacted bilaterally with Western Europe and Japan while Japan and Europe had little mutual interaction. Additionally, the deepening of economic relations between Northeast and Southeast Asia heralds the beginning of an interregional reorganization that may cushion the impact of bilateral trade frictions across the Pacific. In the near term, though, the Pacific will likely remain an American lake in the military, political, and cultural sense, even if the economic Gordian knot that ties East Asia to the United States undergoes continuing attenuation.

In Latin America, where the history of dependence on the United States runs even deeper, John Coatsworth argues in Chapter 8 that the post–Cold War era heralds less a watershed change than a renewal of long-standing historical patterns of subordination. The Cold War in Latin America, he argues, dates back as far as the mid-1920s when the United States intervened in Nicaragua to suppress a Liberal revolt and began to identify opposition to U.S. strategic, political, and economic aims as Communist-inspired—thus generating a transnational political economy of overprotection and persistent inequality, supported by U.S.-dominated multinational corporations, local governments, and industries. As with East Asia, diversification away from dependence on the United States is much needed. But with the incorporation of the former Eastern-bloc countries into the world market, the Latin American hope of attracting sufficient European and Japanese investments to offset the overwhelming American presence is, for now, dashed.

The prospect for Latin America is thus a familiar one, but its hue is a good deal grayer in comparison to either Eastern Europe or East Asia. Eastern Europe is in the orbit of two of the world's most dynamic economies as is East Asia, drawing resources from both Japan and the United States. But the opportunities that such competition generates are mostly lacking in Latin America—leaving it perhaps to repeat history, rather than escape it, in the New World Order.

The final chapter in the book returns us to the examination of the "unwobbling pivot," which was how Ezra Pound translated the Chinese term for the imperial institution. Pound's usage comes close to Franz Schurmann's understanding of the role of the American state in the world system. If the American state and its foreign policy often seem opaque and impenetrable, it is because empires have both interests and ideologies, both of which are frequently incomprehensible in terms of national logic and the discourse of ordinary American politics. The logic that unites imperial interest and ideology resides in the vision of the chief executive, Schurmann argues, making the presidency more than just the sum of the parts that constitute the various bureaucracies responsible for foreign policy. Beneath the level of executive gestalt lie factions that contend for influence and conflict with each other, requiring the analyst to do a kind of sinology to figure out which faction or interest has the president's ear. The case that Schurmann chooses to illustrate his method in this volume, the Gulf War, is just one microcosm of how the United States involves itself with the rest of the world.

Schurmann moves fluidly between factional splits on Middle East policy, from the historical "Israel versus oil" configuration to the shifting coalition inside the "Arabist faction," illustrating how factional politics reflect deeper currents of interests. These conflicts are contrasted with the executive role, or the president's imperial vision, in the Gulf War. The actions taken by George Bush as the imperial commander in chief are related, Schurmann argues, to the emergence of a new configuration in world history: the league of the North, now at peace, and the league of the South, now the prime arena of conflict and rivalry.

The historical background to Franz Schurmann's chapter is unthinkable apart from the state; in fact, it is the story of the state. But it is not history as a conservative force that reflects the consciousness of the powerful, an official narration that binds people to the state. Rather, it is the story of the state as a public realm, whose structures and institutions may be repressive but can also become sources of power, freedom, and heightened consciousness. Such a conception traces to the experience and personal proclivities of the author, who describes himself as a "dissident who was once involved in ideological struggle against certain interest groups active within the 'state site'." This point of view provides an opening for us to reverse the process of examination that we have been engaged in.

We introduced the eight chapters that follow on the premise that the authors were explicit in the way they employed history to understand world politics, and on that basis we have sought to understand the rationale behind each author's choice of the history. But if we can think about history as a consciousness, a "river we all swim in," as Franz Schurmann says, then a different exercise also is possible. *All* social science is historical whether its practitioners know it or not, because the lens through which we observe the world is based on assumptions that are historically derived. Several of the chapters in this volume demonstrate that one's lens is often ground by the region that one studies—by "the river[s] we all swim in."

Bruce Cumings and John Coatsworth are historians of places—East Asia and Latin America—where U.S. policies have profoundly transformed the destinies of the people. The pattern of international history in these places seems a good deal more structured and permanent, with less autonomy imaginable for states in those regions historically dominated by the United States, often unilaterally so, from the Monroe Doctrine onward in Latin America and from the victorious Pacific campaigns of World War II onward in the case of East Asia.

James Kurth and Michael Loriaux excavate quite different patterns for Europe, patterns rooted in the permanence of geopolitics and close-quarter conflict. Much of twentieth century politics in Europe is a struggle to square the circle, to deal with the problem of security and industrial development in a particularly competitive world. For Loriaux, the solution for the old geopolitical problem in the Rhenish corridor rests with European integration, whereas for Kurth it is with the peoples of Central Europe following their cultural and religious telos.

The assumption of permanence sits uncomfortably with Peter Katzenstein. The vision of history that animates his writing emphasizes lessons and the learning of them, a process of complex change and adaptation to new realities: History does not always repeat itself and certainly not as tragedy followed by farce. Postwar Europe has been successfully liberalized after the tragedy of fascism, and German history is thus one of salutary discontinuity, a delinking from a bad past that promises a bright future.

Valerie Bunce's chapter reveals yet another way of thinking about a history rooted in region: the cyclical tendencies in Russia's past. Thus the policies of Mikhail Gorbachev are anticipated in the reforms of Alexander II, many of them owing to the peculiar geopolitical circumstance of Russia. Meredith Woo-Cumings, too, examines periodic recurrences of images and cultural stereotypes, imbedded in and reinforced by power relations in international politics.

Just as people break free of the past to give direction to the future, to fashion freely and spontaneously the New World Order promised by Gorbachev in the mid-1980s and George Bush in the 1990s, they still move forward historically. Just as the political economy of the Cold War lies in wreckage in the former Soviet Union and in the American rust belt, a political economy of allied competition and contention comes to the fore.

Disguised in the new clothes of U.S.-Japan rivalry or an integrated Europe, it runs on well-trodden geopolitical tracks and revives old conflicts just as it creates new unities. It is too early to speak of the history of the making of this New World Order. But it is not too early to ask history to inform us about where we have been so that we might know where we are going.

2

THE END OF THE SEVENTY-YEARS' CRISIS

Trilateralism and the New World Order

For the first time since 1945 it is possible for an American president to speak of constructing a New World Order. For the first time since 1919 it is possible that he might succeed. The onrushing changes of the 1980s curiously recentered the world system circa 1919, minus the three great mistaken outcomes of World War I and the Versailles peace: the failure of the League of Nations, the hard peace that threw a defeated Germany into economic depression, and (from the Western viewpoint) the mistake of the Bolshevik Revolution. As of 1992 the United Nations is reinvigorated, Germany has the "soft" peace of reunification and the most vibrant economy in Europe, and the Bolsheviks have declared themselves to be a mistake.[1]

Seven decades ago, after the terrible bloodletting of "the war to end all wars," Woodrow Wilson and V. I. Lenin offered competing models for a new world system, which nonetheless had much in common: Both held to an internationalist vision, to opposition to Old World imperialism, and to self-determination for colonial peoples. George Bush and Mikhail Gorbachev did not compete so much as unite on principles of collective security, open systems, and a world under law—the last being the personification of the unfulfilled vision of Wilsonian idealism.

The hopes that attended the end of the 1980s, however, have turned to fears. The year 1991 threatened a return to crisis rather than promising the dawning of a new era. Whereas Wilson and Lenin constructed their visions amid the catastrophe of war, George Bush implicitly acted on the principle that the impetus for the New World Order he has spoken of so frequently could be found in war itself, through a punishing, large-scale assault on a Third World upstart, the Iraq of Saddam Hussein. The Gulf

War was another "war to end all wars," and although the fighting ran its course, the ultimate outcome and meaning of this war are not yet clear.

Meanwhile Gorbachev met 1991 with a tilt toward military dictatorship and an uncharacteristic use of force in the Baltic republics; behind these positions is a raging nationalism throughout the former Soviet realm ("self-determination" with a vengeance) and a massive domestic economic crisis. The latter is an acute but common symptom in a world economy still marked by riches and squalor, just as the extremes of nationalism are signs of a global tendency toward splintering micronationalism.

So which general tendency is dominant—a new peace or a new crisis? How can we sort out the seeming contradictions implied in the end of the Cold War, the demise of Stalinism in Eastern Europe, the fall of the Berlin Wall, the hopes for a New World Order, and the distinctly bad news of 1991?

TIME OF ILLUSION

The curious and daunting result of the mercurial turnabouts of the late 1980s and early 1990s is that it is possible to conjure up both the lineages of a new era of peace and cooperation and a new crisis that might mimic the terrible descent of the 1930s: global depression, rising nationalism, war. We live in a time whose essential characteristic, beyond all the others one might mention, is flux and indeterminacy. The dismantling of longstanding Cold War structures has set people free to participate in a lived history—an active, open-ended experiment in which people throw over "history" as a dead weight and rediscover it as an active phenomenon, human beings giving a direction to the future. It is both exhilarating and daunting: Above all, it is something new in the decades since World War II.

There is, of course, no absence of predictions about where we are going and analyses of where we have been. The rubric under which to gather the current flood of diagnoses and prognoses might well be "What's My Illusion?" after the 1950s television show "What's My Line?" Francis Fukuyama can misread Hegel and declare the end of history, just as a forgotten history awakens from long slumber in the Balkans or as Saddam Hussein dusts off a tried-and-true ploy of "history"—aggressive war. At the same time, Richard Gardner can resuscitate Wilsonian internationalism as if we are back to 1919.[2] So are we at the end of history or back to Versailles?

One intellectual finds in the demise of East European communism a "Third Springtime of Nations," a glorious throwback to the "dream of escape from empire" animating people in 1848 and 1919, while another (in the same volume) pictures the same events as "an almost mad race between resurgent nationalism, ethnic hatreds and the counter-force of potential prosperity and free exchange"; he blithely declares George Bush's United States (would-be founder of the new order) to be "now almost surrealistically irrelevant."[3] So are we back to 1919 or 1914? Or 1848, or is it 1815?

Jeane Kirkpatrick can see in "the revolution of '89" a vindication of her well-practiced anticommunism, while conveniently ignoring how the peoples of Eastern Europe demolished her distinction between totalitarian permanence and "authoritarian" temporality. A. M. Rosenthal, in one column after another in the *New York Times*, can go on about how terrible a united Germany or a recrudescent Japan will be,[4] as part of a discourse of eternal mistrust that assumes once a German, always a German (or a Japanese).

One truth about Germany and Japan, at least, is that they won the Cold War and the USSR lost it; the United States may have lost it, too, "if we remember the fate of over-extended empires of the past"—another chic trope, now commonly linked with Paul Kennedy instead of Edward Gibbon. If Germany and Japan won, does this mean a twenty-first century under dual hegemony, a new Berlin-Tokyo axis? Has it all been a horrible mistake, the forty years between 1950 and 1990, in which "those who forgot history are condemned to repeat it"? Above all, has an ahistoric but hegemonic United States contrived to put itself out of the business of hegemony in one brief generation—a mere irrelevancy to a recentered Europe and an insurgent East Asia?

Our dilemma is that although all of us can remember history, we may not all remember the *same* history, and we may not attach the same moral valence to it. Our historical optic ought to be more than grinding an axe, of course, but our assumptions inevitably grind the glass through which we peer. Still, some world views are better than others.

The Gulf War, for example, made the United States appear something more than irrelevant; scholars like Robert Keohane appear premature, at the least, in placing America in a period "after hegemony." Instead, the United States is now the only superpower and likely to remain so for some time. Germany has shrunk from European leadership and pussy-footed so remarkably around the Gulf crisis that Belgian Foreign Minister Mark Eyskens was close to the mark in saying that Europe (read Germany) is "an economic giant, a political dwarf, and a military worm"[5]—and that goes double for Japan, whose leaders wring their hands with their whole bodies when queried about Japan's "contribution" to the Gulf War. Leaders of both countries are all too happy to "let George do it." It also seems that Paul Kennedy rushed to judgment on the causes of American decline—just as Saddam Hussein stimulated a new wave of military Keynesianism, that is, the reigning (if surreptitious) doctrine of American political economy since 1950. But who knows for sure? Maybe Germany and Japan are just playing possum, waiting for the United States to spend and fight itself into oblivion.

A SKETCH OF THE 1990s WORLD SYSTEM

There are ways in which history can help us sort out our current predicament and separate illusion from reality by peering beneath the daily flux of events and looking at structures that condition and shape human action and purpose. If we go back to basics, we can sketch a world system that for the first time since 1917 is structured as follows:

• It is fully capitalist, there no longer being an effective socialist challenge or an alternative socialist common market.

• It has six advanced capitalist economies (the United States, Japan, Germany, England, France, and Italy) that are reasonably prosperous and cooperative and that have no compelling revanchist grievances (unlike Germany at the end of World War I).

• The main threat to the system—the Cold War—is over, ending the system of bipolarity and carrying the potential for a truly multipolar or plural world politics.

• It has a United Nations that is fully inclusive and that is supported by the United States and the former Soviet Union and that in August 1990 successfully implemented a collective security response to Iraq's aggression.

• A divided Europe and a divided Germany, outcomes of the 1945 settlement that represented the greatest threat to peace throughout the Cold War, are now reunited (or reuniting).

• The Third World is fully decolonized, a process also set in motion by the end of World War I and greatly hastened by World War II, and has widely if not completely realized the principle of self-determination.

If we now look at the domestic scene, inside the nations that make up the world system, we find the following:

• All the advanced industrial states are democracies, unlike the traditional autocracies in pre–World War I Western Europe, the post–World War I autocracies in Eastern Europe, or the dictatorships of the 1930s.

• Conflicts between capital and labor are by and large accommodated within established systems and mechanisms for negotiation and accommodation, especially when contrasted to pre–World War II class struggles.

• Ideological cleavages and swings are narrow compared to the pre–World War II situation, caught between a left that cannot but accommodate to capital and a right that cannot but accommodate to social welfare entitlement (if less so in Reaganite America and Thatcherite England).

- In all the advanced industrial countries (if more so in Western Europe) well organized people's movements of various types condition and constrain state power.[6]
- The ongoing technological revolution in communications has made each domestic economy acutely aware of its interdependence with other economies, symbolized by the twenty-four-hour global stock market.

This rosy-fingered dawn for the First World ignores a Third World that remains dominated by the advanced countries and has fewer alternative paths and models than at any point since 1945. It has been largely left out of the prosperity of recent years, furthermore, and thus is the prime source of war, instability, and class conflict. It is also conceivable that West-West conflicts could destroy First World cooperation; some worry that Germany and Japan have not fully learned the lessons of their defeat in World War II or that intercapitalist rivalry will only be deepened by the end of the Cold War and Soviet-American rivalry. The two military superpowers have done exceedingly little to draw down the extensive network of interests that grew fat during the Cold War (although Russia has done more than the United States), leaving in place military-industrial complexes that call forth new wars even as the superpower conflict recedes. Over the long term the capacity of the global environment to sustain continuous industrial development places outer limits on world capitalism, limits that may eventually act back upon the capitalist economies differentially, detonating conflict among them over resources.

Still, the burden of this sketch is that a crisis in the world system lasting seventy years is over and that statesmen now have before them the potential to realize a prolonged period of peace and cooperation. This view does not represent my preferred world—I am far closer to Karl Polanyi's social democratic position, which I discuss below, than to George Bush's New World Order. But a realistic comparison of our 1990s world with that of the past seven decades illustrates why cooperation among the advanced capitalist countries is predictable, at least for the near term of the next decade or two. Now let us look more deeply into this sketch.

ONE CHEER FOR THE MARKET

Why do I speak of a seventy-years' crisis rather than the four decades of the Cold War? Why was it possible to conjure up a New World Order in 1945 but not to create one? It is because the seeds of Soviet-American conflict were sown in the aftermath of World War I and dramatically deepened in the 1930s,[7] and we are only now seeing that fertile if terrible soil plowed under. World War II was part of a European civil war beginning in 1914, and it really ended in Europe only in 1990; both wars were also global, and I will argue that World War II has not yet ended in East Asia.

In *The Great Transformation* Karl Polanyi sought to understand the coming of World War II. He argued that the outbreak of war in 1914 was a symptom of the decline of the "hundred years' peace," dated from the Congress of Vienna in 1815, and that it augured the collapse of nineteenth-century civilization. But that collapse did not finally occur until the early 1930s and the world depression, when one nation after another pulled out of the world system in pursuit of go-it-alone, autarkic strategies of political economy. England was no longer able to pay the costs of keeping the world economy together, and the United States was unwilling to substitute; thus the last vestige of the nineteenth-century system vanished when the United States went off the gold standard in 1933: "The snapping of the golden thread was the signal for a world revolution."[8]

Polanyi located the cause of this collapse in the withdrawal of the British hegemonic hand and, more precisely, in the current panacea for "postcommunism" in the reigning 1980s doctrine of American and British political economy—the Smithean thesis on the unregulated market, "fount and matrix" of the nineteenth-century world system.[9] By "market" Polanyi always meant a system that was capitalist (production for profit rather than use) and that had an inherent tendency toward expansion (who says market says world market) and toward cyclical contraction. The hundred years' peace, he thought, was due to a strong "peace interest" on the part of haute finance and the concert of powers in Europe. Wars between small countries, wars on small countries—which went on throughout the nineteenth-century—could be isolated and contained. War among or between the powers, however, was a dire threat because it threatened the system of world trade. Thus "trade had become linked with peace."[10]

The avatar of the new world system that would replace the nineteenth-century order, for Polanyi, was none other than card-carrying original internationalist, Woodrow Wilson.[11] Wilsonianism was the logical outcome of the spread of market economy, which bred a strong demand for world order and for peace. Perhaps a self-confident United States under Wilson could have accepted the mandate of world leadership that its allies virtually thrust upon it at Versailles and thereby might have changed the course of history. But a fatal gap opened between Great Britain's decline from empire and the willingness of the United States to assume its hegemonic tasks. The result was global depression and then, again, world war.

By "society" Polanyi connoted the actions people take to subordinate and control the market, ranging from poor laws to the minimum wage, Corn Laws to protectionist tariffs, bread laws to industrial unions, utopian to "actually existing" socialism, from the mechanisms of the New Deal to the autarky of fascist political economy. American society was the basic cause of its unwillingness to assume hegemonic leadership, especially the strength in society and in Congress of the isolationist constituency, focused as it was on the vast American national market and not on the world economy.

Polanyi's work gives us a different way of thinking about the contemporary demise of Stalinism and the chances for a New World Order. When the world system collapsed in the 1930s, society reacted on the international level in the form of nations withdrawing from the system, always in idiosyncratic ways: national socialism, the Greater East Asia Co-prosperity Sphere, American isolationism, and Stalinist autarky. The Bolshevik Revolution was perhaps an accident of the outcome of World War I, Polanyi thought; the real Soviet revolution came with Stalin and his "socialism in one country" and, above all, with the forced-pace industrialization of the 1930s, accomplished on a self-reliant basis. This 1930s' revolution was the most violent in world history and yet paradoxically brought the Soviet Union to its most influential position in the world; the USSR "emerged as the representative of a new system which could replace market economy," its industrialization appearing to less modern nations as "an amazing success."[12]

When combined with the Soviet defeat of Hitler's legions on the continent, this system seemed in the early postwar period to have some talisman-like power to transform backwardness overnight and confer national power. The system was imposed with brute force in Eastern Europe (although not without significant domestic support, depending on the country), but its power was more evident as Stalinism became the model for the industrialization of countries where the revolutions were indigenous: China, Vietnam, North Korea, Cuba, and many more. Stalinism had nothing to do with the humane ideals of Marxism and socialism; it had much to do with finding an alternative to the ravages of the market and dependency on the advanced capitalist economies (as perceived in Havana, Beijing, Hanoi). Above all, it was perceived as a way to catch up with the West. Today we know that none of these countries have caught up. Instead, Stalinist development was a kind of wall, intended not just to keep out the West but also to hide underdevelopment. If it was a wall erected against the backwash of the depression in the 1930s,[13] it became a wall against the reality of booming wealth in the postwar capitalist world.

The Great Transformation was written at the end of what E. H. Carr, in another influential treatise, called the twenty-years' crisis, and a sense of crisis permeated the book.[14] Polanyi's optic enables us to see not a two-decades-long crisis, however, but a seventy-years' crisis as the outcome of the actual Versailles "peace": no end to the European civil war, the rise of Bolshevism and fascism, the depression and the breakdown of the world economy, World War II and its "settlement" through a divided and occupied Germany, an occupied Eastern Europe, and a tense bipolarity that came unstuck only in 1989.

In his moving conclusion Polanyi sought to caution the world in 1944 not to forget and thus not to reconstitute international politics on the principles of the unregulated market, the gold standard, and the hegemony of the biggest power but to found a new world based on social democracy, respect for individual freedom, and peaceful cooperation. But no truly new world system emerged after 1945. The United States replaced England as the hegemonic power, and for a generation the grand conflict of the age pitted the more-or-less New Deal United States against more-or-less Stalinist Russia. Meanwhile two main forces in the balance of power of the 1930s, Japan and Germany, remained weak and unimportant to world politics.

In essence, all that is what came unstuck in the 1980s: not just Stalinism, not just the Cold War, but also the New Deal compact, amid resurgent deregulation and revived faith in the unregulated market; dramatically terminated, too, was the breathing space of a world order that did not have to worry about a strong Germany or a strong Japan.

As of 1992 Stalinism and Cold War bipolarity seem to be the only certain casualties of the 1980s. There is still the possibility of global depression as a result of the frantic deregulation of the 1980s, not to mention intercapitalist conflict: Germany and Japan resurgent, the United States in decline. Or perhaps global depression and then withdrawal into regional economic blocs, followed by intercapitalist conflict on the 1930s pattern.

Yet the 1990s promise not only crisis and closure but also prosperity and opening: a genuine common market and the restriction of many national barriers in Europe, the demise of closed economies throughout Eastern Europe and the former Soviet Union, the open possibilities for people throughout Europe who have regained or newly exercised their democratic rights in recent years. Through the optic of the world market we can also see a peace interest today like that of the nineteenth century—and it constitutes our "one cheer for the market."

It is not simply that the antisystem now wants to join up, although the reconnecting of the old USSR and Eastern Europe will mean large new markets for the West (just as China's opening in the 1970s did for the East) and will distinctly reduce the chances for global war. More importantly, as in the long peace of the nineteenth century we also find several great powers of roughly equivalent weight, with a stronger interest in creating wealth than in accumulating power. The new technologies of the information age, speeding labor productivity and expanding service industries so dramatically, combined with the existence of six reasonably dynamic capitalist advanced economies and assuming the creation of new markets in

Central Europe and East Asia, should keep the world from plunging into a new depression. A new boom is more likely, at least in the First World.

It is remarkable that in 1989 Britain, France, and Italy were all economies of about $800 billion GDP; the allegedly gargantuan economy of West Germany was at $950 billion.[15] The addition of East Germany, it now seems, will not do much for the German economy except in the very long run; in the short run it is a distinct drain. Over time Germany may come to dominate its historical terrain in Eastern Europe, but it will have many competitors: American, British, French, and Italian investors, not to mention Japanese and South Korean. In other words, it is unlikely that one nation will have its way in Europe, given that the other industrial economies, whether alone or in concert, are also formidable. This situation augers well for a genuinely cooperative European Community.

The best scholarship on Germany also argues that Germans have learned the lessons of the European civil war and wish not only to live comfortably within a plural and diverse Europe but to have a political system structured to yield that outcome. Peter Katzenstein terms the Federal Republic a "semisovereign state," penetrated by NATO security mechanisms, "deeply enmeshed" in multilateral economic institutions like the European Community, and unyielding to reactionary attempts to rekindle a strong nationalism. It is "semisovereign" at home as well, through a political system that is remarkably decentralized and thoroughly democratized.[16]

The very idiosyncracies through which the 1930s "withdrawals" from the world economy were defined and that detonated fascism in several explosive domestic configurations also no longer exist.[17] These idiosyncracies derived from different social formations in the various countries. As Perry Anderson and others have argued, the European regimes and Japan after World War I were not completed democracies but embodied more or less liberal political forms simultaneously with the intersection or "triangulation" of continued agrarian or aristocratic dominance, the incipient emergence of the second industrial revolution with its new classes and novel technologies (telephones, automobiles, refrigerators, and other consumer durables produced for mass consumption), and "the real or imaginative proximity of social revolution."[18]

If Western Europe's ultimate trajectory was liberal, that outcome was not clear until 1945. Until that time liberal progressivism had to contend with romantic reaction on the right and social revolution on the left, both of them antimarket; out of this collision came Nazi Germany and militarist Japan. World War II finished off this conjuncture, according to Anderson, leaving universal bourgeois democracy in Western Europe. Liberal hegemony had been realized, and the revolutionary prospect slowly faded away. I cite this analysis also to suggest why the "discourse of eternal mistrust" is likely to fade in regard to Japan and Germany: They had their democratic revolutions, even if it took World War II to get them.

In many ways it is not Germany but the United States that is removed from the democratic movements and social safety nets of Western Europe, visible in the attenuation of the contentious "public space" that was one of the best gifts of the bourgeois revolutions or in the small army of homeless people living in the streets of our cities. As Mary Kaldor argues, while Europe moved to the left in the early postwar period, the United States moved to the right; and while popular movements there helped end the Cold War and bring down the East European dictatorships, here a "neo-liberal Right" holds sway and has far more influence over the public than does its counterpart in Europe.[19]

If Germany can be pleased with its newfound status, England and France will have to live with a Europe and a world no longer enthralled with their respective "great modern moments"—the Industrial Revolution and the French Revolution—and no longer subject to English or French imperialism and with a Germany likely to continue outdistancing them economically. All this will be harder for the proud French than for an England long accustomed to a slow decline from global influence, but there is nothing remotely to suggest a level of dissatisfaction that would take this minor discomfort in the direction of major conflict, especially with European economic union just around the corner.

Nor is the European Community likely to be a regional economy that will put the rest of the world in the shade and thus stir regional counteraction elsewhere. Widely touted as having 330 million eager consumers, this community after 1992 will be no larger (and probably smaller) than the combined markets of North America and the middle and laboring classes of Latin America or the Pacific community embracing Northeast Asia, the countries of the Association of Southeast Asian Nations (ASEAN), and Australia.[20] All three markets will be interdependent; if protectionists continue to shoulder Japan out of Europe, they will be opposed not just by Japan but by the United States lest it lead to trade wars, and Japan will continue to invest in local manufacturing to get around trade barriers.

Unlike Germany, the United States and Japan do tower over other industrial economies in their respective regions. Japan has a GDP of nearly $2 trillion, compared to South Korea's nearly $200 billion, one-half the size of Spain's. No economy in the Americas comes close to that of the United States. But Japan and the United States are so interdependent, the American market is still so essential to Japan, that cooperation is much more likely than conflict and the emergence of regional blocs.

Finally, the existence of nuclear weapons carries its own inherent peace interest. These weapons have never been used between nations possessing them, owing to the principle sometimes called Mutual Assured Destruction. All the industrial countries either have nuclear weapons or can acquire them in short order. A small quiver of such weapons and reasonably up-to-date means of delivery are all that is needed for effective deterrence, as the French and the Chinese have shown. This condition suggests a prolonged period of stability, akin to the nineteenth-century balance of power, without the necessity for a furious arms race like that characterizing the period leading up to World War I or the four decades of the Cold War.

TRILATERAL VISIONS

If the above analysis is correct, the tendency in the First World ought now to be toward multilateral great power cooperation rather than unilateralism or the formation of regional blocs. If the United States is in the middle age rather than the alpenglow of hegemony, it ought to do what the British did in the face of incipient but relative decline roughly a century ago: ally with the rising capitalist powers. At that time it meant British cooperation with the United States and alliance with Japan (from 1902 to 1922)— although the British sought outright alliance with the United States as well.[21] (At that time, of course, the strategy also meant hostility to the other rising capitalist power, Germany.) Today the logic suggests a multilateral arrangement focusing on New York, Berlin, and Tokyo, with Washington still hegemonic—that is, what was called "trilateralism," during the brief but instructive return to Wilsonianism of the presidency of Jimmy Carter.

The Trilateral Commission was founded in 1973 by David Rockefeller, then chairman of the Chase Manhattan Bank, and Zbigniew Brzezinski, who later became Carter's national security adviser. It was composed of industrialists, politicians, and self-described technocrats from three continents, with the express purpose of broadening an existing "Atlanticist" constituency to include Japan. Although it quickly became a synonym for capitalist conspiracy, it was essentially a traveling forum geared toward sustaining interdependence (watchword of the 1970s) between the United States, Western Europe, and Japan—a First World condominium that would guarantee the interests of the dominant organizational form of advanced capitalism, the multinational corporation. I use "trilateralism" to signify the consensual ideology that informed the commission and the policies of the subsequent Carter administration that included many trilateralists in its midst.

Trilateralist ideology drew deeply from the well of Wilsonian internationalism, promoting free trade, multilateral cooperation, and a kind of transnational economic planning among the advanced industrial economies (symbolized later by Carter's "three locomotives" strategy); soft-pedaling Cold War anticommunism in favor of an accommodationist strategy toward the socialist world (exemplified in Carter's China-card policy); and trying to co-opt rather than confront a Third World that had accumulated significant power in recent years (symbolized by Andrew Young as the American representative to the United Nations).[22] Trilateralism barely survived the first two years of the Carter presidency, however, and was sharply reversed in the presidency of Ronald Reagan, which was marked by American unilateralism and policies of confrontation toward both Communist and Third World antagonists.

In the late 1980s détente broke out anew, the Cold War ended, and popular movements brought down East European dictatorships. Suddenly the recrudescence of trilateralism was amazing to behold: In September 1989 before anyone dared imagine a rapid German unification, American Ambassador to Bonn Vernon Walters spoke out in its favor, as did Henry Kissinger; overnight the Bush administration switched Germany for England as its "special relationship" in Europe, and soon David Rockefeller was holding closed sessions with Helmut Kohl, emerging to laud the dawning German unity, and with Toshiki Kaifu (emerging to say next to nothing). The alacrity of the American response can be explained only by a trilateral logic in which the United States embraces unified Germany only to constrain it and cooperates with Japan only to corral it in order to ensure that the United States remains primus inter pares in a new world having three poles: Washington, Berlin, and Tokyo.

JAPAN AS TRIPOLE

If we now turn our attention to the third leg of the trilateral system, we find a similar but less altered mise-en-scène in East Asia. Structures elaborated in the wake of World War II still govern; in spite of its world-beating industrial prowess, Japan is still firmly within the constraints of the postwar system. One can see this, of course, in the delicate Kabuki dance carried on by Japan's leadership in regard to the Gulf crisis. Japan gets about 65 percent of its oil from that region, yet even in timidly venturing to send a handful of noncombatant forces to the Middle East, the leadership was quickly forced to backtrack. Then it pledged an additional $9 billion to the effort in January 1991, a substantial sum, only to run into a firestorm of domestic criticism before pushing the measure through the Diet. But one grasps Japan's situation more clearly by imagining this headline: "Tokyo Dispatches Large Naval Task Force to the Gulf." It is still an impossible headline; and if it happened, it would touch off a spate of comment in the United States about Japanese militarism and a frenzy of outrage in Japan's near reaches.

It is perhaps a paradox that although Nazi Germany was more aggressive, violent, and virulent than militarist Japan, its near neighbors are less worried about its new unity than are Japan's about any hint of Tokyo's again taking up a military role—except for Poland, that is, which unlike the United States or England was occupied by Nazi Germany and unlike occupied Vichy France was nearly destroyed by the ordeal. Korea and China look on Japan the way the Poles look on Germany because both were occupied and brutally subjugated. The Communist movements that still govern in China and North Korea were outgrowths of an anti-Japanese struggle and are still governed by Chinese octogenarians and Korean septuagenarians who fought the Japanese. Nor has the general Japanese population shaken off the longstanding (and very welcome) pacifism that was an important residue of military defeat—and long derided by national security pundits as Japan's "nuclear allergy." In this sense, World War II has not ended in East Asia; we are still not in a post-postwar era. And, of course, Japan's leaders pursue the rationality of the German position: Why not "let George do it"?

Trilateralists have not only lauded German unity in recent years, but the brains behind the Trilateral Commission, Zbigniew Brzezinski, spilled oceans of ink conjuring a new condominium called "Amerrippon." For Brzezinski and the trilateralists, after Richard Nixon's 1971 New Economic Policy dealt a *shokku* to Japan, the problem was how to shape the articulation of the new Japan with the world economy, such that what Brzezinski called the "fragile blossom"[23] did not turn into Tokyo Rose. He and his commission became strong and consistent advocates of free trade and partnership with Japan. As the Cold War ended, Brzezinski revived this argument in stunning language. His Amerrippon signified a joint condominium and would stimulate American "revival":

> A greatly revitalized America can be nurtured by policies that exploit the special complementarity of American and Japanese interests, while also providing Japan with the safest route to continued growth. . . . The strengths of one compensate for the weaknesses of the other. . . . Working together ever more closely, they can assure for themselves unrivaled global economic, financial and technological leadership, while reinforcing the protective umbrella of American global military power.
>
> Japan for many years to come will be heavily dependent on American security protection . . . hence the Japanese stake in a globally engaged America will remain great. With America heavily indebted, the American stake in a productive and prosperous Japanese partner will also grow.[24]

Compare now Lord Baldwin in May 1935: "I have always believed that the greatest security against war in any part of the world . . . would be the close collaboration of the British Empire with the United States of America."[25] The logic is the same today: The declining hegemon reaches out to the rising powers, offering the hand of cooperation as a means of restraint.

Brzezinski went on to argue that for Japan "incalculable considerations . . . quite literally a matter of life or death" in its relationship to the United States mean that "Japan would simply not be—nor would it remain— what it is without the American connection." He therefore recommended "the deliberate fostering of a more cooperative, politically more intimate, economically more organic partnership."[26] Because of the "special relationship" between the United States and Japan growing out of World War II, in which the United States held unilateral sway in the Pacific (unlike Europe), Brzezinski does not need to shrink from blunt talk about Japan's defense dependency on the United States. His position would be more nuanced in regard to Germany, of course, but essentially the same stance holds true there, as well, and fills out the trilateral logic implicit in his argument.

For these and other reasons Japan is at least as eager for partnership, cooperation, and continued defense dependency on the United States as is Zbigniew Brzezinski. It is a rising power, and it may one day be the hegemonic power of the Pacific region or even the world, but it is today about where the United States was in regard to England in the first decades of this century—happy to play second fiddle, content to let the hegemon police the world and rule the waves. Nor is this anything new for Japan; as Akira Iriye, the dean of diplomatic historians of East Asia, has shown in several books, through this entire century, except for one (disastrous) decade, Japan has assiduously sought cooperation with the dominant powers in East Asia—first England and then the United States.

Throughout his career Iriye has consistently argued a number of key points that are particularly relevant in the current climate of Japan-bashing in the United States:[27]

1. That Japanese imperialism (conventionally dated from the Sino-Japanese War and the seizure of Taiwan in 1895) was subordinate to British imperialism and coterminous with a similar American thrust toward formal empire in the 1890s, and it was no different in kind from the British or American variety.[28]

2. That Japan got the empire the British and Americans wanted it to have and sought to organize an exclusive regional sphere only when everyone else did the same after the collapse of the world system in the 1930s (and even then, its attempt was half hearted; even then, its development program was "orthodoxly western").[29]

3. That Japan pursued a "cooperative" policy of integration with the world system at all times in the twentieth century, except from the mid-1930s to the mid-1940s when there was no world system.[30]

4. That Japan's presumed neomercantilist political economy of protection at home and export to the free trade realm abroad, with corresponding trade surpluses, has been less important between 1900 and 1990 than an open market at home and a cooperative policy abroad.

The late William Appleman Williams discovered in John Hay's turn-of-the-century "open door notes" a metaphor for American expansion and emphasized that this rising hegemony had its inception in the presumably distant Far East.[31] Williams saw an American empire beginning in the 1890s and maturing under Woodrow Wilson and Warren Harding, with both resisting radical change in the East Asian status quo (in spite of the very different rhetoric employed). American leaders like Hay and Theodore Roosevelt saw an identity of interests with Great Britain in East Asia; meanwhile Japan was the chosen junior partner for both the United States and Britain; Roosevelt "looked to Japan as an advanced country and regional power uniquely qualified to instruct backward China" (and thus defined American policy thereafter toward Japan's colonial and continental dependencies).[32]

Shortly after World War I ended, in 1922 to be exact, the United States came to be the dominant partner in the trilateral hegemonic partnership that had existed in East Asia since the 1890s. This was the time when American banks became dominant in the world economy;[33] Iriye rightly judges the United States, in spite of its isolationism, to have been "the key to postwar international relations . . . its capital, technology, and commodities sustained the world economic system throughout the 1920s . . . as the financial, business, and political center of the world."[34] The Anglo-Japanese alliance had became tattered, and the United States now became more important than England to Japanese diplomacy. The Washington naval system of 1922 was explicitly trilateral in that the United States and England kept their naval superiority, while Japan, the United States, and England all cooperated to keep China a subordinate actor in the East Asian system.

On the critical period from 1941 to 1945 Iriye argues that until the Japanese military's "turn south" in mid-1941 (a decision deeply conditioned by Soviet power), Japan was still dependent on the United States. In 1941 the United States invoked the outer limits of its hegemonic power by embargoing oil to Japan, which came as a tremendous psychological shock to Japan and made its leaders assume that the only alternative was war—yet even in the midst of that terrible war the leaders of Japan's New Order complained that Anglo-American ideas "cling to us like fleas." Japan's failed attempt at unilateral hegemony was visible on the sea after Midway (July 1942) and on land after Guadalcanal (December 1942); within a short time a small cadre of internationalists in Japan and the U.S. State Department were moving on remarkably parallel lines to reintegrate Japan into the American hegemonic regime.[35]

For much of the postwar period the United States has given every support to Japan and the other East Asian capitalist economies. If in the 1940s the United States structured a situation in which Japanese industry could revive, in the 1960s the administration of John Kennedy placed strong pressures on Japan and its near neighbors (especially South Korea) to restore Japan's economic influence in the region. This policy resulted in the normalization of relations between South Korea and Japan in 1965 and a bundle of Japanese grants and loans that helped the economy of the Republic of Korea (ROK) take off. It was also in the Kennedy period, however, that for the first time American leaders began criticizing Japan for its "free ride" in security affairs.[36] It is daunting to realize that this rhetoric now is entering its third decade, with Japan still recalcitrantly limiting defense spending to about 1 percent of its GNP and American politicians still carping about it. But what is the alternative—a Japanese fleet in the Gulf?

Elsewhere in East Asia we also see continuity rather than change. Even the Communists have failed again—this time, to understand that according to the Americans their system has failed. The East is still Red, with Communist leaderships that emerged in the 1930s and pursued revolutionary-nationalist strategies still holding power in China, North Korea, and Vietnam. But perhaps because of the nationalist credentials of these leaders, most of them have found it easier to open themselves to capitalist interests (especially Japanese) than have their counterparts in the Soviet Union or the more hard-line East European states before the changes of the late 1980s.

Japan seems to be hedging against its possible exclusion from the European Community after 1992 by building its position in East and Southeast Asia. Its direct investment in the region has grown sixfold since 1985, its trade with Taiwan tripled in the same period, and its manufactured imports from the Asian region as a whole more than doubled from 1985 to 1988 (contrary to pundits who argue that its economy is basically closed). Japanese investors have been especially active in Thailand; on the average, one new Japanese factory opened every working day in 1989.[37]

The Pacific region including Northeast Asia, the ASEAN countries, and Australia will have a GNP of $7.2 trillion by the year 2,000, according to current projections, which will be bigger than that of the EC; as stated earlier, the number of effective consumers in the region will be at least as large as in Europe.[38] Japan has also been assiduous in breaking barriers to trade with the Asian Communist countries: It is North Korea's biggest capitalist trading partner and may normalize relations with P'yongyang soon; it went back into China much more quickly than did other investors in the wake of the Tiananmen bloodletting in June 1989.

All this regional investment is grist for the mill of those who find a developing tendency toward regional economic blocs. But as I have argued, such blocs are unlikely short of a major world depression; a trilateral regime of cooperation and free trade linking Europe with the Far East and the Americas is much more likely, with the three great markets of each region underpinning and stabilizing intercapitalist rivalry in the world system and encouraging interdependence rather than go-it-alone strategies that would be deleterious to all.

If partnership and cooperation are the trilateral watchwords, however, why is Germany still a member of NATO, in spite of the collapse of the Warsaw Pact? Why do American military bases still dot the Japanese archipelago, even though North Korea is almost the only remaining "threat" in the East? In thinking through the problems of Japan and Germany today, we can grasp that a kind of trilateral cooperation has been the name of the game since the late 1940s. Furthermore, although the Cold War had ended by 1990, the project of American hegemony did not, and that project was always trilateral. How so?

WHAT WAS THE COLD WAR?

The ostensible conflict in the years of the Cold War was a global struggle between communism and capitalism, with frightening military formations arrayed along the central front in Europe. In fact, this was a shadow conflict, and the shadow obscured the real history of the four decades of the Cold War. Hardly any lives were lost along the central axis of conflict in Europe, leading historians like John Gaddis to speak of a "long peace" in our time.[39] Following his much-beloved George Kennan, Gaddis argued for the success of the containment doctrine, conceived as a long twilight struggle to hold the existing lines of the postwar settlement, until the Soviet Union saw the error of its ways and reformed itself. When Gorbachev proceeded to dismantle the Soviet empire, Kennan's wisdom seemed triumphant.

There was a curiosity in Kennan's strategy, however, in an unspoken premise: the doctrine was meant to contain both the enemy—the USSR—and the allies—mainly West Germany and Japan. Kennan was an architect of a strategy in which West Germany and Japan were shorn of their previous military and political clout during the period of American occupation, but their industrial economies were encouraged to revive, and they were posted as engines of growth in the world economy. Meanwhile the United States kept both countries as defense dependencies and shaped the flow of essential resources to each in order to accumulate a diffuse leverage over all their policies and to retain an outer-limit veto on their global orientation. This strategy was articulated precisely at the time of the formal onset of the Cold War in spring 1947.

The major wars in the period of the ostensible long peace (in which millions of lives were lost, including nearly 100,000 American soldiers in Korea and Vietnam combined) were part of the American hegemonic project. In Korea the United States picked up the glove of the Japanese empire and sought to keep South Korea and Taiwan within Japan's historical economic area and thus to aid its reviving industry. In Vietnam the United States picked up the French glove but again for reasons connected to the needs of the French and Japanese economies.[40] Lesser interventions, like those in Greece in 1947 and Iran in 1953, were similarly connected to the revival of the advanced industrial economies and the American desire to police the lines of resource flow to the advanced industrial states.

The real reason for the long peace between the superpowers was that the Soviet Union shared the American perspective to a much greater degree than is generally recognized. Stalin's doctrine, which became the lifelong doctrine of Foreign Minister Andrei Gromyko, was to contain not just the United States but also any hint of revanche in Germany and Japan, to contain an Eastern Europe that had been fertile ground for conflict before both world wars (Soviet domination froze the Balkan problem that so vexed the allies at Versailles), and to contain a restive Third World with clients that might draw Soviet might and prestige into unwanted peripheral clashes with the United States. When push came to shove, the Soviet Union pulled its forces out of northern Iran in 1946, cut off the Greek guerrillas, distanced itself from direct involvement in the wars in Korea and Vietnam, and withdrew from the brink over Cuba in 1962. Meanwhile it laid siege against West Germany and Japan.

Thus when the United States found itself in the best of all possible worlds in 1990, having won the Cold War but still retaining immense leverage vis-à-vis Germany and Japan, it was not by accident, because the Cold War consisted of two systems: the containment project, providing security against both the enemy and the ally; and the hegemonic project, providing for American leverage over the necessary resources of our industrial rivals. Both the hegemonic project and the allied-containment system have survived.

The shadow conflict of the Cold War period shaded our vision, obscuring the hegemonic project and highlighting threats that could never stand the glare of realpolitik analysis—above all, the obsession with China growing out of the Korean War, which for a generation made the People's Republic seem far more important than it really was, both to the Nixon who clamored about its expansionism in the 1950s and the Nixon who inflated it into a strategic ally in the 1970s. Notice how China has faded from view as a strategic asset, coterminous with the end of the Cold War. More importantly, Russia is now seen for what many revisionists always argued it to be: a regional power of the second rank (except in regard to inherently unusable nuclear weapons), inflated out of all proportion by the heat of Cold War ideology. Finally, the United States can now be seen to be what it always has been since the 1940s: the only hegemon, the England of our time.

From the onset of the Cold War into the mid-1960s, American industrial and military dominance was so complete and American allies so relatively weak that an expensive unilateral role was the only one available to American policy, creating an era of indulgence in which the United States transferred enormous resources in the form of capital, aid, and technology to the industrial allies. But that was an anomalous period, sure to end when the other industrial allies revived after the war and sure to spawn a move toward multilateralism when that revival occurred.

The intractibility, stupidity, and gross expense of the Vietnam War hastened this process, and it hastened a modest American retreat from empire—known as the Nixon Doctrine for a while and articulated by trilateralists in the Carter administration as a move from being the world's policeman to being the world's "night watchman."[41] The more important watchwords of the 1970s, however, were free trade and interdependence, as responses to Nixon's brief flirtation with neomercantilism in his New Economic Policy. And if Republicans experimented with détente in the early 1970s and then declared it a nonword in the administration of Gerald Ford, Jimmy Carter revived the policy during the first years of his administration. Trilateralists correctly gauged the Communist weakness to be primarily economic and technical and understood that nearly everywhere in the Communist sphere revolutionary socialism had given way to bureaucratic conservatism; they thought that through loans, aid, and open markets the Communist nations could be tamed and brought into the world system. There was, in fact, supreme confidence that these nations would sooner or later join the world economy, largely on American terms. Although trilateral strategy failed with the Soviet Union by 1979, it succeeded in enveloping China in a broad-ranging economic relationship (with the key Chinese internal reforms coming at the end of 1978) and in making unprecedented inroads into the Soviet sphere in Eastern Europe (especially through big loans to Poland, Hungary, Romania, and others).

As similar policies mushroom before our eyes in the 1990s, we can look back on the period between 1979 and 1989 and see, in effect, ten lost years. The Cold War had ended in most of East Asia by the late 1970s, trilateral policies headed off the danger of trade wars, and new thinking in regard to the Third World made major advances in the late 1970s. But by 1979 we were steaming into the Second Cold War, as Fred Halliday termed it. The Soviets invaded Afghanistan in a move that seemed for the first time in the

postwar period to mimic American attempts to stifle Third World guer-
rilla movements, and hard-liners in the Carter administration triumphed
over détenteniks (and also incorporated the Gulf in the "zone of containment," as Brzezinski called it, lest that important change be forgotten).
Thereafter a five-year period of confrontation ensued in which both
Reagan and successive Soviet leaders were deeply implicated.

The third and final phase of the Cold War began with Gorbachev's assumption of power in 1985 and quickly carried Reagan's confrontational
policies forward to oblivion. Although Reaganites argue that their rapid
buildup forced the Soviet retreat-cum-capitulation that characterized the
last half of the 1980s, it was obviously the rise to power of reformers under
Gorbachev who understood the futility and danger of Soviet imperial
overstretch and who thus took a number of truly remarkable decisions
that ended the Cold War: the unconditional withdrawal from Afghanistan, flexible solutions to a series of regional problems in 1987–1988, and
the dismantling of the Soviet empire in Eastern Europe in 1989.

That the Cold War came to an end essentially through the unilateral acts
of the Soviet Union[42] also helps to explain why the American projects of
global hegemony and allied containment continue: Nothing really
changed in American policy. It was as if while two horses were racing
around a track, one broke its leg, and the other kept on running. But my
treatment of U.S. global policy is not sufficient to explain why Bush kept
on racing. The rise of the Cold War system had a domestic corollary, as
well, in the emergence of mechanisms that served the twin projects of containment and hegemony: a military-industrial complex and a national security state. Although the twin projects were conceived in 1947, the system
necessary to service them was not in place for several years.

A diverse American coalition of left and right, located in small business, labor, and farming constituencies and known colloquially as isola-
tionists, resisted the march of Franklin D. Roosevelt and Harry Truman toward world power and up until 1950 had been unwilling to countenance
the major defense expenditures deemed necessary to service the new
global commitments. It was the Korean War that "came along and saved
us," as Secretary of State Dean Acheson later remarked, a necessary crisis
that galvanized Congress and the public toward a near quadrupling of
military expenditure in the six months from June to December 1950. Only
then did the mechanisms and bureaucracies of hegemonic maintenance
proliferate in the federal government and the defense industries (the CIA,
for example, was still little more than a rump operation in early 1950).

This domestic system, like the hegemonic project, showed little effect
from the much-vaunted end of the Cold War. Although the first months of
1990 were filled with optimism about a big "peace dividend" just around
the corner, Iraq's invasion of Kuwait had an evil genius: Just in time, it

snatched defense contracts and military production lines from the jaws of oblivion. As Michael Klare and others have pointed out, the American response to this invasion also bore close comparison with Korea: After years of warning about threats to Third World resources, contingency plans for intervening in the Middle East, the elaboration of rapid deployment forces and the like, Saddam Hussein's invasion touched off an astonishingly rapid intervention, as if the forces had been preplaced at the ready. But there is nothing surprising in this, either: The end of the shadow conflict with the Soviet Union has merely revealed what the Cold War was really about for Americans—interventions in the Third World, from Korea through Iran, Guatemala, and Cuba to the debacle in Vietnam. Like Soviet interventions in Eastern Europe, the United States was trying to keep its side in line and to prevent losses defined by movement to the other side.

This analysis of what the Cold War was really about, then, provides us with the best explanation for the sudden materialization of half a million American troops in the Gulf in 1990. The only aspect of the Gulf crisis that really bespoke the end of the Cold War was this: Iraq felt free to invade Kuwait not because the United States was likely to respond in some way but because the Soviet Union was *not*. At any previous time Iraq's invasion would have invoked Soviet credibility and a distinct threat of superpower conflict. And so Saddam knew that the Soviets or the Americans or both would have stepped in to prevent it.

Otherwise, this crisis partook of the untouched elements of the Cold War system: First, it is part of the longstanding hegemonic project to shape the flow of resources to Japan and Western Europe and thereby to retain leverage on our economically worrisome allies. Second, it is part and parcel of the real conflict we have fought during the past four decades—that between the United States and the Third World. Third, and most important, if Korea was the alpha of the military-industrial complex, Iraq was the omega. The end of the Cold War had done nothing by mid-1990 to dismantle the enormous machine set in motion in the 1950s, a perpetual-motion machine that was built for war and that advances its interests in making war. Joseph Schumpeter's famous interpretation of imperialism as an atavism is precisely relevant here: Institutions built for service to empire continue onward with a clanking automaticity in spite of dramatic changes in the world or strong constituencies calling for an end to empire. Made to fight old wars, the systems call forth new ones.

The postwar American empire has not rested on territorial exclusivity, like the old European colonies. It has been an open-door empire, policed by a far-flung military basing system and penetration of allied defense organizations (for example, American command of the West German or Korean militaries).[43] This global system necessitates constant maintenance by the domestic military-industrial complex and is in many ways its foreign expression and replica. Little or nothing has been done to dismantle it since the Cold War ended because it is the deep structure enabling continuing leverage over our capitalist allies.

The Schumpeterian perspective makes understandable the atavism of American behavior amid the welter of transformations in Europe; it is why the Bush horse keeps running. At the precise moment when Gorbachev was dismantling his empire and calling for a New World Order and when the last of the East European Stalinist systems was crumbling, George Bush decided to invade Panama; for the umpteenth time in this century American forces intervened in Central America as if nothing whatever had changed.

Bush's initial reaction to the invasion of Kuwait was more modestly defensive and widely supported by the world community (including the Soviet Union). It fit a reasonable definition of collective security, operating through United Nations mechanisms. Thus American opinion was for a few weeks thrown into the anomaly of left-wing critics like Noam Chomsky and Alexander Cockburn supporting the intervention and right-wing critics like Patrick Buchanan opposing it. But then came the November elections and, as Thomas Ferguson has argued, "the great puzzle" of the move from the defensive to the offensive, from Desert Shield to Desert Storm, as the American commitment doubled in size overnight.[44] What goal was so compelling, so urgent, that the passage of time and the application of sanctions could not be allowed to work their will on Saddam Hussein?

Ferguson's answer is fiscal—that burgeoning deficits and a swamp of domestic problems meant that the Gulf crisis had to be ended quickly and decisively, lest it spill over and infect everything else from the bailout of the savings-and-loan fiasco to bankrupt cities to the foreign aid necessary to keep the Soviet Union and Eastern Europe from falling apart. This is a shrewd and important answer at the level of policy. For a variety of reasons this war had to be funded out of the current account, without new taxes or drains from other programs. At the structural level, however, the American commitment cannot be understood apart from the Pentagon's perpetual-motion machine, the dire situation of several big defense contractors, a four-decade history of military Keynesianism, and the need to maintain the global hegemonic project.

The atavism of Bush administration policy is seen in its extraordinary continuity, as the USSR collapsed: The Soviets slashed defense spending, Bush increased it. The Soviets withdrew troops and closed bases in Eastern Europe, the United States kept its troops and bases in Western Europe. The Soviets dismantled the Warsaw Pact, and the United States placed unified Germany in NATO. The Soviets disabused themselves of a client state in Iraq, whereupon it was immediately embroiled in war with the United States. The Soviets removed a major logjam in another grave trouble spot by opening diplomatic relations with South Korea (in September 1990), and the United States continued to lay siege against North Korea, hoping for its collapse on the Romanian model. Why would it be surprising if the atavism known as the Russian military-industrial complex springs to life again?

The ultimate atavism of Bush administration policy and the real meaning of its New World Order, however, rests in its remarkable desire to have its cake and eat it, too—that is, to continue in place the domestic and global structures of the Cold War period while moving toward trilateral accommodation with a newly emerging Europe and Japan. Thus we get multilateralism in the First World and unilateralism in the Third, accommodation of the (formerly socialist) Second World and confrontation with the Third, perestroika and arms control for Moscow and Indian summer for the American military-industrial complex.

To the extent that this program persists over time, we will have to designate it not a holdover from the Cold War but the post–Cold War program itself. In other words, the new trilateralism would mean cooperation among the advanced capitalist states, accommodation and envelopment of the formerly socialist regions, and heightened domination and exploitation of the Third World in everyone's interest—except that of Third World peoples themselves. This program may explain why the Soviet Union was so eager to wash its hands of its own Third World involvements (in Africa, Afghanistan, Vietnam and North Korea, Cuba, and the Middle East) and may be the best explanation for the high level of allied support for the American effort to subdue Iraq.

CONCLUSION

In August 1990 a rare moment of true collective security materialized, unlike any other moment since Versailles, in a United Nations coalition embracing all the powers and determined on a patient defensive effort to reverse Iraq's invasion—itself an event far worse than anything North Korea or North Vietnam did, because Saddam's army crossed well-recognized international boundaries and had no pretense of fighting a civil conflict. But precisely because the would-be father of the New World Order could not understand that if Cold War politics were to end anywhere they had to end everywhere, George Bush in November 1990 moved to the offensive, transformed the multilateral effort into a unilateral American war, and deepened the long-standing project of American hegemony in the Middle East. He did this not because he is a warmonger but because he had not begun to learn the lessons that Gorbachev had and thus did not start the process of dismantling the policies and the domestic systems of Cold War maintenance. Instead his actions were propelled by these same policies and systems.

The result, as in Korea and Vietnam, was unrestrained American punishing of a small and weak Third World country and a tragic diversion of the world away from the idealistic hopes of early 1990. It may be, as I have suggested, that the First World is content to unite against a restive Third World—to dominate it rather than accommodate its demands for a sharing of power and resources. It is even possible that the atavism of Washington's policies will cause the worst calamity—a return to power of hardline military forces in Russia and thus a return to superpower conflict. It wouldn't be surprising, as U.S. hardliners need their hardliners and vice versa. At home the Gulf War set back a long postponed project now recognized as necessary by all sides of the political spectrum, the American perestroika needed to set our own house in order and dismantle the systems built up during the four decades of the Cold War, in order to get about our real task of peaceful economic competition with Europe and Japan.

Yet the argument of this chapter is that the atavism of American policies since November 1990 need not have happened and can be reversed. Domination of the Third World, too, is an atavism of imperialism and the Cold War; it cannot continue without undermining world peace. The American people are unlikely to bring about the reversal because of the fatal gap that, I have argued, has opened between Europe and the United States: The rise of West European societies with at least a good start at social democracy is not matched by the United States, which is still in thrall to the unregulated market and to a pale version of democratic participation.

If that were not the case, if the United States were not so disastrously removed from the left-liberal consensus that is emerging in a unified Europe, we might hope to realize Polanyi's vision of a truly New World Order based in social democracy, respect for individual freedom, and an end to hegemony and a real era of peaceful cooperation. Instead, as I have argued, we should expect another period of American hegemony and trilateral partnership with Germany and Japan, the nearest rivals of the United States.

A reversal of policy can occur if we understand that the chances for realizing the ideals of cooperation and partnership among the powers are better than at any time since 1919 and that America's main problems are at home. This prescription was, after all, what one father of the realist school in international relations sought at the end of the twenty-years' crisis: "Ultimately the best hope of progress towards international conciliation seems to lie along the path of economic reconstruction."[45] Americans, like the Russians we fought for so long, should understand that this project must begin at home, in our own form of perestroika; it is the only way to bring the Cold War system to a close.

3

MITTELEUROPA AND EAST ASIA

The Return of History and the Redefinition of Security

The three years from 1989 to 1991 saw more history made, and unmade, than did the previous two generations. The great events in Eastern Europe—the East European revolution, the end of the Cold War, the unification of Germany, and the disunification of the Soviet Union—together add up to the greatest transformation in Europe since the end of World War II. Indeed, these events reversed many of the results of that war. The great events in the Gulf during 1990 and 1991—the invasion of Kuwait, the Gulf War, the defeat of Iraq, and the pronouncement of a New World Order— together add up to the greatest transformation of the United States' international reputation since the Vietnam War and the revolution of the Organization of Petroleum Exporting Countries (OPEC). Here, too, the events reversed many of the results of that war and that revolution.

With so much history in so short a time, it is not surprising that there is no agreement on what it will all mean for the American role in the world. In the year between the collapse of the Soviet empire in 1989 and the invasion of Kuwait in 1990, it seemed that economic power would dominate the future, with leadership falling to Japan and Germany. Then, in the months after the invasion of Kuwait and the ensuing Gulf War, it seemed that military power would again dominate the future, with leadership returning to the United States. Now that both the dust from the fall of the wall and the sand from Desert Storm have settled, there is an opportunity, and a necessity, to try to perceive the shape of things to come.

In this chapter, I argue that we shall soon see a great drama involving two distinct conceptions or paradigms of international order. The first is a global conception, expounded by the United States for much of this century and now expounded once again as the New World Order. The second is a regional conception or, more exactly, two variations on a regional

33

theme. One of these centers on Germany and Central Europe, and the other centers on Japan and East Asia.

THE NEW WORLD ORDER
AND THE REPEAL OF HISTORY

Many political commentators think that the phrase New World Order means nothing at all; it comes, after all, from a president famous for his ridicule of "the vision thing." Yet the phrase is only the latest in a series of expressions of the most solid and established American tradition in world affairs. The phrases used have changed with the circumstances of the times and have included "a world safe for democracy," One World, Free World, and finally, New World Order. But the content of that tradition has largely remained the same for the last half century or, in yet another of these phrases, the American Century.[1]

That tradition addresses both the organization of the international economy, and the organization of international security. In the international economy the tradition has been international liberalism: Liberal states, particularly those in North America and Western Europe, support market forces within an open international economy. This tradition might be termed the GATT model, after the General Agreement on Tariffs and Trade, which was established in 1948. Similarly, in international security, the tradition has been collective security and nuclear deterrence: The United States contains Soviet military aggression, particularly in Western Europe, by the threat of nuclear escalation in response. This tradition might be termed the NATO model, after the North Atlantic Treaty Organization, which was established in 1949.

In 1945, of course, the United States had hoped that its great victory in World War II would bring about a liberal international order that would truly be One World in its scope. But the completeness of the American triumph and the liberal order was ruined first by the Soviet Union and then by the Communist revolutions in Asia. By 1950 the visions of the United Nations and One World had been reduced to the realities of GATT, NATO, and the Free World. Indeed, by 1960 the One World had been split into the First, Second, and Third Worlds.

The events of the three years from 1989 to 1991 have reversed this melancholy history. The collapse of the Soviet threat has meant the removal of the major obstacle in the Second World to the American conception of One World. Similarly, the defeat of Iraq in 1991 in the Gulf War has meant the removal of a major obstacle in the Third World to that conception. But these events not only have removed external obstacles; they have also dissolved internal obstacles in the United States itself. The collapse of the Soviet threat reversed the great disappointment of the Cold War; it removed the historical burden of the 1940s and 1950s. The defeat of Iraq reversed the great debacle of the Vietnam War; it removed the historical burden of the 1960s and 1970s. Together these two events, in effect, rolled history back to that great moment of American triumph in 1945, the beginning of the American half century, which quickly became only an American half world. It appeared a fitting time indeed to pronounce a New World Order, to announce the Second Coming of One World.

The security and economic pillars of the New World Order appear to have much in common with those of the world order set up in 1945. After 1945 the American international security order was based on American high-tech weaponry, in that case the atomic bomb, and the strategy of nuclear deterrence. This order provided a secure framework for the political reconstruction of Western Europe and Japan. After the Gulf War, an American international security order could again be based on American high-tech weaponry—in this case smart bombs, precision missiles, and stealth aircraft—and the strategy of conventional deterrence.[2] And this strategy of conventional deterrence could have a good deal more credibility than did the strategy of nuclear deterrence for much of the American half century.

Similarly, after 1945 the American international economic order was based on American dominance of Middle East oil,[3] which provided a secure fuel supply for the industrial reconstruction of Western Europe and Japan. After the Gulf War, an American international economic order could again be based on a heavy American influence over Gulf oil. It has been observed that one of the results of the war was to make the United States, in effect, a new and important member of OPEC.

Together, the American credibility in military operations and the American influence over Gulf oil could provide the United States with substantial bargaining power in its economic negotiations with its principal economic rivals, Germany and Japan. Given the collapse of the Soviet empire, these two nations appear to be the only candidates, other than the United States itself, for shaping the world order of the future. However, the hesitant and reluctant behavior of Germany and Japan during the Gulf War confirmed for many the perception that the two countries were incapable of taking initiative and exercising power in international affairs. And in fact, Germany and Japan are incapable of employing military power; they are also incapable of exercising any political influence on a global scale or even within the Middle East. The only global power for some time to come will be the United States, and the only world order will be an American world order.

The German and Japanese roles in the New World Order are those of merely regional powers. But by being the regional powers in Central Europe and in East Asia, they will actually transform, and perhaps hollow out, the meaning of the New World Order itself. I shall therefore look at that other great conception of international order, the regional paradigm, and at the regions where it can unfold, giving particular attention to Central Europe, or Mitteleuropa.

The revolution in Eastern Europe in 1989 abolished the Soviet empire in Europe and thus, in effect, abolished Eastern Europe itself, which had existed as a separate, and separated, region since the Soviet conquest and communization at the end of World War II. In the place of Eastern Europe, there is now Central Europe, the region that had been there for centuries. The abolition of Eastern Europe has meant the resurrection and return of Mitteleuropa.

THE ORIGINS OF THE EAST EUROPEAN REVOLUTION: FROM STEEL COMMUNISM TO YUPPIE COMMUNISM

The great and sudden transformation in the Soviet empire in Eastern Europe in 1989 had its origins in the great, long trajectory of Soviet-style industrialization from the 1950s to the 1980s. Undermining the apparent stability of the Communist political system was a steady decline in its industrial performance and therefore in its legitimacy. Each successive decade in this period saw a decline in the rates of economic growth of the Soviet Union and of its East European allies.

For the Soviet bloc the 1950s was a decade that perfectly fit the Stalin formula and, indeed, might be called the decade of steel communism. (Stalin had chosen his pseudonym because it meant "steel," and for the rest of his life he saw steel as the solution to virtually every military or economic problem.) It was the true and pure decade of forced-draft industrialization and of rapid growth in heavy capital-goods industries. The decade also brought into being a large class of industrial workers, supposedly the suitable mass base for Communist rule.

During the 1950s Soviet and East European annual growth rates often exceeded 6 percent and were among the highest in the world. This impressive economic performance gave great legitimacy to the Soviet model. When the Soviet Union exceeded the United States in steel production in 1958, it seemed as if the Communist system might indeed "overtake and surpass the West." But the great project of capital-goods industrialization—of steel communism—was already reaching its limits.

The 1960s might be called the decade of Sputnik communism, after the dramatic success of the Sputnik space program in 1957. The emphasis then was on high-technology industrialization, and there was also a vast expansion of higher education and the creation of a large class of managers and professionals. The annual economic growth rates remained high in this period (4–5 percent), but they were lower than they had been in the

1950s. In fact, they were not much higher than the growth rates in Western Europe and were exceeded by those of Japan and the newly industrializing countries of East Asia. The Soviets had adopted a standard of legitimacy that was closer to the values of the West, and their advantage on this standard was much less pronounced.

The 1970s might be called the decade of goulash communism, after Nikita Khrushchev's description of János Kádár's Hungary, which Khrushchev saw as something of a model. At that time, the emphasis was on consumer-durables industrialization. In order to bring about this level of industrialization, the Soviet bloc opened itself to Western loans, investments, joint ventures, and licensing agreements—that is, to the first beachheads of the world market. A prime example was the arrangement with the giant Italian enterprise, Fiat, to reorganize and expand Soviet production of automobiles (the Lada). During the 1970s the annual growth rates of the Soviet bloc fell to 3–4 percent. The new standard of legitimacy was virtually identical to the consumerism that constituted one of the central values of the West and the new world market, but on this standard the Soviet bloc was at a marked disadvantage.

Finally, the 1980s might be called the decade of yuppie communism. During this decade the annual growth rates of the Soviet bloc economies had fallen to 1–2 percent or less. It became clear that the Communist regimes were not able to fulfill the promise of mass consumption, and they retreated to the promise of elite consumption, that is, consumption by the "new class" of bureaucrats, managers, and professionals, most of whom were products of the great expansion of higher education in the 1960s. The Communist parties of the Soviet bloc had always been a grand coalition of the old class—industrial workers—and the new class—organizational bureaucrats. But in the beginning most of the bureaucrats were former workers and made up a rather thin stratum on top of a large worker mass. By the 1980s, however, the new class had expanded enormously in size, partly because of the vast expansion of higher education. It had expanded considerably in scope to include professionals and managers as well as bureaucrats. And it had expanded significantly in depth to include young people whose parents had been members of the new class and who thus were second-generation members.

By the late 1980s the youngest two-thirds of Communist party members had been born after World War II, had become adolescents after Stalin's death, had been university students in the 1960s or later, and were in mid-career or middle management positions. They were thoroughly imbued with the aspirations, tastes, and desires of professional people, not those of industrial workers; they identified specifically and intensely with their counterpart professionals in the West; and they craved the benefits of international trade. In form, they were members of the Communist party;

in fact, they were members of what might be called the yuppie internatio-
nale. Red on the outside, white on the inside, numbering in the millions,
they appeared on the political landscape as a vast field of radish Communists.

In the 1980s the Communist parties had become a thin stratum of ger-
ontocracy on top of a large mass of yuppies. The only growing and dynamic force in these otherwise stagnant societies was this professional-
managerial class, and in the course of the decade the aging Communist
leadership began to yield more and more to their demands. At first, the
professionals demanded cultural liberation, and the Communist governments gave it to them by spending large sums on the restoration of cultural monuments of the past and by virtually eliminating restrictions on
cultural imports from the West. Then the professionals demanded consumer liberation, and the Communist governments gave them a larger
and larger share of a smaller and smaller economic pie; they paid off the
new class at the expense of the old class of industrial workers. Finally, in
the epic and epoch-making year of 1989, the professionals demanded political liberation. The Communist governments, after years of yielding to
professional demands and ignoring worker problems, found themselves
utterly without loyal support. The governments gave into this ultimate
demand with a suddenness and a completeness that astonished the world.

THE CONSEQUENCES OF THE EAST EUROPEAN
REVOLUTION: THE RETURN OF MITTELEUROPA

The East European revolution of 1989 was the third East European revolution in this century. Like the two earlier revolutions of 1918 and 1945, the
revolution of 1989 came at the end of a world war, in this case, the Cold
War. The settlement following each of these wars and revolutions has
brought about great shifts in power—both international and internal, strategic and economic. In understanding the consequences of the end of the
Cold War and the revolution in Eastern Europe, it will be helpful to place
the consequences in the historical perspective of the two earlier postwar
and postrevolutionary settlements. It is useful here to distinguish between
the apparent and the real victors of the war. For in each of the three cases
discussed, those who appeared to be the victors in the great struggle immediately afterward were not those who emerged as the real victors from
the perspective of later years.

The Post–World War I Settlement

In 1918–1919 it certainly appeared that the Western allies—particularly
France, Britain, and the United States—were the victors over Germany,
and this perception was certified in the Treaty of Versailles and in the sys-

tem that it established. But France and Britain had fought the war so long and so hard that they were exhausted by their victory, and by the 1920s it was clear that the real inheritor of the fruits of victory was the United States. The United States created the League of Nations (which it almost immediately abandoned) and then the Dawes Plan (large-scale bank loans) for reconstructing Central Europe, especially Germany, in its own liberal-democratic and liberal-capitalist image. At the end of the 1920s, however, it turned out that the U.S. victory, too, was only apparent. With the onset of the Great Depression in 1929, the Dawes Plan and the American project for Germany collapsed.[4]

The real and fundamental strategic legacy of 1918 was then revealed. Before 1914 Germany had been haunted by the "nightmare of encirclement" and was trapped between France and Russia. During World War I, however, Germany had defeated Russia, as demonstrated in the "forgotten peace" of Brest-Litovsk in March 1918, and for two decades thereafter the Soviet Union remained isolated behind the cordon sanitaire of new, weak states and preoccupied with its "socialism in one country." Thus after 1918 Germany was confronted with only one major continental adversary, France, rather than with two. The economic legacy of 1918 was much the same. Despite Germany's long succession of economic miseries—defeat, revolution, occupation, inflation, depression—the underlying reality of the German economy was that it remained the largest, the most advanced, the most efficient, and the most competitive industrial complex in Europe, just as it was before 1914.

When the Weimar Republic was displaced by the Nazi regime in 1933, it was not long before these underlying strategic and economic strengths were recognized and realized. While Adolf Hitler and the Nazi elite fixated on the strategic strengths, the conservative elites of German industry and finance understood well the economic strengths. These elites soon composed the Schacht Plan (based on organized foreign trade and controlled currency exchange) for reconstructing Central Europe, or Mitteleuropa, in their own corporatist-authoritarian and organized-capitalist image. This grand project for German hegemony in Mitteleuropa through economic power, which very well might have succeeded, was instead overtaken by Hitler's own ambition for German domination of all of Europe through military conquest.

The Post–World War II Settlement

A similar but simpler pattern of apparent and real victors occurred after World War II. In 1945 Britain, the United States, and the Soviet Union were the obvious victors over Germany and Japan, as was demonstrated in the Yalta-Potsdam system. But Britain had fought World War II longer and harder than any of the other Western allies, so long and hard, in fact, that it was again exhausted by its victory, and the real victor was again the United States. The United States then developed the Marshall Plan and the NATO alliance for reconstructing Western Europe in its own liberal-democratic and liberal-capitalist image, modified by the New Deal welfare state. In this grand project Britain had a special relationship but played only the secondary role.

There was also no doubt that the other real victor was the Soviet Union, which proceeded to carry out the East European revolution of 1945, a revolution from above and from outside.[5] The USSR also imposed forced-draft industrialization and created the Molotov Plan to reorient the East European economies toward the Soviet model. The Soviet Union thus reconstructed Eastern Europe in its own Stalinist and state-Communist image. More precisely, it created an Eastern Europe in much of what had previously been Central Europe, or Mitteleuropa. In extinguishing the old Central Europe and creating a new Eastern Europe, the Soviets severed it from the rest of Europe, which thereby became Western Europe (even if Stockholm remained east of East Berlin, Vienna east of Prague, and Athens east of Sofia).

The Post–Cold War Settlement

Political commentators have repeatedly proclaimed that the United States has won the Cold War (as famously argued by Francis Fukuyama).[6] But in a pattern similar to that of Britain earlier, the United States fought the Cold War longer and harder than any of the other Western allies, so long and hard, in fact, that it was depleted by its military expenditures (as famously argued by Paul Kennedy),[7] and in many ways the advantages of victory have gone to Germany and Japan. It is likely that Germany will eventually compose a Mitteleuropa project, if not quite a Kohl plan, reconstructing Eastern Europe in its own liberal-democratic and social-market image (and thereby converting Eastern Europe back into Central Europe). In this grand project, the United States will have a special relationship but will play only a secondary role.

This Mitteleuropa project might recapitulate the economic goals and methods of the German industrial and financial conservatives from the 1880s to the 1930s and the political goals and methods of the German Social Democrats of the 1920s and the 1940s to the 1980s. The project would also represent the reversal of the military defeats of the 1940s with the economic achievements of the 1990s. De-Stalinization would reach its logical culmination in the reversal of Stalingrad not long after 1992, the fiftieth anniversary of that great climactic battle (and the unification year of the European Community).

MITTELEUROPA AND THE RETURN OF HISTORY

The notion of a return of Mitteleuropa must certainly give one pause. Of all the regions that have generated international conflict in this century, Central Europe has generated the most momentous, having been at the center of the two world wars and the Cold War. Indeed, it was not only at the center of these conflicts but in large measure the source. Out of Central Europe came a destructive energy that threw much of the rest of the world into war and turmoil. Onto Central Europe then came a deterrence system erected by the two superpowers, the United States and the Soviet Union. It has been remarked that Central Europe has to export its history, because it produces too much for it all to be consumed locally.

Of all the international security systems of the past half century, easily the most important and the most institutionalized have been NATO and the Warsaw Pact, which by partitioning Europe into Eastern and Western blocs appeared to have put an end to Central Europe as an assortment of independent actors and a mass producer of international insecurity. With the collapse of half of the old security system—the Soviet bloc and the Warsaw Pact—and the transformation of Eastern Europe back into Central Europe, the ancient problem of the international security of Mitteleuropa confronts us once again.

What will be the nature of the new Mitteleuropa, which has the new Germany as its core? Here, again, it is useful to look at the old Mitteleuropa, which had first Austria and then Germany as its core.[8] And just as the problem of Mitteleuropa has returned with the departure of a multinational military state—the Soviet Union—part of the solution may lie in the return of a multinational religious institution, the Roman Catholic church.

Habsburg Legacy and Catholic Vision

For most of the past half millennium, the history of Mitteleuropa was defined by the grand alliance between a multinational religious institution—the Roman Catholic church—and a multinational empire—the Habsburg monarchy. Together these two great institutions shaped the society, the culture, and the life-style of Central Europe into forms that were distinct from those of the Europe to the west and the Europe to the east.

This half millennium, which corresponds to the modern era, is often seen as the story of the rise of secular national states whose prototypes were England and France. Seen from the other side of the coin, however, it is the story of the decline of the two great multinational institutions, the Roman Catholic church and the Habsburg monarchy.

The decline of the Habsburg monarchy culminated in its destruction in 1918. That destruction in turn led to revolutions and wars until a new order of sorts was imposed on Central Europe by powers that were neither central nor even European but rather by the superpower to the west of Europe (the United States) and the superpower to the east of Europe (the Soviet Union). Indeed, these two superpowers were not even national states in the conventional sense but were themselves multinational states or even transnational empires. The decline of the Catholic church, in contrast, has been punctuated by a long series of reforms and revivals, of transfigurations and resurrections, so that it remains a vital multinational institution. It is probably the most significant multinational institution operating in what was until recently Eastern Europe.

The Polish Model:
Social Solidarity Versus Communist Regime

The collapse of the Soviet bloc was in some part inspired and initiated by the Catholic church in Poland and by a Catholic pope from Poland, John Paul II. In Poland (as in Ireland), because of the long history of foreign occupation and persecution of both the Catholic church and local nationalists, there has long been a greater unity between the hierarchy and the society than in most other Catholic countries. From 1945 to 1989 the national state was rejected in Poland as a foreign imposition, and the local branch of a universal church was accepted as the fullest embodiment of the national ideal. Conversely, the Polish nation was probably the most Catholic in the world—in a sense, the fullest embodiment of the Catholic ideal. For several decades, the Polish church has been the perfect example of that "integral" Catholicism that was the Catholic project in Latin Europe (Spain, Portugal, and Italy) in the first half of the twentieth century.

The Polish hierarchy and John Paul II readily developed the conception that the Catholic church, social solidarity (expressed in the union, Solidarity), and "civil society" represented the real Poland, whereas the Communist state merely represented the formal, or even a phony, Poland. In the peculiar conditions of a nation subjected to a foreign power, a multinational religious institution can become the most authentic and dynamic national institution, more so than the national state itself. Thus over time the civil society, or real Poland, relentlessly hollowed out the Communist state, or formal Poland, until in August 1989 the Polish regime became the first Communist government to give up power to an anti-Communist movement.

The Mitteleuropa Model:
A Third Way Between East and West

At the present time, the conventional wisdom holds that the countries of the old Eastern Europe, or new Central Europe, aspire to become like

Western Europe or even like the United States, that is, to become not only civil societies but liberal democracies and capitalist economies. This judgment is the famous "end of history."[9] The great transformation from Eastern to Western, authoritarian to liberal, Communist to capitalist, however, shows more and more signs of being a great deformation instead. It is probably only a matter of time before the nations of Mitteleuropa reject the extreme of liberal capitalism as decisively as they have rejected the extreme of state socialism and seek a third way. An alternative scenario is that the former Eastern Europe—the new Central Europe—will become rather like the old Mitteleuropa, representing the return, rather than the end, of history.

The civil society, the cultural standards, and even the life-styles of much of Mitteleuropa were shaped either by the Catholic church (in Poland), by the Habsburg empire (in the Czech lands of Bohemia and Moravia), or by church and empire acting together (in Hungary, Slovakia, Croatia, and Slovenia). These countries have long found their social and cultural models in Germany (whose southern region is Catholic) and Austria and are looking there for their economic and political models, as well. Their economic model is not the free market but the social market as it has existed in West Germany and Austria since the early 1950s. This market includes (1) a substantial part (40–50 percent) of the gross national product passing through the state sector, that is, through either federal, state, or local governments; (2) "societal corporatism," or close and continuous cooperation between state agencies, business corporations, and labor organizations; and (3) a universal system of social welfare benefits.

The principal political model is the Christian Democratic party as it has existed in most of West Germany (Christian Democratic Union [CDU]), in Bavaria (Christian Social Union [CSU]), and in Austria (People's party) since the late 1940s. Governments led by Christian Democratic parties have been elected in Hungary, Slovakia, Croatia, and Slovenia. As it happens, these countries were once both Habsburg and Catholic. The German Christian Democratic party, the political leader and the financial power of the Christian Democratic International, has provided substantial guidance and support to these new Christian Democratic parties to the East. A political model at another level is the federal republic, as it also has existed in West Germany (officially the Federal Republic of Germany) and Austria (the Federal Republic of Austria) since the late 1940s. Czechoslovakia has reconstituted itself officially into the Czech and Slovak Federal Republic.

Catholic Social Teaching

The ideas of civil society, social-market economy, Christian democracy, and federal republic are completely in accord with Catholic social teaching as articulated in a century-old tradition of papal encyclicals.[10] The first papal encyclical on social questions, *Rerum novarum* (On the condition of the working classes), was promulgated in 1891 by Pope Leo XIII. It has been followed by a half-dozen comparable encyclicals focusing on the social questions of their times, including *Quadregesimo anno* (Social reconstruction, 1931) by Pius XI, *Mater et magistra* (Christianity and social progress, 1961) by John XXIII, and *Laborem exercens* (On human work, 1981) by John Paul II. To commemorate the centennial of *Rerum novarum* and to direct the application of this Catholic social tradition to the new emerging Europe, Pope John Paul II designated 1991 as the Year of Catholic Social Teaching, during which he promulgated a new encyclical on contemporary social questions, *Centesimus annus,* and convened a synod of bishops that formulated a social project for the new Europe.

The papal encyclicals and the social teaching of the Catholic church have consistently criticized both state socialism and liberal capitalism as incomplete and flawed ideologies. In their place the Church advocates such conceptions as society's need to have both business organizations and labor unions but also the "principle of the priority of labor over capital"; the need for meaningful work and a "just wage" for the full development of the human person; and the need to limit state power to its proper role by the "principle of subsidiarity," which devolves power and responsibilities to intermediate institutions between the state and the individual.

The 1991 encyclical of John Paul II continues and expands on this tradition. *Centesimus annus* celebrates the fall of communism in Eastern Europe in 1989. But it also condemns two forms of capitalism, the "national security state" (such as existed in Latin America from the 1960s until the 1980s) and "consumer society" (such as exists in the United States and increasingly in Western Europe). Instead, the pope praises "a democratic society inspired by social justice" (such as that pursued in much of Western Europe for most of the period since World War II). As John Paul sees it, such societies

> endeavour to preserve free market mechanisms, ensuring, by means of a stable currency and the harmony of social relations, the conditions for steady and healthy economic growth in which people through their own work can build a better future for themselves and their families. At the same time, these attempts try to avoid making market mechanisms the only point of reference for social life, and they tend to subject them to public control which upholds the principle of the common destination of material goods. In this context, an abundance of work opportunities, a solid system of social security and professional training, the freedom to join trade unions and the effective actions of unions, the assistance provided in cases of unemployment, the opportunities for democratic participation in the life of society—all these are meant to deliver work from the mere condition of "a commodity," and to guarantee its dignity.[11]

The papal encyclicals and the social teaching of the Catholic church will fit the economic realities of the new Mitteleuropa for many years to come and could provide an intellectual order, political legitimation, and policy guidance to governments in Mitteleuropa after the collapse of state socialism and out of the turmoil of liberal capitalism.

THE NEW GERMANY IN THE NEW MITTELEUROPA

The German Magnet

The new united Germany will be the national state that will most shape and influence the new Mitteleuropa. This role will be a fulfillment of the vision and the *Westpolitik* of Konrad Adenauer, chancellor and Christian Democratic leader, in 1950. Adenauer conceived that a West Germany fully integrated into a Catholic Western Europe (France, Italy, Belgium, and the Netherlands) would become a "magnet" that would gradually but steadily draw the countries of Eastern Europe to it by its economic, social, and cultural lines of force. This role will also be a fulfillment of the vision and the *Ostpolitik* of Willy Brandt, chancellor and Social Democratic leader, in 1970. Brandt conceived of removing the iron curtain that stood between Eastern and Western Europe in the way of the iron magnet's lines of force. The unification strategy and *Deutschlandpolitik* of Helmut Kohl, chancellor and Christian Democratic leader, in 1990 nicely combined East and West in many senses of the words.

The German Christian Democrats, however, are no longer a very good example of Catholic social teaching. At least since the end of the Adenauer era in 1963, they have been more capitalist than Catholic. Moreover, it may turn out that the Christian Democrats will be in power in the new united Germany less often than they were in the old West Germany. In West Germany Catholics composed about 50 percent of the population; in East Germany they were about 10 percent; and in united Germany they are about 40 percent. In any event, the economic depression in eastern Germany since unification has extinguished the earlier enthusiasm of East Germans for Kohl and the Christian Democrats. When the Christian Democrats give up power, however, it will probably be to the Social Democrats, as it has been in the past in both West Germany and in Austria. For more than three decades, the Social Democrats also have adhered to the principles of civil society, social-market economy, electoral democracy, and federal republic, similar to those articulated in the papal social encyclicals.

Catholic social teaching helps to make Catholic capitalists more social in their economic activities, and it helps to make Social Democratic policies more acceptable to a Catholic population. The social teaching of the papacy has provided a common denominator and ideological consensus for the Christian Democratic and Social Democratic parties of Germany and Austria. In the future it could function similarly in the other nations of the new Mitteleuropa, as well. Thus the papacy probably will play a significant role in the way that the nations of Mitteleuropa come to define their social policies, their national identities, and their international security in the decade of the 1990s, that is, until the next millennium. Obviously, this is most likely with the papacy of John Paul II, the Pope from Mitteleuropa. (Indeed, he is from Polish Galicia, that part of Poland once ruled by the Habsburgs.) But it will probably be true of his successor as well. The roles of the Roman papacy and the German state in Mitteleuropa, and the relations between them, will bear some resemblance to the roles of and relations between the Roman papacy and the Habsburg monarchy in the lost era that until recently seemed so long ago.

A Tale of Three Cities: Bonn, Brussels, and Berlin

The history of Germany since the end of World War II can be seen as a development of three successive German personas or characters. It is also a journey between three cities and a trajectory over three generations.

The first Germany is the Germany of Bonn, of the Federal Republic. The earliest and weakest Germany, it was also the American Germany. Its historical moment was the 1950s and 1960s, but this particular German character still survives in Germany's military dependence within NATO.

The second Germany is the Germany of Brussels, of the European Community. As one of several equal West European states, it is the West European Germany. Its historical moment was the 1970s and 1980s, and thus this particular German character not only came to overshadow the first Germany but still appears as the most prominent German character.

The third Germany is the Germany of Berlin, of Mitteleuropa. As the largest and easternmost Germany, it is the Central European Germany. But as we have seen, to a degree it also means a German Central Europe. Its historical moment will be the 1990s and 2000s.

When Germany faces east toward Mitteleuropa, its role will be that of the dominant partner in a series of bilateral relationships with each of the Central European states, as the hub with spokes radiating outward. Conversely, as Germany faces west toward the European Community, its role will continue to be that of the first among several equal West European states but now more manifestly the first than before. Germany will also be the bridge and the broker—indeed, in large measure the gatekeeper—between the European Community and Mitteleuropa. Direct investment and foreign aid from the Community and from its member states will find their way into Mitteleuropa but within a framework of German practices, as junior partners to German firms, and perhaps subject to the veto of the German government.

Germany will seek a basic standard of political stability and predictability within the Central European states. It will pursue this goal by bringing about a basic standard of economic stability and predictability within the region, including preferential trade, investment, and aid arrangements. The German conception of the international economy will become primarily a continental, rather than a global, one.

To the Brandenburg Gate

Great international orders have their great cities, and great cities have their essential symbols. The city of the liberal international order has been New York, and its symbol is the Statue of Liberty. The city of the Communist international order was Moscow, and its symbol was Lenin's tomb. The city of the international order of Mitteleuropa will be Berlin, and its symbol is the Brandenburg Gate.

In 1991 the Brandenburg Gate was two centuries old. It was one of the first of the great neoclassical monuments that distinguished the Prussian capital in the first half of the nineteenth century. But it is surrounded on all sides by monuments that express different styles and different parts of the German experience and achievement. Two monuments in particular express the values of the liberal, the western, Germany. To the west of the Brandenburg Gate is the Kurfurstendamm, the symbol of capitalist Germany; also to the west is the Reichstag, the symbol of democratic Germany. Similarly, two monuments in particular express the values of the traditional, the eastern, Germany. To the east of the Brandenburg Gate is the statue of Frederick the Great, the symbol of military Germany; also to the east is the Museum Island, the symbol of cultural Germany.

The Brandenburg Gate is at the center of Berlin and therefore of Mittleleuropa. It is also at the center of the four great talents of the German past—capitalist, democratic, military, and cultural—and the four great promises of the German future. The tragedies of the German past and of the old Mitteleuropa occurred when these four powers fell out of balance and ran out of control. On top of the Brandenburg Gate stands the Quadriga, the chariot drawn by four horses, and at its center stands the charioteer, the symbol of classical order harnessing, balancing, and directing dynamic powers. In our time it may again be the symbol of order harnessing powers, of organized capitalism, of the social market, of the civil society. The order of Mitteleuropa will depend on the German charioteer's prowess and skill. And so will the order of the New World Order as well.

THE NEW JAPAN IN THE NEW EAST ASIA

The Japanese Coprosperity Sphere

The potentialities for Germany and Mitteleuropa in the 1990s have a good deal in common with what already had become the realities of Japan and East Asia in the 1980s. East Asia, of course, is not a region in quite the same sense as Central Europe. In particular, Japan has provided much less of a historical and cultural model for East Asia than Germany has for Mitteleuropa (although imperial China once provided a model in some ways similar to that which was provided by the Habsburg empire). In the 1980s, however, Japan's example and investments have helped inspire much of East Asia—especially South Korea, Taiwan, and Singapore—to emulate Japan's own model of dominant-party politics (for example, rule by the Liberal-Democratic party for forty years) and organized capitalism.[12]

Japan's role in East Asia has often been described by critics as a new version of the Greater East Asia Co-prosperity Sphere that existed during World War II. By evoking the wartime memories of military conquest, domination, and exploitation, these critics intend to condemn Japan's role in East Asia today. But in fact, if the wartime connotations are forgotten and if some of the uppercase letters of the phrase are replaced by lowercase letters, the term "greater East Asia coprosperity sphere" becomes a quite accurate description of the results of Japan's role in the region in the early 1990s. That role conforms to a particular Japanese vision of international order; it includes both a conception of the economy, which can be termed international mercantilism, and a conception of security, which the Japanese have called comprehensive security.

International Mercantilism

The international mercantilism of Japan and other East Asian states conceives of the state as guiding society toward effective competition in the world market for the purpose of increasing the power and wealth of the state and society. It also conceives of this competition as taking place within a context of dynamic, not static, comparative advantage, with the state helping society to move progressively higher up the ladder of technology, to shift out of low-technology and low-wage industries into high-technology and high-wage industries. As one country moves up from a lower rung on the technological ladder, other countries—especially the newly industrializing countries (NICs) of East Asia—will move onto it. Thus international mercantilism conceives the world economic competition to be not a zero-sum but a positive-sum game; not only one but many countries will benefit, and these benefits will be not only short-term gains but long-term development. However, this mutually beneficial process requires the more advanced countries to be continually developing new technologies and new industries so that they can devolve their old industries to less developed countries. This, in turn, the Japanese believe, requires the guidance of a strong and coherent state.

This international mercantilism has fulfilled the economic goals and methods of the Japanese industrial and financial conservatives, first in the 1920s and then in the period since the 1950s; it also has fulfilled the political goals and methods of their liberal-democratic partners of the 1920s and of the period since the 1950s. It is a cliché that Japan has already reversed the military defeats of the 1940s with the economic achievements of the 1980s and that U.S. trade and budget deficits have brought about the reversal of Midway, that other great climactic battle of 1942.

Comprehensive Security

Japan has also developed a particular conception of international security. After World War II Japan was not permitted to provide for its own security, a condition institutionalized in the famous Article 9 of the new constitution that placed severe limits on Japan's military ("self-defense forces"). Accordingly, the Japanese army was in effect replaced by the U.S. Army, which performed some of the roles of the Japanese army—that is, it fought and remained in Korea in large measure to ensure the military security of Japan. Similarly, the Japanese navy was replaced by the U.S. Navy, which performed some of the roles of the Japanese navy—it secured access to markets for Japanese goods in Southeast Asia and ensured the free flow of oil to Japan from Indonesia and the Gulf. (It was actually the oil embargo by the United States, the leading oil exporter in 1941 and the Saudi Arabia of the day, that drove the Japanese government to seize the oil of the Dutch East Indies, the predecessor to Indonesia, and to protect the strategic flank of that oil lifeline with a preventive strike on the U.S. Pacific Fleet at Pearl Harbor.)

By the 1980s Japan had arrived at its own distinct conception of international security based on a combination of U.S. military power and Japan's own economic power and low-posture diplomacy, a combination that has become known as the concept of comprehensive security. The core of the concept, however, has been economic power. Comprehensive security is obtained by an implicit grand bargain between political and economic leaders in Japan and their counterparts in the United States, involving both economic and military dimensions. The Japanese continue to provide capital to the United States, most obviously in the purchase of U.S. Treasury notes, and the United States continues to provide military protection to Japan and to East Asian countries that are of vital interest to Japan, especially South Korea.

THE RISE AND FALL AND RISE AGAIN
OF GREAT POWERS

Kennedy and Fukuyama

The potentialities of Mitteleuropa and the realities of East Asia mean that two intellectual fashions of the late 1980s (Paul Kennedy and great-power decline, 1988; Francis Fukuyama and liberal triumphalism, 1989) will have to be revised. Each, it turns out, was half right and half wrong. Kennedy was perfectly right about the impact of military spending and "imperial over-stretch" on the economic decline of the Soviet Union, so much so that the Soviet empire collapsed for those reasons in the next year, 1989. But this same rapid collapse made less plausible and more debatable the other half of Kennedy's argument, which was that there was also underway an economic decline of the United States owing to military spending and imperial over-stretch.

Conversely, although Fukuyama was perfectly right about communism, he was wrong about liberalism. Fukuyama's history ends with liberalism, but the world's history will not. The next stage of history will certainly not be dominated by state communism, but it probably won't be dominated by liberal capitalism either. It is more likely that it will be shaped in major ways by states practicing the social market and organized capitalism. In the terms used by Richard Rosecrance, it will be led not by the "military-political state" but by the "trading state."[13] The next stage of history will also be a return to history, to an era when Germany and Japan were leading powers and Mitteleuropa and East Asia were leading regions of the world.

It seems, then, that the Cold War was the era of the military-political state, whose exemplars were the Soviet Union and the United States, and that the period after the Cold War might be the era of the trading state, whose exemplars are Germany and Japan (just as they were the exemplars of the military-political state in the era of the Great Depression and World War II). With the unification of Germany and with the end of the Soviet Union, Germany became the third largest economy in the world, following the United States and Japan. Germany is now the major power in Europe, Japan the major power in Asia, and the two together the major powers in Eurasia.

The New Russia in the New Eurasia

Lying between Germany and Japan are the ruins of the Soviet Union: an impoverished Russia surrounded by a slew of poor, weak states. But this mendicant Russia, like its superpower predecessor, still possesses more than 20,000 nuclear warheads.

The Soviet Union clearly was the big loser of the Cold War. While Germany achieved union, the Soviet Union underwent disunion. The Soviet government lost the old Eastern Europe, which has become the new Central Europe, and the old Warsaw Pact, which has become a new cordon sanitaire. It then lost the new Eastern Europe, which was Soviet Europe (Estonia, Latvia, Lithuania, the western portion of the Ukraine, and Moldavia), and finally the Soviet Union itself. In December 1991, the Soviet Union broke down into its component national parts, like the Russian Empire for a few years (1918–1921) after the Russian Revolution and the treaty of Brest-Litovsk. After the dust has settled, what will the new Russia look like? One possibility, the benign one, is that Russia will remain economically dependent on the democratic and capitalist states, especially on a Europe guided by Germany, and that it will develop some form of democratic political system and market economy. Russia would be something like a larger Poland or perhaps a colder Brazil.

Another possibility, a malign one, is more in keeping with Russian history, however. There will remain in the middle of Eurasia the same irreducible mass that has existed many times in the past—a Russian state, most likely ruled by a populist or an authoritarian regime, inspired by a nationalist ideology, capable of only a closed and controlled economy, and still possessing the largest army in the world and more than 20,000 nuclear warheads. A brief period of Weimar Russia will be followed by a more permanent period of national-socialist Russia (with the *n* and *s* in lowercase, however). Such a Russia would likely bring into being a new Cold War (more precisely, the Third Cold War, after the First Cold War of circa 1945–1965 and the Second Cold War of circa 1979–1985). This new Cold War between Russia and Europe would not look much like the earlier Cold War between the Soviet Union and the West. But the most important of the old familiar features—ideological conflict, containment policy, nuclear deterrence, and credible response—would again be there.

The New United States in the New Global Market

The United States clearly is not a military-political state in the same sense as was the Soviet Union. However, it is not a trading state in the sense that Germany and Japan are. What it has become is something else, that is, a postindustrial economy based on financial operations and service occupations rather than on industrial production. A postindustrial country, even if it is the leading power, is not the same thing as a postindustrial world, however. The world will continue to have industrial countries existing along with postindustrial countries.

When certain countries (for example, Britain) became industrial (and postagricultural) economies, it did not mean that the world became postagricultural. Indeed, there was an even greater demand for agricultural commodities than before (fibers for industrial products, food for industrial workers), except that now these items were supplied by the most efficient producers in a global market (for example, the United States). Similarly, when certain countries (for example, the United States) become service or financial (postindustrial) economies, there is an even greater demand for industrial products than before, and these products, too, are supplied by the most efficient producers in a global market. The countries in which efficient industrial production takes place are well known: Japan and the newly industrializing countries, or "little tigers," of East Asia; and Germany and the specialty countries or "niche-occupiers" of Western Europe.

These efficient producers and success stories in the global market have received a good deal of attention from social scientists, who have sought to define their distinctive nature. In addition to being called "trading states" as opposed to "military-political states" (Richard Rosecrance), they have also been termed "corporatist states" as opposed to "liberal states" (Peter Katzenstein), "strong states" as opposed to "weak states" (Stephen Krasner), and "late developers" as opposed to "early developers" (Alexander Gerschenkron). Each of these terms captures an aspect of the distinctive nature of these states. Most of these states also happen to be the clearest examples of the nation-state in the world today. It turns out that the most successful competitors in the global market of the postindustrial era are nation-states, a distinctive creation of the industrial era,[14] providing yet another chapter, on a higher stage, of the well-known saga of "the advantages of backwardness."

It is a saga in which Germany and Japan, the perfect nation-states, have been the leading characters for a century, and characters with dual personalities and dual capabilities at that. In the 1940s, the term "trading state" would not have been the first to come to mind when one thought of Germany and Japan. "Military-political state" would have been more like it. But in the 1920s Germany and Japan were widely recognized as highly efficient industrial producers and traders. And in the 1900s Germany and Japan were widely recognized as highly efficient in both industrial production and military operations.

The United States seems to be a case of the disadvantages of forwardness. In addition to being a postindustrial economy, it is the prototypical postmodern society and even postliterate culture. The United States is also no longer a nation-state. Perhaps it never really was one. In any event, since the 1960s it has steadily become less a nation and more a multicultural society. It also has steadily become less a state and more a divided and stalemated government. The United States is now a multicultural society with a divided government led by a political class whose interests are as much international as they are national. It is not a nation-state but a multicultural regime. This postindustrial, postmodern, postliterate, and postnational United States, however, will probably still have a role to play in international security. Indeed, it may be the only international role it will be able to play at all. What will this role look like in the post–Cold War world?

MITTELEUROPA AND EAST ASIA IN THE NEW WORLD ORDER: THE SECURITY ROLE OF THE UNITED STATES

If the benign possibility regarding Russia—that is, existing in cooperative association with Europe—develops, the United States will no longer be so necessary for European, including German, security. How, then, will Germany and Mitteleuropa fit into the New World Order, particularly into its old institutions of NATO and GATT?

A Return to the Original NATO

The departure of Russian troops from German territory will probably be followed by the departure of American troops from German territory, as well. But Germany and Mitteleuropa will still want some residual security, some insurance, against potential conflicts with a still unstable and unpredictable Russia.

The most stable equilibrium would be gained through nuclear deterrence provided by U.S. naval forces stationed in the waters around Europe, perhaps supplemented by other U.S. military forces based in Britain. This nuclear protectorate could be organized within a NATO framework in which the U.S. security role was more like that in the original NATO of 1949–1951, that is, an Atlantic alliance centered on U.S. nuclear and naval forces, rather than the NATO since 1951, which has been an integrated organization centered on national ground forces under the overall command of an American general.

A Voyage to Post-Vietnam East Asia

This redefinition of the possible U.S. security role with regard to Germany and Europe would have much in common with the U.S. security role with regard to Japan and much of East Asia since the end of the Vietnam War. In the East Asia of recent years, as in the Mitteleuropa of the future, there has been little expectation of either an invasion by Soviet ground forces or (Korea apart) the use of American ground forces. Rather, U.S. nuclear and naval forces have provided insurance against unspecified but potentially disastrous events. Of course, U.S. military forces may not be based in Germany in the future; even in Japan, however, they were never based in the region (Hokkaido) closest to the Soviet Union and thus most subject to Soviet invasion. There was no "forward strategy," "flexible-response doctrine," or "nuclear trip-wire" in Japan as there was in West Germany (and, to a large degree, in South Korea). But it is precisely these features of the U.S. security role that have now disappeared in united Germany.

The malign possibility—of an authoritarian, autarkic, nationalist, and heavily armed Russia—would lead to a new Cold War, as I have noted. It would lead also to a renewed recognition of the need for a U.S. security role. What this role would be in the new Europe remains clouded, given the vast changes that have already occurred with the revolution in Eastern Europe, the unification of Germany, the dissolution of the Warsaw Pact, and the dissolution of the Soviet Union itself. However, what this role would be in the new East Asia is easier to discern, given that the new East Asia would not be that different from the old.

There has been no East Asian counterpart to the unification of Germany or the dissolution of the Warsaw Pact, and the East Asian counterpart of the East European revolution has been the Mongolian revolution, such as it is. As for the dissolution of the Soviet Union itself, what is momentous when viewed from Europe is marginal when viewed from East Asia. Europe now borders on seven former Soviet republics; East Asia borders on only one—Russia itself. In East Asia the Third Cold War would look much like the Second.

A Grand German-American Bargain:
NATO for GATT

What could be the incentives for the United States to assume the burden of providing a nuclear deterrent for German economic hegemony in Mitteleuropa? One incentive might simply be the inertia of military and security institutions, such as NATO, that could carry the old nuclear deterrent for West Germany during the Cold War into the new conditions of united Germany in the post–Cold War era. Institutional inertia can explain a great deal about international security, including U.S. military bases and defense spending for East Asia, as well as for Europe.

In addition, however, there have emerged the elements of a grand bargain between economic and political leaders in the United States and their counterparts in Germany, a bargain comparable to the prior one between economic and political leaders in the United States and Japan. The bargain involves the economic dimension as well as the security dimension—the GATT institution as well as the NATO institution—of the liberal international order. At the same time (1989–1990) that the United States strongly supported the unification of Germany, it hoped and expected that Germany would strongly support a continued American economic presence in the European Community. The 1992 deadline and the prospect of a unified Community excluding American corporations, banks, and products have wonderfully concentrated the minds of American economic and political leaders. The East European revolution and the prospect of new market economies, in which the United States could easily lose out to German competition, have concentrated the minds of these leaders even more. With German support rather than opposition, however, the prospects become brighter. The American economic presence in the new European Community and in the new Mitteleuropa would not be nearly as prominent as the German presence, but it would be substantial and profitable nonetheless. The obvious bargain to be struck is for American economic and political leaders to continue to support a U.S. nuclear deterrent for Europe while their German counterparts support an American economic presence in Europe.

FOUR CONCEPTS OF SECURITY

These speculations about the possible U.S. security role in the future lead to more systematical consideration of four different concepts of international security: (1) collective security, (2) comprehensive security, (3) common security, and (4) compound security.

The American Concept: Collective Security

Since World War I the American conception of international security has been collective security, successively expressed in the League of Nations (abortive), the United Nations (paralyzed), and the North Atlantic Treaty Organization (partial but successful). In practice, collective security has worked only when the United States performed the leading, even hegemonic, role and provided a core of military power. By definition, collective security is founded on extended deterrence; the core power must extend its military guarantee to cover the lesser and peripheral states. Extended deterrence in turn requires credibility, which is buttressed with such doctrines and devices as treaty commitments, forward defense, flexible response, and nuclear trip-wires. Collective security is clearly security as defined by a military-political state.

The United States created collective security in Europe, where, as NATO, it fit and functioned rather well. The United States then attempted to extend it to East Asia, where it fit awkwardly (the Southeast Asia Treaty Organization [SEATO]) or not at all (Northeast Asia) and functioned poorly (Korea) or disastrously (Vietnam). What has remained of U.S. collective security in East Asia is a series of bilateral security treaties, extended deterrence, and credibility. But because a Soviet blitzkrieg in East Asia was always less probable and more likely to be defeated than it was in Europe, the buttressing devices for credibility were not really necessary.

The Japanese Concept: Comprehensive Security

The misfit of the American concept in the East Asian context has encouraged the Japanese, as in so many other areas, to invent a better product—in this case, the concept of comprehensive security. After World War II Japan was largely permanently demilitarized, as expressed in the famous Article 9 of its new constitution. Because Japan could no longer provide for its own security with its own military, it had to construct a functional equivalent with a combination of U.S. military power, its own economic power, and in cases where neither of these was very useful (for example, the Middle East), its own low-posture diplomacy. This comprehensive combination has become the concept of comprehensive security, but the core of comprehensive security has been economic power. Comprehensive security is clearly security as defined by a trading state.

Within the framework of comprehensive security, the concept of finite deterrence, rather than extended deterrence, can be reasonable. Because of its insular geography, Japan has been a much less likely target of Soviet attack than was West Germany and, more generally, Western Europe. The problem of deterrence of Soviet military aggression against Japan has been more soluble and the solution more stable than was the case with Europe.

Of course, finite deterrence for Japan could not include reliance on a national nuclear force (unlike China and France, which have developed their own versions of finite deterrence). The nuclear explosions over Hiroshima and Nagasaki produced in Japan an enduring nuclear allergy, so it is likely that there will be no Japanese nuclear deterrent. Further, Japanese finite deterrence would really be extended deterrence, that is, it would have to be extended beyond the national territory to include South Korea. But this action would nevertheless represent extension only into a rather small country against a rather small adversary, North Korea. South Korea is now a plausible target only of a North Korean attack.

The European-Left Concept: Common Security

The Japanese concept of comprehensive security can be compared with a concept developed in the 1980s by the left in Europe and especially in West Germany, that is, the concept of common security. The core component of common security is economic interdependence; the military component is "defensive defense"; and the workings of the economic and military components are supplemented and smoothed by an emphasis on a diplomacy of consultations and consensus.

It is one thing to adhere to comprehensive security when one is the most successful trading state in the world, as well as being an island country. It would be quite another thing to adhere to common security when one is living on the same continent not only with other trading states but with the Soviet Union or even Russia, which remains the largest military-political state in the world. It is not surprising that before the fall of the Berlin Wall the West German government did not adopt the security definition of the West German left. If the new united Germany had to deal only with the states of Mitteleuropa, however, a redefinition in the direction of comprehensive or common security likely would occur. Because a united Germany will have to deal also with a still unstable and unpredictable Russia, however, the need for some features of collective security and extended deterrence will remain.

The Japanese-American Reality: Compound Security

The actual result in Europe might be a combination or compound of comprehensive and collective, trading-state and military-political state, definitions of security. As I have suggested, this concept of compound security would have at its core German economic power and U.S. nuclear and naval forces. As such, it becomes clear that the concept of compound security has long been expressed in the actual practice of Japanese-American security relations, where Japan carries out its trading-state activities within the military-political framework provided by the United States. But the end of the Soviet threat to Japan may permit the Japanese to reduce their reliance on U.S. military forces. The result could be a shift from compound security to comprehensive security proper.

Conclusion: The End of Security?

The revolution in Eastern Europe, the collapse of the Warsaw Pact, and the end of the Soviet Union meant the end of a fifth concept of security—the Soviet concept of coercive security. This great transformation likely will bring about the redefinition of security for other powers and other regions. For Germany and much of Europe the likely redefinition will be from collective security to compound security. For Japan and some of East Asia the likely redefinition will be from compound to comprehensive security. For the United States the likely refocus will be from continental strategy to maritime strategy, but the definition of security as collective security will likely persist. And for Russia, the likely redefinition will be from coercive security to very little security, and very little definition, at all. But in the longer run, as for much of the twentieth century, a Russia that has very little security means that the rest of us will have very little, as well.

4

TAMING OF POWER

German Unification, 1989–1990

In thinking about Germany the past as prelude evokes, at best, an ambivalent reaction.[1] Most Germans and their neighbors view modern German history as an enormous disaster for Germany and for Europe. Germany's Faustian bargaining with modern technology was sealed during the empire and became the basis for a reckless policy of aiming to establish German hegemony over Europe. The result was Germany's second Thirty Years' War (1914–1945), interrupted by an armistice during the "golden twenties." As was the case in the seventeenth century, Germany was totally shattered by the war. The genocide and militarism of its totalitarian regime were so evil in intent and so horrible in consequence that any repetition of this German past is dreaded by Germany's neighbors and by the Germans themselves.

But other parts of the German past, both distant and recent, are a source of hope for the future. The German states were centers of culture in the Augustan age of modern Germany in the eighteenth century. In the nineteenth century German science and technology flourished in a university system that was among the best in the world. And the Weimar Republic, for a brief period, succeeded in making Berlin and Germany a vibrant center of European culture. These strands of German history make the prospect of a second coming of Central Europe deeply appealing.

This chapter presents a disagreement with these two views of German history. The relevant past that helps us to interpret the unification process and assess its likely consequences is the recent past. The German revolution of 1989 and German unification in 1990 point to the importance of discontinuities rather than continuities in modern German history. The effects of the Nazi regime and the loss of World War II were profound. And so were the effects of the integration of the two Germanies into two hostile blocs led after 1949 by the United States and the Soviet Union. These forces have had a very deep effect on the political structures and practices of contemporary Germany and are likely to continue to do so for some time.

German unification in 1990 resulted from a combination of domestic and international forces shaping German, European, and international politics. The strategic retreat of the Soviet Union from Central Europe was an event of decisive importance that paved the way for German unity. But the events of 1990 were also shaped by the fact that Chancellor Helmut Kohl and Foreign Minister Hans Dietrich Genscher wagered everything on early unification. The chancellor, in particular, had grasped early on that the basic decision for unity was being made by 16 million East Germans rather than 60 million West Germans. And in international affairs it was clear to both men that the growing instabilities in Soviet domestic politics were opening a brief window of opportunity for unity in 1990 that a subsequent reversal of reform policies in the Soviet Union might quickly close. The Social Democratic party (SPD) candidate for chancellor, Oskar LaFontaine, in contrast, believed that the hesitation of 60 million West Germans would outweigh the vote for unification by 16 million East Germans. Honed to the postnationalist era of the West European integration process, his political instincts were simply insufficient to appreciate the short-term intensity of German nationalism. And LaFontaine had little understanding of the severity of the nationality conflict in the Soviet Union and its likely consequences for Soviet domestic and foreign policy. The policies of the Christian Democratic Union/Christian Social Union–Free Democratic party (FDP) coalition government thus were important for Germany's unification in hastening the strategic retreat of the Soviet Union from Central Europe.

This confluence of international and domestic factors in 1990 has been characteristic of Germany's position in Europe and of German foreign policy since 1949. Konrad Adenauer's successful policy of Western integration in the early 1950s agreed with the political realities of the Cold War. But would Adenauer have seen these realities without the Western orientation that he acquired in his distinguished political career in local politics during the Weimar Republic? Similarly, the success of Willy Brandt's Eastern policy depended on the climate of détente between the United States and the Soviet Union in the late 1960s. But would Brandt have developed his strong Eastern political sensibilities without his career as mayor of the besieged city of West Berlin? With a few years' delay the SPD in the 1950s and the CDU/CSU in the 1970s adjusted to the new political realities created by this interaction between foreign and domestic policy. The SPD will undoubtedly also soon adjust to the political realities of the 1990s.

The end of the Cold War and Germany's rapid unification pose three important questions. Why is it implausible to make the case for long-term continuities in German history, whether for ill or for good, the baseline from which to evaluate German unification in 1989–1990? Secondly, which political structures have developed in West Germany since 1949? How much will these structures be altered in a united Germany? Finally, how has the Federal Republic evolved in the international system since 1949 and how will its international position change in the coming years? I shall try to answer each of these questions in the following four sections of this chapter before reaching some tentative conclusions in the final section.

THE GERMAN PAST AS PRELUDE?

John Mearsheimer's essay, "Why We Will Soon Miss the Cold War," interprets Germany's position in Europe in structural rather than historical terms.[2] Mearsheimer is a pessimist. The withdrawal of the armed forces of the United States and the Soviet Union from Central Europe and from the brink of a nuclear confrontation made possible by German unification, he argues, is not moving Europe forward to 1992 but back to 1912. The long peace of the Cold War was artificially imposed on an inherently war-prone Europe. Because it is too strong for Europe and because of the existential insecurities that exist in an anarchic international system, Germany must acquire nuclear weapons to assure its security. Backed by its new military might German economic expansion will eventually translate into old territorial demands, first directed at Poland and eventually perhaps also at other Central or West European states. For international conflict and war are a constant in history. "Without a common Soviet threat or an American night watchman, Western European states will do what they did for centuries before the onset of the Cold War—look upon one another with abiding suspicion."[3] States cannot learn. They are condemned to repeat their national catastrophes. For Mearsheimer German unification in 1990 is the opening chapter of the third edition of the German Catastrophe.[4]

This prediction is not due to any political attribute of the Germans themselves or their politics. Indeed, Mearsheimer, a military strategist, downgrades the importance of German or European politics. He has no interest in the character of the international society of states. Multipolarity in the 1890s is for him the same thing as multipolarity in the 1990s. What matters to him is a parsimonious, deductive theory of international politics that abstracts from the social characteristics of states and the environment in which they act.

The breakup of a bipolar world that is a probable consequence of German unification and the return to multipolarity will greatly enhance the risk of war in Europe. Mearsheimer recognizes that factors, such as nuclear weapons, also influence whether states choose peace or war. Indeed, with the spread of ethnic conflict in Eastern Europe and the former Soviet Union his theory predicts that a united Germany will feel so threatened in an unstable Europe that it will acquire a national nuclear capability, as is becoming to an important power in a multipolar world. To preempt this unavoidable German yearning for security and stability in an insecure and unstable multipolar world, Mearsheimer recommends a policy of "well-managed proliferation."[5] He advocates giving the Germans access to nuclear weapons within a political framework that is less destabilizing, both politically and militarily, than the mad rush to a first-strike capability that would ensue in a Europe seething with ethnic conflicts and a Germany arming with nuclear weapons.

Mearsheimer's essay is brilliantly wrongheaded. His austere sense of what makes for social science theory leads him to empty the categories of his analysis of all social and political content. The state actors moving around in his abstract systemic structures are little automata, programmed to achieve only one overriding objective—the minimization of insecurity in an insecure world through military means. Properties of the international state system are postulated to have effects on actors that the actors themselves can interpret in only one way. But what happens if on account of their past experiences Germans think of security not only in military terms? To the extent that the Germans themselves do not feel as insecure as the structural theory of international politics predicts, according to Mearsheimer, we are dealing not with a distinctive national practice in the system of international self-help but with the inevitable lags in human consciousness that need time to adjust to the new structural imperatives of a multipolar world.

Mearsheimer's argument is not new. It is, however, startling in the boldness with which it claims that structures determine, rather than help shape, policy choices. And it is notable for the brashness with which it moves from theory construction to policy prescription. Critics were quick to point out that in the Cold War bipolarity itself may have been less important than the effects of nuclear weapons, the character of the two superpowers, or a host of other variables, some of which Mearsheimer considers in the development of his argument.[6] I am agnostic about the empirical validity of Mearsheimer's theoretical claims, which, as he readily acknowledges, have not yet been tested against a comprehensive survey of multipolar and bipolar systems in history.[7] It is particularly difficult to support these claims empirically for the period after 1945 for the simple reason that we have had only one bipolar system with nuclear weapons in history. How to disentangle what may be parallel, moderating effects is a difficult problem.

But we are safe to conclude that without knowledge of the actors and the stakes involved in international conflicts it is impossible to deduce anything sufficiently concrete from structural theories to warrant Mearsheimer's policy prescriptions. An exclusive focus on the character of international structures is unlikely to illuminate the likely future of Germany and Europe as long as no attention is paid to the character of German and European politics.[8] Important domestic reasons that propelled Germany and European societies toward war in the nineteenth century—territorial ambition, irredentist nationalism, autonomous militaries, archaic social structures coupled with rapid social changes, and a tradition of authoritarian forms of politics—characterize parts of Central and Eastern Europe as well as the former Soviet Union and are a likely breeding ground for war and dislocation just as Mearsheimer predicts.[9] But the social and political attributes of these societies are likely to be more important than the effects of multipolarity in determining the choice for war or peace. International structure by itself is inadequate as a determinant.

Western Europe and Germany differ from Central and Eastern Europe. They have substituted a demand of access to markets for territorial ambitions, a nationalism of·social entitlement for irredentism, internationally constrained militaries for autonomous militaries, modern social structures and slow social changes for archaic social structures and rapid social changes, and a democratic for an authoritarian politics. Most importantly, only a small segment of German national conservatives see German national security enhanced by nuclear weapons. The broad social and political consensus in Germany has learned from the disasters of two lost wars that the search for international, political solutions rather than national, military solutions serves German security interests best. And there is nothing in the history of either the post–World War II world or the post-reunification world that dissuades most Germans from that view.

It is, of course, conceivable that Mearsheimer's pessimism will in the end be born out by future events. German interest in nuclear weapons is affected not only by what the Germans wish but by what the Russians, Americans, French, and British do. But what does "in the end" mean concretely? The Cold War is not yet really over and, according to Mearsheimer's theoretical arguments, probably will not end in Europe for quite some time.[10] There is, after all, widespread agreement on both sides of the Atlantic on keeping some American military presence on the European continent for the foreseeable future—according to Mearsheimer, a legacy of the Cold War; and Russia as the successor to the Soviet Union will remain a military superpower in Europe. The deductive rigor of the theory and its ahistorical character thus are quite likely to make it very difficult to test its claims empirically. Furthermore, for a theory designed to cover centuries, lack of empirical support during a few decades is a matter of little consequence.

Other difficulties arise in testing this structural theory. For such a theory is cast in terms of comparative statics. For the period of transition from one international system to another history will have an effect on actors making choices in emerging political structures. Political behavior not attuned to the logic of the emerging multipolar world may well be "dysfunctional" and, as Mearsheimer and other realists claim, subject the actor to eventual extinction. But much depends on the length of the transition and the political experiences actors have. If Germany were to succeed in its foreign policy objectives without acquiring nuclear weapons in the coming years, it would not only shape the future behavior of German governments, it would also alter the character of the emerging international system. The political dynamics of a period of transition, that is, have an effect on international structures that structural theory does not capture. Structural analysis cast in the terms of comparative statics is ill suited to capture dynamic political processes.

Confronted with individual and social learning and adaptation in history, Mearsheimer himself recognizes in the end that structural theory is reduced to possibilistic and "soft" rather than deterministic and "hard" projections of the future. "Is it not possible, for example, that German thinking about the benefits of controlling Eastern Europe will change markedly once American forces are withdrawn from Central Europe and the Germans are left to provide for their own security? Is it not possible that they would countenance a conventional war against a substantially weaker Eastern European state to enhance their position vis-à-vis the Soviet Union? Finally only one country need decide that war is thinkable to make war possible."[11]

Everything is indeed possible. Individuals or collectivities will learn lessons from the past and adapt to new circumstances. They may learn the wrong lessons and adapt unsuccessfully. We can move from possibilistic to probabilistic reasoning only by including in the analysis the very aspects that Mearsheimer's parsimonious structural theory deliberately neglects: the qualities of states and the domestic and international social context in which they act.

There is a final ambiguity in Mearsheimer's analysis. Structural theory predicts that after the end of the Cold War European states will try to fashion a balance of power. It does not predict how they will define such a balance of power. Mearsheimer assumes that Germany will try to counterbalance France and thus bring about the breakup of the EC; Kenneth Waltz assumes that Europe as a whole will try to counterbalance the United States.[12] In either case, predictions about the direction of the balancing behavior are based on the application of structural theorizing, that is, knowledge of political context and content. They do not inhere in the structural theory of international politics, which is entirely free of empirical content. This ambiguity is the unavoidable price that structuralism pays for its theoretical parsimony.

Another variant of structuralism leads to a less gloomy view of the future and to more plausible policy conclusions, perhaps because it is less abstract. In a brief rebuttal of his critics Mearsheimer articulates this view. It does not look to the distribution of capabilities as the sole cause of peace and war. Instead, Mearsheimer writes, "If the Germans cause trouble in the new Europe, it will not be a consequence of peculiar aggressive traits. Germans are *not* born to aggress. An acute sense of insecurity is instead likely to be the source of trouble. The root causes of it will be Germany's exposed location in the center of the Continent and its non-nuclear status."[13] In a brilliant book published in 1978 David Calleo developed this geostrategic thesis (a style of analysis represented in this volume also by Valerie Bunce and Michael Loriaux) that its geographic position in the center of Europe and the fear of a two-front war rather than any inherent German attributes were the main cause for Germany's aggressive and illiberal political tendencies. Surrounded by strong neighbors and with few natural barriers to invasion, Germany's geography, not polarity, determined policy.[14] I have argued elsewhere that Calleo's argument, though brilliant in conception and development, fails to account for very important aspects of German policy and politics.[15] But toward the end of his book Calleo holds forth the prospect of a European solution to the German problem in a more plural world, a view that is theoretically less rigorous than Mearsheimer's but that is empirically more plausible.

Other observers of German unification have not looked to the international structures that shape Germany but instead to attributes of Germans and Germany. During the months in which the German unification process unfolded, the "past as prelude" was a theme that reverberated through the German, European, and American press. The German left viewed unification as a mixed blessing at best. It had never been seriously interested in real socialism in the German Democratic Republic (GDR). But the crumbling of socialism in the GDR and throughout Central and Eastern Europe expressed a fundamental change in the world that Marxist categories trained on a crisis-ridden system of capitalism did not accommodate easily. Furthermore, the fear spread quickly that German nationalism might again become a political force for mass mobilization and the revival of a neo-Nazi movement, especially in newly liberated East Germany. Furthermore, critics from the left felt ill at ease with the takeover of an entire country by the two most powerful institutions of West Germany, the political parties and the deutsche mark. As had been true of the wars leading to Germany's unification in 1871, the peaceful unification of 1989–1990 threatened to install for a generation a conservative government under whose auspices unification had occurred.

In Europe the quiet unease that existed in many quarters was expressed most clearly by Nicholas Ridley, then British secretary of state for industry. In an interview that eventually cost him his job, Ridley articulated the deep fears of a united Germany that were apparently shared by a sizable segment of the Tories, including Margaret Thatcher.[16] Former NATO Secretary Joseph Luns warned in a similar vein that a united Germany might once again become a threat to Europe: "Ridley said out loud what many Europeans think. We all know about the German character, don't we? Germans naturally become a little arrogant when they are powerful."[17] Similar views were published also in American newspapers. Leopold Bellak, for example, argued that he fears Germans because they abuse their children more often than do parents in other societies, and these children grow up to become aggressive adults who cannot be trusted to be peaceful.[18]

Other observers, however, drawing on other strains of the German past are less pessimistic. In Chapter 3 of this volume, for example, James Kurth invokes Mitteleuropa as a new paradigm for a global politics that will take on a more distinct regional form. "This Mitteleuropa project," writes Kurth, "might recapitulate the economic goals and methods of the German industrial and financial conservatives from the 1880s to the 1930s and the political goals and methods of the German Social Democrats of the 1920s and the 1940s to the 1980s. . . . The new Central Europe will become rather like the old Central Europe, Mitteleuropa. . . . The German conception of the international economy will become primarily a continental, rather than a global, one." In Kurth's view the social teaching of the Catholic church provides the basis for an ideological consensus that has united Christian and Social Democrats in Germany and Austria and that offers to do the same throughout Central Europe with consequences that will affect global politics.

There is a world of difference between these two styles of analysis that focus on the characteristics of Germans and Germany. Psychoanalyzing the Germans and inferring political consequences from some assumed typical trait, such as the tendency toward child abuse, makes for good copy on the op-ed page of a national newspaper. But in the social sciences it is risky business and fraught with difficult and often insurmountable problems of evidence and inference. Analyzing, as does Kurth, the institutions, ideologies, and political practices of Germany and Central Europe is a more likely source of insight into the future.

But the two styles of analysis share a characteristic that offers a dubious basis for an analysis of possible German and Central European futures. They underestimate the effect of change, especially the change since 1949. We know, for example, from survey data that the political culture of Germany has changed substantially since the early 1960s.[19] This change is mirrored not only in the revival of democracy in schools and in local politics but also in numerous citizen initiatives and social movements at all levels of politics in the 1970s and 1980s. In politics, as in other spheres of German life, it makes little sense therefore to stipulate a fixed German character that predisposes Germany toward aggressive, overbearing, and militarist patterns of behavior.[20] The Gulf War, for example, illustrated in 1991 a deep ambivalence about Germany's participation in a multinational military force, even though that force was sanctioned by the United Nations. Apparently Germans have been affected deeply by the loss of World War II and the successful, and at times unsavory, policies of a trading state. German confusion was perhaps greatest when it became clear that German firms secretly had been deeply involved in helping equip the Iraqi armed forces with advanced weapons technologies. Meanwhile the German government was very slow to meet, in a halfhearted way, its obligation to render assistance to its NATO ally, Turkey.

Kurth's argument presumes a future that extends directly the institutions and practices of the Central European past. From Berlin financial conservatives will spin a web of bilateral relations; Social Democrats will adhere to the Keynesian prescriptions that characterized their policies between the 1940s and 1980s; Central Europe will embody Germany's return to a continental vision of the international economy; and the Catholic church will offer moral cement for the social-market economy as a viable "third way" in Central Europe.

These arguments neglect the changes that have transformed Germany since 1949 and make the prospects of European regionalism quite different from the version that Kurth extracts from the past. Bilateralism will be an important element of the new links forged between German corporations and those in Central and Eastern Europe. But multilateralism is likely to be an attractive method in Germany's relationships with Central and Eastern Europe. It diversifies economic risks and minimizes political exposure. Social Democrats and Germany's strong unions may continue to adhere to the Keynesian paradigm but, even if in power, they will lack the resources to finance their version of a "grand bargain" in Central Europe. The capital requirements for reforming East Germany (estimated roughly at 1 trillion deutsche marks during the decade of the 1990s) will strain German capital markets. It is difficult to conceive of a political scenario in which German Social Democrats would provide a multiple of that sum in order to help reform the economies of Central and Eastern Europe. Furthermore, as the second largest exporter in the world in 1989 German business has an overwhelming interest in the richest and most rapidly growing markets. These markets exist not in Central and Eastern Europe but in Western Europe, the United States, and Asia. And the German social-market economy and welfare state, shaped in part by the doctrines of Catholic social reformers in the nineteenth century, are unlikely to be affected by a Catholic church that has been on the political defensive in West Germany for a

generation. Instead these institutions will evolve under the impact of national and supranational policies responding to the changing requirements of international competitiveness and political balances of power in
national and international affairs.

In recent years German historians have had sharp debates about the
past.[21] I argue that an interpretation of the events of 1989–1990 should turn
to Germany's most recent past as a prelude to its future. The sharp break in
German history in 1945 and the relative longevity of the Federal Republic
makes this argument compelling. The loss of World War II, the division of
Germany, and the strong influence that the United States and the Soviet
Union exercised over the shape of West and East Germany reduced or
eliminated altogether the premodern social structures that Thorsten
Veblen, Joseph Schumpeter, Eckart Kehr, and Barrington Moore, among
others, had singled out as a major factor in the authoritarian and militarist
policy and politics of Germany.[22] And the institutional features of postwar
West Germany created a predilection for incremental and gradual political
and economic change that made any dramatic policy change highly unlikely.[23] Germany's return to the risky foreign policy experimentation of
prior German regimes, as Mearsheimer correctly points out, was made impossible by the Cold War that massed hundreds of thousands of foreign
troops and thousands of tactical nuclear weapons on German soil. The institutionalization of a new type of politics and the implantation of a new
world view thus could proceed to gather strength for decades. For we tend
to forget too quickly that the forty years' history of the Federal Republic is
about three times longer than the history of either the Nazi government
(1933–1945) or the Weimar Republic (1919–1933). Specific features of the
international system and distinctive features of Germany's domestic
structures after 1949, as well as the world views that these features helped
create and sustain, are the factors that make the past most relevant as a
prelude for Germany's future.

THE TAMING OF POWER
IN GERMANY'S DOMESTIC POLITICS

Scholarly and journalistic assessments of the character of modern Germany have been remarkably consensual compared, for example, to the
sharp divergences in American interpretations of Japanese or Soviet domestic politics. The major interpretations differ only on questions of detail.[24] The political structures and processes that have evolved in West
Germany are distinguished by the central fact that power has been tamed.
The important political actors—parties, the state bureaucracy, interest
groups, the federal reserve, individual states, the supreme court, and the

media, among others—through a variety of political institutions and practices, are so closely tied to one another that it is rare for them to develop autonomous political strategies for large-scale political change. Chained to important actors and institutions, political adversaries in domestic politics can take only small steps.

This taming of political power in domestic affairs characterizes not only West German politics since 1945 but is also typical of the small, rich states in northwest Europe. The system of social partnership and a thick web of institutions and practices facilitate trade-offs between different issues in economic and social policy in a system of democratic corporatism. These social and political arrangements are not well known in other countries, such as the United States, Britain, Japan, and France.[25] Despite some notable differences, among all of the larger industrial states German domestic politics shows the greatest affinity with the politics of democratic corporatism.

This characterization is true not only of everyday politics. Even important West German reform policies are normally broken down into smaller parts and then adjusted significantly before they become politically viable. Basic reorientations in policy thus have typically been no more than minor alterations. The policy of "domestic reform" that the SPD-FDP coalition championed in the early 1970s and the "big change" that the CDU/CSU-FDP coalition advocated in the early 1980s did offer some modest policy changes. But these changes simply fell short of the high expectations raised by the political rhetoric in the electoral competitions between the major parties. Compared to the Reagan revolution in the United States, Thatcherism in Britain, experimentation with socialist and social democratic policies in France, and important rationalizations in Japan's public sector, West German politics in the 1980s were marked by great continuity. Basic innovations in West German politics have occurred only twice since 1949. In the early years of the Federal Republic the government made a number of basic policy decisions that had a lasting effect. And between 1966 and 1969 the CDU/CSU-SPD Great Coalition did pass several important reform proposals that had been blocked for a long time.

Will politics in a unified Germany introduce substantial changes in policy, as was true in the years 1949–1953 and 1966–1969? Or will power continue to be tamed as was true throughout most of West Germany's history? The politics of unification in 1990 were characterized by what appeared to be an inexorable extension of West German institutions, norms and practices into East Germany. The *Anschluß* (annexation) of the GDR amounts to an enlargement of the Federal Republic rather than a basic alteration in Germany's political arrangement. The political parties, the big interest groups, the federal reserve, the institution of federalism, the court system, the education system, cultural affairs, and media are all "made in West Germany" rather than in "united Germany."

It would, however, be a serious mistake to think that the Federal Republic will have as easy a time in digesting the territories of the former GDR as it had in swallowing them. New problems and institutions may still end up making the united Germany quite different from its West German predecessor. For example, the German government took over a parapublic organization created by the German Democratic Republic in 1989, the Treuhand, charged with the privatization of about 10,000 East German firms. Its mission is to operate for about five years before liquidating all unsold firms as well as itself. This is the official scenario. Equally plausible is the expectation of the long-term existence of a very large bureaucracy running parts of the East German economy. A German version of Italy's impoverished Mezzogiorno region and a German version of Italy's Institute for Industrial Reconstruction would surely alter Germany's federalism, its regional policy, and its stance in European and international negotiations. Furthermore, the new German (old West German) institutions will pose for all East Germans, and thus for all Germans, questions of identity that may facilitate a broadening of the political spectrum and a deepening of experimentation with new policies (in local and regional politics as well as through social movements). Feminist and environmental social movements have already experienced this phenomenon firsthand. However, this development began in West Germany in the 1970s and gained strength in the 1980s. Such a development, should it materialize, thus would not be a product only of the unification process of 1990.

THE INTERNATIONAL POSITION OF GERMANY

The concept of the taming of power is also useful for labeling important developments in the evolution of West Germany's international position. For good reasons West Germany has been described as a country that, to an unusual degree, is penetrated by international structures. What a prominent American specialist of West German foreign policy called a "penetrated system," West German scholars have dubbed the "entanglement" of West Germany in its international setting.[26] Regardless of the particular way in which scholars have described this political condition, there exists virtual unanimity on one point. West Germany's rearmament within the context of the Western alliance and the European integration process have embedded the Federal Republic much more deeply in the international state system than was true of various German regimes before 1945.

The Western Alliance

West Germany's rearmament in NATO and under direct NATO supervision was the result of a policy that had two aims. It sought both to protect Western Europe from an attack by the Soviet Union and to prevent the emergence of a politically autonomous West German military.[27] These have been the basic premises of Western security policy since 1949. Forward defense at the River Elbe was guaranteed by NATO divisions deliberately positioned so that they could easily have encircled the divisions of the Bundeswehr interspersed between Allied troops. The Bundeswehr did not become, as many members of the German left had feared, "a state within the state." It became instead an integral part of an internationally organized alliance that was dominated by the United States.[28] To be sure, the presence of thirteen other NATO members was of enormous importance politically, psychologically, and militarily. But in essence the alliance revolved around the nuclear deterrence provided by the American strategic and tactical weapons and the conventional defense offered by German and American ground forces.

The taming of West German power was accelerated by the fact that after 1950 NATO gradually evolved into an alliance that not only planned for the eventuality of war but began to integrate its military operations already in times of peace. It is, in fact, the first alliance in modern history that has an internationally organized and integrated structure. Its general secretary, in 1992 a former West German minister of defense, Manfred Wörner, chairs the NATO Council and the Defense Planning Committee. The foreign and defense ministers as well as the chiefs of staff of the various national military forces meet several times a year.

The military integration of West Germany into NATO operations was more far-reaching than was true for any other member state. With the exception of a few paramilitary units, all forces of the Bundeswehr are under NATO command. Virtually all important questions involving Bundeswehr training, procurement, organization, planning, and leadership are decided within NATO committees. NATO's Supreme Allied Commander Europe (SACEUR) has the power to inspect West German troops and to assume the military leadership of the Bundeswehr in times of crisis. The Bundeswehr is in uninterrupted contact with other troops operating under NATO auspices. And West German defense specialists sit on all important committees in which NATO strategy is being planned.

This structural integration of the Bundeswehr into the Western alliance has eventually resulted in a curious fact. Although it has lived on the front line of the Cold War, West Germany lacks an independent national profile on virtually all defense issues. "External actors and preferences penetrate German deliberations at every stage."[29] The fragmentation and bureaucratization of defense policy are certainly not restricted to West Germany.

But the structural integration of the Bundeswehr into NATO magnifies immensely the problem of national and transnational policy coordination.[30]

West Germany's integration into NATO has also had important consequences for the evolution of the Western alliance. These consequences are most notable in the relative weights attached to the military and political aspects of the alliance. For American foreign policy elites NATO was typically an instrument for enhancing the military security of the West. This interpretation may have been derived from the historical experience of Pearl Harbor. But it also agreed with the interests of the United States as the strongest military power in NATO. The situation was more complicated for West German governments. The military threat from the East, successive West German governments insisted with increasing urgency, called for a political as well as a military response. This dual purpose was, according to West Germany, the foundation of NATO, its raison d'être. The West German view reflected Germany's experience in World War II, the realities of the Cold War, and a policy that accepted as a last resort national suicide in the form of a limited nuclear war to be fought in Central Europe. But the insistence on NATO's dual mission also supported West German interests in furthering good relations with the Soviet Union and the Eastern European members of the Soviet bloc. Such a policy helped improve the relations between the two Germanies and hedged against the ever-present threat of a partial or total withdrawal of the United States from Europe.[31]

With the rise in West German power this basic difference in the American and West German outlooks has increasingly shaped the alliance since the mid-1960s. As early as 1956 the political aspect of NATO's mission had been the subject of a report drafted by a commission during the first thaw in the Cold War.[32] One consequence was the founding of a commission of political advisors to NATO. But the commission proved to be particularly weak in dealing with questions of arms control and disarmament. West Germany and Denmark thus succeeded in 1965 in convincing the other allies to institutionalize meetings of political experts under NATO auspices. This was "the first West German attempt, to break a hole in the wall which the Cold War had created in Europe."[33] In the end it was the Harmel Report of 1967 that contributed to an important political reorientation of NATO. It advocated that deterrence and détente should become the two most important instruments of NATO's security policy. These policies constituted the international platform that permitted Willy Brandt's Eastern policy. In the 1970s West German diplomacy contributed much to the institutionalization in 1975 of the Conference on Security and Cooperation in Europe (CSCE). And in the 1980s West Germany's coalition government, headed by Chancellor Kohl, never left a shred of doubt that

"Genscherism"—a modern synonym for "Rapallo" and "Schaukelpolitik" inside Washington's Beltway and on the editorial pages of the *Wall Street Journal*—articulated a fundamental political interest of West Germany in search of good relations with its neighbors in the East.[34]

European Integration

The fundamental entanglement of the Federal Republic occurred also in the European integration process along political, economic, and social dimensions.[35] In many respects the foreign policies of the Allies aimed from the very beginning at anchoring West Germany as deeply as possible in Europe. Thus, it was hoped, one could prevent future German governments from ever again waging an independent, aggressive foreign policy. The European Coal and Steel Community (ECSC) was dedicated to this task in a particularly farsighted manner. It imposed limitations on the sovereignty of all of its members rather than only on West Germany. The European integration process was shaped by a number of accelerating and retarding forces. The failure of the European Defense Community (EDC) in the French parliament in 1954 was followed, as a sort of salvage operation, by the founding of the European Community in 1957. And Britain's foreign policy, which aimed at the European Free Trade Area (EFTA) rather than the EC, threatened to split Western Europe into two economic blocs, especially after Charles de Gaulle vetoed Britain's application to join the EC. By insisting that they would never want to choose between a European and an Atlantic option, West German governments prevented the split between France and Britain from deepening.

Despite some exceptions West Germany has remained an active proponent of European integration in the 1970s and 1980s. West German governments actively supported the evolving system of European Political Cooperation (EPC). The West German hard currency policy was the core of the European Monetary System (EMS) that, in close European cooperation, has offered one of the most dynamic and politically sensitive institutions for a further integration of Europe in the 1990s. And in the 1980s the West German government supported vigorously the project to complete the commercial and monetary integration of the community by 1992 (EC92). It did so diplomatically when the project got launched in 1985 and financially in 1988 when it offered to finance a compromise on the contentious issue of agriculture so that further progress toward 1992 would not be blocked by that long-standing conflict. At the European summit in Maastricht, Netherlands, in December 1991 Germany continued to push hard for greater powers for the European Parliament and for far-reaching monetary integration by the end of the decade. With France opposed to the first initiative and Britain opposed to the second, Chancellor Kohl had, at best, limited success on both fronts.

It is, of course, true that the most important reason for the move toward 1992 did not lie in an unchanging West German but in a changing French foreign policy. The irrelevance of a nationally autonomous foreign economic policy in an integrated Western Europe was a lesson that a Socialist government in France may have learned reluctantly in the early 1980s. But it was a lesson well learned. The prospect of a Germany increasingly oriented toward the Soviet Union and Eastern Europe converted President François Mitterrand after 1986 into a strong proponent of an acceleration of the European integration process, with a compatriot and political ally, Jacques Delors, operating in Brussels to achieve that difficult task. Only Britain's Margaret Thatcher warned against unseemly haste—as, for example, in her speech in Bruges, Belgium, in September 1988—and remained hesitant without any noticeable effect on the acceleration of European integration brought about jointly by France and West Germany.

West Germany's entanglement in the process of European integration has also had important consequences for Europe. It has been a basic premise of West German foreign policy since 1949 to sidestep the choice between the United States and France as major allies. And it has been a basic premise of West German foreign economic policy to create conditions favoring easy access to markets anywhere in the world. West German foreign policy thus has always aimed at an "open" Europe. De Gaulle's offer in the early 1960s to create a smaller and more cohesive Europe did little to change that basic orientation, despite the deep fissures the general succeeded in creating in West Germany's conservative camp. West Germany's Gaullists were always a small minority. Chancellor Ludwig Erhard was deeply committed to the program of Atlanticism, worked strenuously against the split between the EC and the EFTA, and had reestablished this foreign policy line unambiguously in Bonn and Brussels by late 1965. The political summit in The Hague in 1969 confirmed that the foreign policy of the new SPD-FDP coalition government was also firmly committed to the vision of an open Europe. In the 1970s and 1980s the West German government was an active proponent of the southern enlargement of the EC. The Central European enlargement in the 1990s that has been discussed throughout Europe since 1989 may take different political forms. But there can be no doubt that the West German government is an enthusiastic supporter of such a policy initiative. Contrary to American and Japanese fears, German policy maintains that EC92 is not a political attempt to throw up barriers around Europe but a further step toward the liberalization of a global economy that also has assumed regional forms. The "fortress Europe" that is frequently criticized in American business publications is an unacceptable vision for Germans—and not only because the term was originally coined by Josef Goebbels. From the perspective of Bonn it would be sheer economic nonsense for the second largest export economy in the world to devote its political resources to building economic walls. And for a country that gained so much from its reliance on the American deterrence, it would be an act of great political foolishness permanently to antagonize the United States.

GERMAN UNIFICATION 1989–1990 AND THE NEW POSITION OF GERMANY IN THE INTERNATIONAL SYSTEM

In comparison to the historical experiences of the German Empire, the Weimar Republic, and the Third Reich the international entanglement of West Germany has been unique. The alliances that Germany had joined before 1945 were driven by state interests that did not impinge on the daily experiences of important institutions, such as the armed forces. And there is no historical parallel before 1945 to the dynamism of the European integration process that has so deeply affected the political, economic, and social affairs of West Germany in the postwar era.

The entanglement of West Germany in the institutions and markets of the international system is considerably stronger than is true for other Western powers. This assertion could be easily supported with reference to the United States and Japan. But it is also true in comparison to Britain and France. France, for example, left the military, as opposed to the political, arm of NATO in 1966. And its strong support of European integration has existed for less than a decade. Under Conservative governments Britain has been a strong supporter of the Atlantic alliance. But the issue of European integration has been a vexing one for British politicians, both in the 1950s and 1980s. Indeed, during the 1980s it has often looked as though Britain was trying to stage a contemporary version of its traditional policy of "splendid isolation" just as the process of European integration gained additional momentum.

In comparison to the German past as well as the historical experiences of other Western states, the history of West Germany is marked decisively by international structures, such as the Atlantic alliance, and international processes, such as European integration. The radical changes in the bipolar system that have occurred since 1986, and in particular in 1989–1990, have not altered but rather deepened this defining condition of German politics.

The conception of national interest that has informed West German foreign policy is shaped not only by the constraints and opportunities that result from West Germany's deep international entanglements. As part of a process of historical experience and learning, these international entanglements have contributed also to the growing strength of the norm of peaceful international cooperation and dynamic economic expansion. And that norm has been validated by the success that the Federal Republic has enjoyed in the last four decades. It would be an important mistake to neglect the importance of this norm and the unstated political premises that it informs. For the norm of a liberal lawful state that is actively engaged in furthering international cooperation is essential for the newly found and voluntarily accepted self-limitations of German power.

The tacit recognition of this fact inside and outside Germany is the main reason that the rush to unification did not create a more severe political backlash among the critics of unification both at home and abroad. For what is striking about the unification process is the difference between its international and multilateral form and its national and unilateral substance. The four-plus-two framework for negotiations between the four Allied powers and the two German states was in fact largely superseded by the one-on-one negotiations between the Soviet Union and West Germany. The intensity of these bilateral negotiations was extraordinary. Between January and July 1990 the two foreign ministers, Hans Dietrich Genscher and Eduard Shevardnadze, met a dozen times, and the frequency of meetings between high-ranking personal advisors of Chancellor Helmut Kohl and President Mikhail Gorbachev was probably much greater before the two leaders signed the historical accord in July 1990 sealing German unification under specific terms: membership of the united Germany in NATO, limitations on the size and character of Germany's Bundeswehr, generous economic and technological German assistance to the Soviet Union, and the departure of Soviet forces from Germany and of Allied forces from Berlin. What was striking about Kohl's leadership was "his decision to make German unity an issue for the Germans alone and to act accordingly. . . . At every turn, including in NATO summit meetings, he has preempted or evaded control, while providing what might be called sovereign reassurance about his intentions and destination."[36] The political reassurance that Kohl and Genscher could offer indicated the wide-spread assumption in most European capitals that the West German political leadership had in fact internalized the norm of peaceful international cooperation. For Kohl and Genscher repeatedly insisted in public that the terms of German unification that they were negotiating with the Soviet Union would have to be acceptable not only to all of the Allied powers but, more importantly, to all members of the CSCE and, in particular, to Poland. In their minds German unification was as much a European as a national issue.

In 1989 and 1990 almost everything was astonishing.[37] One of the few exceptions was the fact that the structural integration and historical experience of West Germany were reflected clearly in the German unification process. Secretary of State James Baker spoke in Berlin in December 1989 of a new political architecture in Europe. His speech was a far-reaching affirmation of West German foreign policy in a rapidly changing Europe.

The upgrading of the political component of the Atlantic alliance, actively pushed by West German governments since the mid-1960s, is an essential part of this new architecture. The same is true of the American acceptance of the CSCE process and its possible further institutionalization as an additional element of a European security arrangement. The basic demand of the West German government, the United States, and most Western and Eastern European states aimed at preventing the reemergence of a neutral, autonomous, united Germany at the center of Europe, shifting between East and West. Soviet acceptance of this demand in July 1990 paved the way to unification in December, years sooner than even the greatest German optimists, including the chancellor, had hoped for in January 1990.

Similarly the European integration process in the year 1990 reflected the deep entanglement of Germany. In fall 1989 throughout European capitals the fear was widespread that German unification would seriously delay or possibly derail altogether the accelerating movement toward European integration. This fear was nourished by the West German government's request to put temporarily on ice the Schengen negotiations concerning the abolishment of internal borders between Germany, France, and the Benelux countries. But this fear proved to be unfounded. Within a few months the West German government resumed its old policy that aims, according to a much-quoted dictum by Thomas Mann, at Europeanizing the Germans rather than Germanizing Europe. German unification and European integration apparently reinforce each other in part because only an integrated Europe, not a united Germany, can cope with some of the most vexing problems of the 1990s. Policies that a united Germany simply could not impose for reasons of both domestic and international politics, such as a strict immigration policy to curtail the flow of economic refugees from the East, can be made acceptable politically—as an active step toward European integration. Even in areas that impinge on Germany's newly won sovereignty, European integration is seen as the best way of furthering German interests within a normative framework that informs German choices. The skeptic on questions of European integration remains Britain, not Germany. Despite German unification, the expectations about the extent of political, economic, and monetary integration far exceed those held when the EC92 process was launched in earnest in 1987–1988.

Project 1992 is acquiring greater political importance because of Germany's unification. But the architecture of this new Europe does not revolve around only a more powerful core. It also takes the form of several concentric circles. It is permissive of different forms of association of West European states still debating the merits of EC membership or waiting to be admitted, as well as a number of Central European states that are seeking to master the transition from socialism to capitalism under democratic auspices.

According to German views this new European architecture should also incorporate the United States and the successor states of the Soviet Union, especially Russia. The United States has been closely tied to Europe for decades, both economically and politically. The economic ties will tighten further after 1992. But the political relations between Europe and the United States are bound to become more complicated. Will American ground forces continue to have a symbolic presence in Germany? Will the American air force and navy provide a deterrent threat as part of a reorganized NATO? And what will happen to the political weight of the United States in Europe as the American military presence diminishes? Nobody knows the answers to these questions. But the German view of the future European order is inclusive, not exclusive, and is likely to continue to support strongly the U.S. political engagement in European affairs without, however, accepting any longer American leadership on all vital issues. The weight of German and European interests will undoubtedly increase.

Although the successor states to the Soviet Union are not members of NATO or the EC, in geographic terms most of them are part of Europe. German policy assumes that it should apply to these states the same political formula that it has seen work so well in the West German past, a formula that it applied to southern Europe in the 1970s and that it is seeking to extend to Central and Eastern Europe in the 1990s. The successor states to the Soviet Union are to be tied politically to Germany and Europe through far-reaching economic, technological, scientific, and cultural ties. In the CSCE Russia is predestined, as the largest European nuclear power, to assume a position of leadership, together with the United States. Although this is a blueprint, not reality, the German vision of Europe, it appears, extends from San Francisco to Vladivostok.

CONCLUSION

I have argued in this chapter that what matters most for understanding the new Germany is its recent past. The four decades since 1949 have created political structures and norms that have moderated German politics and policies. No one knows whether future developments will reinforce or undermine this feature of German politics. We know, however, that future events will have to overcome the legacies of Germany's recent past. History thus makes it highly improbable that German politics and policy would simply extend the various strands of the past that pessimists and optimists are tracing back to decades and centuries predating the two great wars of this century.

The taming of power in German domestic politics is rooted in what the Germans call a system of "social partnership" between the major interest groups. The taming of German power in the international system, heartily endorsed by big and small states in East and West and embraced by the Germans themselves, is best summarized by the term "security partnership." Social partnership and security partnership are the sum total of diverse structural ties, political practices, and norms that have gradually emerged in West Germany since 1949. They are likely to shape the future political course a united Germany will try to steer.

These concepts mirror not only a fundamental political consensus among the major political groups inside Germany. They point also to differences in political ideologies and interests. In a system where most groups cluster in the political center, the concept of social partnership for those on the right is interpreted quite restrictively to exclude many economic issues. In sharp contrast, Germany's left interprets this concept quite broadly to refer to a system of social and economic partnership. This is the reason that the unions and the SPD insist so strongly on the continued viability of Germany's system of codetermination, which assures labor a voice in the boardrooms of major corporations. Similarly, the concept of security partnership means for those on the right a secure anchoring of Germany in the Western alliance and in the process of European integration. On the left, by way of contrast, the concept of security partnership extends beyond the process of European integration to include as well the creation of a pan-European peace order that conceivably might become a complement or alternative to the Western alliance.

One can trace the effects of structural entanglements and norms that have shaped the German concept of security partnership in the decisive stages of the unification process of 1990. The unambiguous vote of the East Germans for unification, reinforced by the unstoppable expansion of the West German party system and the West German currency, created fears, especially in Britain and Poland, that a united Germany would seek a hegemonic position in Europe. But even a united Germany controls only about one-third of the economic resources of Western Europe. And the German capital market is simply too small to finance by itself the economic development projects that are needed in the eastern parts of a united Germany, Central Europe, and the Soviet Union. Germany's willingness to broker the conflict between Japan and Russia expresses the awareness that substantial Japanese aid would help stabilize conditions in Russia and thus enhance German security.[38]

The foreign policy adhered to by the West German government to achieve unification was distinguished by a readiness to accept limitations on German power. Against the backdrop of recent German history this was not an act of national sacrifice but of rational calculation. A security partnership is a marriage of convenience. It is utterly rational for a couple that hopes to lose weight to equip the refrigerator with a lock that can be opened only with two keys; nobody can gorge alone. History has taught the Germans that it is in the German interest to have German security and power aspirations as deeply anchored in international arrangements as possible. This historical lesson is readily accepted both inside and outside Germany.

Even though the events of 1989–1990, applied to Germany, contradict the essential insights of structural realism, we should be cautious. The new Europe, especially in the East, contains many old conflicts. The political theory of realism, a product of nineteenth century Germany, counts for much in the major capitals of the world. Gorbachev, for example, announced with a broad smile in July 1990 that he and Chancellor Kohl had just presented a masterful piece of realpolitik. President Mitterrand refused, despite intense German efforts, to have France join again the military part of NATO, apparently for *raison d'état*. Finally Prime Minister Thatcher made it abundantly clear in 1990 that Britain's foreign policy would continue to seek to defend Britain's sovereignty in a rapidly changing Europe. Informed by different historical experiences and exposed to less far-reaching international entanglements compared to Germany, other major states are to some extent interpreting the new conditions in Europe through old analytical and political lenses. Under these conditions it is not inconceivable that the Germans may begin to pay less heed to their recent history. Although there is no evidence to support this view, should political developments move in that direction, it might indeed lead to new tragedies.

But in 1989–1990 old-style power politics appeared to the Germans like a farce. The treaty that Germany and Poland signed in 1991 promises a reconciliation in a European context modeled along Franco-German lines. And the Gulf War showed that two defeats in the two world wars that Germany started have left a deep mark. Germans regard war as an obsolete institution for settling conflict. This explains perhaps why to Anglo-Saxon eyes Germans appeared to be so surprised and so provincial in their reaction to the crisis in the Gulf. To the extent that Germany is drawn in the future into military conflicts, it is likely to participate only under UN or international auspices. It would take enormous upheavals in the international system and in German domestic politics for Germany to let go of the internationalism of a trading state and to return once again to the unilateralism of a warfare state. Since nothing in history is impossible, neither is such a dramatic reorientation. But developments since 1949 make such a change highly improbable.

The unification of Germany illustrates that a policy of taming German power is in Germany's national interest. The political reforms in Central and Eastern Europe toward liberal-democratic states and systems of social partnerships, that is, reforms modeled along German lines, are to be assisted by a Germany that is securely anchored in a variety of international political arrangements. Germany does not seek to withdraw from the stage of world politics, as did Sweden in the eighteenth century. Rather, it seeks to apply what it regards as the important lessons from the last century to manage a successful transition to the next. For Germany the central lesson is unambiguous. Political power should neither become an obsession nor should it be forgotten. Rather political power needs to be tamed.[39] The fruits that the system of social partnership brought to West German domestic politics, the Germans expect the system of security partnership to bring to Germany and its European neighbors in international politics. It remains to be seen how this vision will fare when it is exposed to possible upheavals in Eastern Europe and the Soviet Union and how it will fit with the New World Order casting the New World in the role of a global policeman. But a taming of politics in the Old World, this much we can conclude safely, would signify a very important historical change with ramifications that are likely to extend beyond Europe.

5

THE RIDDLE OF THE RHINE

*France, Germany, and the Geopolitics
of European Integration, 1919–1992*

There can be no denying the dramatic change of course that political and economic integration has imposed on European history. Since the seventeenth century Europe has been the scene of the most murderous, geographically widespread, and destructive wars in human history. In the 1950s Europe's erstwhile fratricidal powers embarked on the most ambitious effort to reform the nature and logic of international relations that human societies have attempted since the Treaty of Westphalia. Neither can one deny the impression, however, of déjà vu. The Europeanism of Valéry Giscard-d'Estaing and François Mitterrand curiously resembles that of Aristide Briand. The efforts of Helmut Schmidt and Helmut Kohl to improve ties with France seem to echo those of Gustav Stresemann. Similarly, the nationalism of Charles de Gaulle at the close of World War II reminds us of the nationalism of Georges Clemenceau and Raymond Poincaré at the close of World War I. Are the resemblances fortuitous?

I argue that they are not, that they are revelatory of a geopolitical logic that has presided over the international politics of Western Europe since 1919. That logic has its source in the economic preeminence of the Rhineland. The dominance of Rhenish industry in the economy of Europe has been such that the most powerful nations of the West staked claims on the fate of the Rhineland in 1919 and again in 1945. The French wanted to keep it away from the Germans, the British wanted to keep it away from the French, and the Americans wanted to keep it away from the Russians. European integration, informed by the canons of economic liberalism, was the path on which the great powers eventually embarked as a means of adjusting their incompatible geopolitical claims. European integration, in other words, was the only way the great powers found to divide the Rhineland in four. I argue in the conclusion that any prognosis regarding

83

the future of the European Community and the EC's place in the world must take into account its geopolitical birth.

THE RHENISH CORRIDOR

There is a golden triangle within the European Community, whose vertices are at Milan, London, and Frankfurt. Within this triangle hums the economic motor of the European Community. One finds here an astonishing concentration of economic power: financial power in Frankfurt and Zurich, London and Paris; manufacturing power in Milan, Düsseldorf, and Stuttgart; commercial power in London, Duisburg, and Rotterdam. Here one also finds one of the great concentrations of cities in the world, matched only by the Great Lakes region and the Boston-Washington corridor in the United States and the Tokyo-Kobe conurbation in Japan.

Running almost the entire length of this golden triangle is the Rhine. Navigable by ocean-going freighter from Rotterdam to Duisburg and by heavy barge-train from Duisburg to Basel, it links the near extremities of the triangle like an artery and a nerve. Through its affluents—the Meuse, the Moselle, the Neckar, and their canals—it draws into its thick web of traffic such cities as Metz and Nancy, Brussels and Antwerp, Stuttgart and Amsterdam. From its seaports at Rotterdam, Amsterdam, and Antwerp, the Rhine extends its reach to southern England. In the south, through a series of Alpine passes—notably the Simplon and the St. Gotthard—it extends to Milan, Turin, Genoa, and Italy's industrialized north, and the valleys of the Saône and the Rhône link the Rhineland to Lyon and Marseille. At the core of this Rhenish triangle, Western Europe's steel-producing heartland extends from Lorraine to the Ruhr, encompassing the Saar, Luxemburg, and half of Belgium. It is no accident that the original six countries of the European Common Market all belong to this Rhenish fraternity.

The Rhine's fortunes flow from an accident of physical geography that placed a north-south depression across a continent that topography has ordered latitudinally. Topographically, Europe consists of a broad plain in the north that extends from Paris to Moscow, wooded plateaus and deep valleys deployed along a central band from the Massif Central to Bohemia, and finally the high peaks of the Alps and its sister ranges—the Pyrenees and the Carpathians—to the south. Cutting across these three geographical zones are the depressions of the Rhine and the Saône-Rhône. These depressions facilitated the exchange of goods between the North Sea and the Mediterranean from prehistoric times, and they channeled east-west traffic through bridgeable fords across the rivers. At the crossroads, cities arose—Basel, Strasbourg, Mainz, Frankfurt, Cologne—feeding on the commercial and industrial opportunities that geography created. Geography nurtured the development of a commercial, industrial civilization buttressed by a network of cities that was as dense in premodern times as it is today.[1]

Geography smiled on the economic development of the cities of the Rhine but frowned on their political development. The Rhineland entered the modern era in political disorder. With the exception of the ephemeral fifteenth-century Duchy of Burgundy, the Rhineland's close association with imperial and military power—as in the days of imperial Rome or of the "new Rome" of Charlemagne—was a thing of the past. The typical form of political organization was the city-state, which the Rhineland shared with its sister civilizations in northern Italy and among the Hanseatic cities of the North Sea and the Baltic. This city-state civilization was by the sixteenth century threatened with obsolescence by the rise of the national monarchies.

The national monarchies arose in regions where cities were weak: France in the wheat plains of the Paris basin; Spain in the forests and dry plateaus of northern Iberia, whence it expanded by crusades directed against the flourishing cities of the Saracen south; England in the wool-producing heaths of Britain, which were lifted to prosperity when the merchants of the Rhine linked them to the textile towns of northern Italy; and Brandenburg in the poor rye fields of Europe's great northern plain. The Habsburgs owed their disparate empire less to geographical accident than to marital opportunism.

Stein Rokkan describes an urbanized, romanized region extending from the Rhine southward to northern Italy, which he identifies as the economic and cultural center of premodern Western Europe. He goes on to explore the paradox that the history of Europe was one of state formation at the "periphery of a network of strong and independent cities," where the typical sequence was one of "gradual build-up at the ethnic center, rapid imperial expansion, consolidation within a more homogeneous territory." The political economy of the monarchical states was founded on their ability to control and to exploit the movement of goods and persons across their frontiers, whereas the political economy of the merchant city-states was predicated on the ease and openness of such movement. The resultant incompatibility of interests nourished the desire of the monarchs to extend their control, and wherever "the cities were weak and isolated, the territorial centralizers succeeded." The monarchies extended their reach from periphery to core, encountering one another and competing to integrate this urban political society into their kingdoms. War was endemic in the Rhineland from the seventeenth to the early nineteenth century. Only the cities of Holland and Switzerland forged a successful defensive alliance that held the monarchical aggrandizers at bay.[2]

The Treaty of Vienna in 1815 completed the integration of the Rhineland within the now triumphant nation-state system. France, though the
loser of the war, retained its conquests and acquisitions in Lorraine and
Alsace. The Habsburgs retained their influence—or lack of it—over the
principalities of southern Germany. England was recognized as the guar-
antor of the sovereignty and integrity of the Netherlands (which for a
short time included Belgium). Switzerland had long since won its claim to
the headwaters of the Rhine, and Spain had long since been evicted from
the contest. Finally, the youngest monarchy, Prussia, was installed on the
banks of the Rhine between Bingen (downstream from Frankfurt) and the
Dutch border.

The solution achieved at Vienna was shortlived, coming as it did at precisely the wrong time. The industrial era had dawned, and industrialization brought with it the exploitation of riches that hitherto had played
only a secondary role in the Rhineland's prosperity: coal and iron. The
valley of the Ruhr harbored one of the richest reserves of coal in the entire
world, and the coal produced by its mines was of high quality, easily
transformed into the coke required by late nineteenth-century steel mills.
Coal of lesser quality was abundant in the valley of the Saar, and iron had
long been mined in the valley of the Wupper and in the area surrounding
Liège.[3]

France, which had thought of the Rhine only as a "natural frontier"
from the mid-seventeenth century on, began to develop a real interest in
its economic potential during the Napoleonic period. French engineers
and functionaries were dispatched to examine the possibility of exploiting
the mineral wealth of the region. In the 1830s it was French and Belgian
capitalists who first began to invest heavily in Rhenish mines, and indeed,
French and Belgians supplied the first contingent of steel workers in the
Ruhr.[4]

It was Prussia, however, that was to reap the industrial bounty of the
middle Rhine, which the Treaty of Vienna had surrendered to its jurisdiction. Prussia's fortune was not due solely to diplomatic accident. Its government worked hard to develop the industrial potential of the middle
Rhine and to yoke that wealth to its military machine. It pieced together a
German tariff union, the Zollverein, that promoted commerce. It raised
levees along the Rhine and dug canals that allowed large barges to reach
Mannheim in 1830 and Strasbourg in 1890. Germany, unified under Prussia's leadership in 1871, financed the St. Gotthard tunnel, making communication by rail possible between the Rhine and the Mediterranean. It also
financed the Nieuwe Waterweg in 1872, creating the infrastructure that
propelled Rotterdam to its present-day status as busiest port in the world.
The German government encouraged mine owners to form cartels, of
which the most powerful, the Rheinisch-Westfälisches Kohlensyndikat,

eventually controlled 80 percent of the coal production of the Ruhr. Verti-
cal concentrations, linking mines to steel mills, were also encouraged, giving rise to the great steel empires: Krupp and Thyssen.[5]

The mines of the Ruhr, which were producing 12 million metric tons of
coal in 1870, were producing ten times that amount by 1913. The mineral
wealth and industrial development of the Ruhr and the Rhenish provinces
that surrounded it provided the foundation for the development of other
manufactures: automobiles, electrical goods, machine tools, and precision
tools. The chemical industry, based first on the transformation of coal and
later on the transformation of petroleum imported through the port of
Rotterdam, provided the impetus that put Germany ahead of Great Britain as the premier industrial power of Europe in the last years of the nineteenth century. By 1898 German levels of production outstripped those of
Great Britain in most basic industries. German industries supplied 24 percent of the world's production of chemical goods in 1913 while Great Britain produced only 11 percent (and the United States 34 percent). "Made in
Germany" resounded in English ears then in much the same way that
"made in Japan" resounds in American ears today.[6]

Industrial growth stimulated rapid population growth at a time when
military power was measured by the numbers that could be conscripted
into service. The population of Germany grew from 25 million in 1816 to
36 million in 1871 to more than 56 million in 1911. The Rhenish provinces
of Prussia and Westphalia grew from 2 million to 9 million during the
same period. As Germany waxed, France waned. A century before, France
was the most populous country of Western Europe, but between 1871 and
1911 its population grew by only 2.5 percent. Although it occupied fourth
place among the world's commercial powers, its foreign trade grew by
only 16 percent between 1895 and 1905, while that of Germany during the
same period grew by 66 percent.[7]

As the French gazed across the Rhine, they felt fear as they looked upon
the greatest threat to their security and predominance in Europe since the
days of Habsburg encirclement in the sixteenth century.

COMPETITION FOR CONTROL OF THE RHINELAND

German ascendance in European affairs was heralded by Prussia's victory
over the French in 1871. That victory created the conditions for the political unification of the new German Reich, to which were awarded the
Rhenish provinces of France: Alsace and Lorraine. Germany now ruled
both banks of the Rhine from the Swiss to the Dutch borders, bringing
most of the productive capacity of the region within the dominion of a single sovereign. In the end, however, German supremacy (and post-
Bismarckian diplomatic errors) resulted in Germany's isolation and defeat

at the hands of the principal economic powers of the world acting in coalition.

The defeat of the German Reich in 1919 created the opportunity for the nations of Europe and the United States to negotiate a new settlement concerning the Rhineland. That solution would not be a Viennese solution, however—that is, a territorial solution of the type achieved by the great peace conferences of past centuries. Two of the victorious states that now claimed a stake in the fate of the Rhineland, Great Britain and the United States, were not contiguous to it. Nor, given the economic nature of their interest in the region, could they be satisfied with a solution that, as at Vienna, addressed their claims by creating buffer states like Holland and Belgium that prevented the Rhine from feeding the expansionist ambitions of other powerful militarized states, namely France and the German Reich. The only feasible solution required the liberalization of economic ties among the interested countries as well as the development of supranational institutions that curtailed German and French sovereignty in the region.

French policy provides a window through which to observe the process that brought integration to Europe as a solution to the geopolitical puzzle of the Rhine. French policy—from 1919 to 1992—was characterized by a clear and stable set of preferences regarding the fate of the Rhineland:

1. To reclaim Alsace and Lorraine, to annex the Saar, and to detach the Ruhr from Prussia.

2. Failing which, to enter actively and constructively into some more or less exclusivist and mercantilist arrangement with Germany such that France's claims on the wealth of the Rhineland were given some satisfaction and such that German sovereignty over the Ruhr was constrained.

3. Failing which, to enter actively and constructively into some more liberal arrangement with Germany, Great Britain, and the United States that constrained German sovereignty over the Ruhr, even though it obliged the French to compete within a more open market with more competitive economies.

4. Rounding off this set of preferences, a final outcome—the one the French consistently sought to avoid—the return of the Ruhr to the sovereign control of a unified Germany.

The pursuit of these preferences after both world wars generated parallel histories, as the French were denied successively their first and second preferences and obliged to cultivate the third. These parallel histories attest to the geopolitical logic of European integration, a logic unleashed prior to the post–World War II imperium of the United States. One can distinguish three periods in French diplomacy after both wars, one of territorial expansionism, one of economic mercantilism, and one of political and economic internationalism. It is this third period that interests us the most, because it is this third period in which we are living today. Let us retrace these parallel histories from the cessation of hostilities in 1918 and 1945.

First Period: French Territorial Claims,
1919–1923 and 1945–1947

At Versailles, the French claimed that their military security required, at a minimum, the return of Alsace-Lorraine, the demilitarization of the Rhineland, the annexation of the Saar, and complete indemnification of the costs of the war. Beyond these minimum demands, Clemenceau advanced a more ambitious claim that sought to reestablish the status quo ante—not as it existed prior to World War I but as it existed prior to the creation of the German Reich in 1871. Clemenceau wanted to create a new state, a Rhenish republic, forbidden by treaty from adhering to a revived German federation but exonerated from the payment of war indemnities. Reparations were to be born only by the "bad Germans" to the East, leaving the new republic economically intact and beholden to its benefactor, much as the independent German principalities were subjected to French influence throughout the seventeenth and eighteenth centuries.

Clemenceau's demands encountered stiff resistance from the British and the Americans, who objected to a territorial settlement that rewarded the French but contained nothing for them.[8] The British were particularly clear on this point. France could not be allowed to win territory and influence in the Rhineland as if it had won the war alone. This was inequitable and, moreover, would merely have substituted French ascendancy in Europe for German ascendancy. But because the British were prevented by geography from balancing French territorial gains by gains of their own, they voiced support for Wilson's idealist reform schemes—"peace without victory"—though in a manner consonant with their interests as an imperial power.

The American position, however, was hardly one of unadulterated idealism. Although the United States had entered the war with the express aim of using victory to reform the very nature of international relations, U.S. diplomacy assigned clear limits to Wilsonian internationalism. It did not extend, for example, to collaborating with Great Britain and France in a cooperative manner to resolve the problem of the Allied debt. Nor did it prevent the United States from giving its approval to the cynical carving up of Germany's small colonial empire. Finally, U.S. internationalism vaporized completely when it became apparent that "perpetual peace" might require the Monroe doctrine to be revoked in order to make aggression in the Western hemisphere subject to collective jurisdiction.[9] Just as the British interpreted Wilson's new order as ending at the frontiers of the British empire, so did the Americans exclude from its scope their own quasi empire in Latin America. U.S. "internationalism" was thus "geographically circumscribed"—and focused primarily on the future status of the Ruhr.

The French, to bolster their claims, stationed troops at key bridgeheads on the Rhine and stood ready to occupy the right bank. The military strength of their position, however, was sapped by their financial weakness. They needed and expected American financial aid and were unable to secure their military advantage on the ground without economic and diplomatic support from their allies. Their position was further weakened by the Bolshevik Revolution and the specter of revolution in Germany and even at home.

The British proposed that the French relinquish their demands regarding the Ruhr in exchange for a British-American security guarantee. Clemenceau agreed to the proposal but sought to strengthen it with a thirty-year military occupation of the Rhineland, the creation of a demilitarized zone extending 50 kilometers east of the Rhine, and on-site inspections to assure German compliance. French Chief of Staff Ferdinand Foch argued: "If you are master of the Rhine, you are master of the whole country. But if you are not on the Rhine, you have lost everything."[10] The final compromise provided for the demilitarized zone and an occupation period limited to fifteen years.

With regard to the Saar, the combination of France's dominance on the ground and its need for American financial and diplomatic benevolence again gave rise to compromise. The Saar was placed under the protection of the League of Nations but united to France through a customs union. After fifteen years a plebiscite was to decide the Saar's ultimate fate, France being assured of financial compensation if the people of the Saar should decide to join Germany.[11]

The only things that now stood between the French army and occupation of the right bank were the British-American security guarantee, reparations, and the expectation of U.S. financial aid. In the years following the signature of the treaty, those expectations were dashed one by one, leaving France with nothing to restrain it from reasserting its claims. With regard to financial aid, the United States refused to entertain seriously any request of supplementary aid to help with reconstruction and rejected suggestions that international trade and financial arrangements be tinkered with to facilitate reconstruction. The tripartite security agreement with France and Great Britain failed to win U.S. Senate ratification. Finally, the issue of reparations was left unresolved. The United States wanted to assess reparations at a level that was within Germany's capacity to pay while restoring its economy. The restoration of the German market was in the economic interest of the United States and was seen as well as a bulwark against the spread of bolshevism.

When German troops intervened in the Ruhr in April 1920 to quell a revolutionary uprising, the French cried foul and crossed the Rhine without informing the Allies, occupying Frankfurt and Darmstadt for the next six weeks. Both the United States and Great Britain voiced strong disapproval. A year later the French accused the Germans of defaulting on reparations payments and spearheaded an allied occupation of Düsseldorf, Duisburg, and Ruhrort. Raymond Poincaré, who became prime minister in 1922, gave an even more decidedly unilateralist thrust to French foreign policy. As a former general counsel of the French steel trust, the Comité des Forges, he was keenly aware of the geopolitics of the situation. Despite renewed U.S. warnings against an occupation of the Ruhr, France and Belgium sent "control missions" into the Ruhr in January 1923, again alleging Germany's failure to make good on deliveries of coal and wood in payment of reparations. Germany's policy of passive resistance to the occupation, though effective, collapsed after nine months—France was victorious. The French celebrated by proclaiming the independence of a Rhineland Republic in October.[12]

French diplomacy following World War II was the twin of that pursued by Clemenceau and Poincaré. The Provisional Government of France, offspring of the French resistance and presided over by General Charles de Gaulle, focused much of its attention and energy on the future status of the Rhineland. It demanded that Alsace, Lorraine, and the Saar revert to France, that the Ruhr be internationalized, and that heavy reparations in coal, machines, and money be exacted from the defeated power. In order to prosecute its claims, the government demanded that French forces be allowed to occupy the contested areas.

Despite similarities with the interwar period, France's capacity to prosecute its demands was much weaker. In World War I the French army was victorious. In 1945, French forces had played only a minor role in the Allied victory. Diplomatic claims were not sustained by French military dominance on the ground as they had been at the end of the previous war. But the French added three new cards to their negotiating hand that compensated for their military weakness: British solicitude for the interests of a kindred imperial power, growing American concern over Communist influence in France and Italy, and the presence of Soviet occupation troops in East Germany.

With these cards France's fortunes at the negotiating table grew rather than shrank. Franklin Roosevelt initially excluded the French from negotiations at Yalta, San Francisco, and Potsdam. Roosevelt even wanted to deny France a seat on the Security Council of the newly founded United Nations, as well as to exclude French troops from the occupation of Germany. It was the insistent demands of Winston Churchill that won France admission to the Security Council and a share in the occupation. For the

British the specter of French hegemony in Europe had all but disappeared, given France's military and economic weakness. On the contrary, the presence of a fellow imperial power at the postwar negotiating table was welcome as a check on the liberalizing thrust of U.S. policy. Nonetheless, Great Britain was not supportive of French claims to the Rhine and defended, as it had after World War I, German political unification and economic restoration.

There was much ambivalence and considerable confusion in the American position. The Morgenthau plan had called for the "pastoralization" of Germany through the destruction or transferral of its industrial capital to Allied countries. This plan concurred with French designs. By the war's end, however, it was apparent that American officials had come to share Great Britain's concern for Germany's future as an economic power. The United States began to criticize the expropriation of German capital in payment of reparations and to advocate a cash settlement, which it conceived not as a lump sum, as in the 1920s, but as a function—to be determined—of Germany's capacity to pay. By the summer of 1945 both the Americans and British were taking measures to halt the decline in the living standard in their sectors.

But France's occupation zone now gave it veto power over German unification. It used its veto in 1945 to block efforts on the part of Great Britain and the United States to define and implement economic restrictions that required coordination of policy and exchange of goods among the separate occupation zones—a possible prelude to reunification. The French insisted particularly that restrictions not apply to the Rhineland or the Ruhr and that those regions be removed from the area that was to be included under any eventual central administration. "The French veto was perhaps the first postwar example of France's capacity for surprising its allies by bold use of such power as it possessed to promote its distinctive policies."[13]

In October 1945 the French advanced their own claims regarding the Ruhr. They demanded that it become a separate state whose government, though independent, would be supervised by an international authority made up of French, British, and Benelux representatives and whose independence and neutrality would be guaranteed by the United States and the Soviet Union. Though this Rhenish state would have its own currency and its own trade policy, its foreign supervisors would assure that its mineral wealth was used to pay reparations and to reconstruct the Allied economies.

These demands went counter to U.S. ambitions, which were now oriented more decisively toward German economic reconstruction and political reunification. Although the Allied Control Council had agreed in March 1946 to limit German industrial production to one-half its 1938 level, the United States stopped dismantling factories in May as part of the reparations arrangement and in December decided to merge its occupation zone with that of Great Britain. The United States began to count on an economically strong and united Germany to play a key role in its capacity to contain Soviet power. A restored Germany, even amputated of its eastern territories, would create a powerful buffer against further Soviet expansion and contribute to a level of economic prosperity that would secure Europe against the threat of communism. This policy involved the United States directly in the administration of the Ruhr (which was in the British sector) and thus in permanent dispute with the French.

In order to speed German economic reconstruction, the United States began to advocate that steel production in the Ruhr be allowed to rise. France objected strenuously, not only because U.S. demands sounded the death knell of its own claims on the Ruhr but because they would increase German demand for coal and coke sorely needed in France and increase the supply of German products to markets that France wanted to conquer. France's claims regarding the Ruhr were motivated not only by high politics but by the ambition to use Germany's defeat to transfer resources and productive capital from Germany to France. The French wanted to use German resources not only to pay for the reconstruction of their economy but to ensure privileged access to the Ruhr to catapult their own economy to industrial preeminence. Behind this ambition was the shock of defeat in 1940 and the realization of the extent to which France had stagnated as a world power. The resistance forces wanted to use the Allied victory to achieve a radical aggiornamento of French society and economic life. This modernization required that levels of production achieved before the war not only be restored but transcended. This goal in turn required the accelerated development of France's basic industries, nourished by a plentiful supply of American money, German coke, and a large export market for its products.

French ambitions were set out in the Modernization and Reequipment Plan authored by Jean Monnet (who, significantly, would soon become the most active advocate of European integration) and adopted by the French government in March 1946. Alan Milward writes:

> If the Monnet Plan was to be fully realizable, [it required] permanently maintaining the German economy at so low a level of industrial output as to guarantee the availability for the future, not just of the 3 million [metric] tonnes of coke and 1.8 million [metric] tonnes of coking coal on which the French steel industry had depended before the war, but of at least twice those quantities. Far from being based on a liberal internationalism, the Monnet Plan was based on the crudest possible expression of mercantilist principles. It was aimed at seizing German resources in order to capture German markets.[14]

Thus by 1947 France, the United States, and Great Britain had all staked out radically incompatible claims on the Ruhr. The French sought to separate it from Germany and exploit it to modernize their economy to become the principal economic power on the continent. The British sought to prevent such a unilateral exploitation of the Ruhr's wealth. The Americans wanted to incorporate the Rhineland in their own sphere of influence and exploit its wealth in the service of their policy of containment.

Second Period: Bilateral Mercantilism—1923 and 1952–1973

France's claims to certain regions of the Rhineland were honored following both wars. Alsace and Lorraine were returned to the French, and French influence and privileges in the Saar were eventually (though temporarily) recognized. The French failed to detach the Ruhr on both occasions, however, because of British and U.S. opposition. Thus the French were obliged to adapt again to the presence of a reunified Germany on their eastern frontier within whose frontiers lay the industrial powerhouse of the Ruhr. On both occasions France's fallback position was to explore the possibility of entering into a tight bilateral, mercantilistic relationship with Germany. Success eluded French efforts after World War I but their success was great after World War II. Both outcomes were predicated on U.S. policy.

France's efforts to create such a bilateral arrangement were little more than embryonic in 1923. As the French became aware that their victory in the occupation of the Ruhr was a Pyrrhic one, some began to argue that the answer to France's problems, indeed to Europe's problems, lay in Franco-German cooperation rather than in French supremacy. This was the position eventually adopted by the Comité des Forges. Even before the Ruhr occupation representatives of French steel enterprises had approached their counterpart organization, the Verein Deutscher Eisen- und Stahlindustrieller, to explore solutions to the reparations problem that might prove beneficial to both parties. Their efforts were supported by the very able and influential foreign ministry official, Jacques Seydoux. The Comité des Forges produced a plan that called for the transfer of a number of Ruhr mines sufficient to meet French steel industry needs and to credit that transfer to the reparations account. Lack of German enthusiasm for such outright despoilment led the Comité des Forges to produce a second plan that met with greater German interest. According to this plan a smaller number of mines would be transferred in payment of reparations, but the Germans would sign a long-term contract guaranteeing the delivery of German coke to French mills. This agreement would be accompanied by a second long-term contract whereby German mills would agree to buy a part of the semifinished goods produced by French mills. Finally, the Comité des Forges proposed that French and German steelmasters enter into a cartel with their British, Belgian, and Luxemburger counterparts to divide up the European market for steel rails. [15]

The potential impact of Franco-German industrial cooperation on U.S. interests was recognized by U.S. businessmen before it was recognized by the U.S. government. Charles Schwab, president of the Bethlehem Steel Corporation, responded to France's occupation of the Ruhr by offering to purchase German steel firms himself. And the effect of such rumors was not foreign to the efforts of American businessmen to find and finance some solution to the reparations problem. Indeed, the initial impetus behind the Dawes Plan came not from the U.S. government but rather from the U.S. business community. Henry Blumenthal writes:

> Disturbing as [the immediate economic] consequences of the occupation were, they paled by comparison with the potential problems growing out of the gigantic struggle for control of the steel industry. As long as neither France nor Germany singly controlled the coal, iron, and steel plants of the Rhine, Ruhr, and Saar regions, their industrial, military, and political power remained limited. As matters now stood, full control of all these resources by France, or by a combination of France and Germany with France in the driver's seat, promised to assure the French the "security" they coveted. For whoever was absolute master of this region was in a geopolitical position to guide the destiny of Europe. Indeed, by seizing the Ruhr, France threatened not only the interests of Germany, but those of England and the United States as well. France would be able to compete with their steel industries and act in the world-political arena with greater independence from them than in the past. Henceforth, the policies of Britain and the United States, and those of the American steel industry, would strive to block the emergence of such a colossal competitor.[16]

The Comité des Forges got nowhere with its efforts. The financial position of the French government in 1923–1924 was such that it could not pursue this policy against the opposition of the Americans. Conceptually similar efforts after World War II met with greater success, however, and ironically it was U.S. policy toward France that made the second preference more viable. Rapid decay in U.S.-Soviet relations turned openly conflictual when the United States intervened financially in the Greek civil war. The Cold War caused the United States to reassess its attitude toward French ambitions and to develop greater sympathy for France's mercantilist efforts to restore and modernize the French economy. This reassessment caused the United States to place greater importance on finding some way to accommodate French interests in the German question.

At the London Conference of February 1948 both the United States and Great Britain made a substantial concession to the French by agreeing to the creation of an International Authority of the Ruhr to oversee and control the economic reconstruction of the region. The conference also awarded France temporary control over the Saar.[17]

This outcome made it possible for the French to buy Saar coal with francs and facilitated the implementation of the Monnet Plan. The London Conference laid the cornerstone of the hegemonic edifice that the United States was now actively constructing, the raison d'être of which was to provide a solution, through the development of international arrangements and institutions, to the vexing problem of persistent competitive national claims to the Ruhr.[18]

In summer 1947 George Marshall proposed American financial support for European reconstruction on a massive scale. Aid was made conditional, however, on the ability of the Europeans to allocate aid collectively, to which effect the Marshall Plan proposed the creation of an Organization for European Economic Cooperation (OEEC). The United States hoped that the OEEC would make German economic reconstruction and reunification palatable by subjecting it to international supervision.

Although a compromise between France and the United States over the status of the Ruhr had been reached at London, differences between the two countries remained great. The United States tried unsuccessfully to include German technicians and representatives in the OEEC's deliberations and had still not won French acceptance for an increase in German steel production. France was just as adamant in its opposition to U.S. efforts to promote German economic reconstruction. In support of its claims France was able to use its power effectively to obstruct the work of the International Authority of the Ruhr as well as to slow down the proceedings of the OEEC in collusion with other powers such as Great Britain.[19]

No compromise on the Ruhr was in sight as late as March 1949 when European foreign ministers were preparing to meet in Washington to lay the ground for a defensive alliance, the North Atlantic Treaty Organization. The "high" political goal of the United States of yoking an economically powerful Germany to its policy of containment was effectively being held hostage by the "low" politics of the coke trade or, more precisely, by France's "high" political goal of yoking the Ruhr to its own strategy of political and economic restoration. Secretary of State Dean Acheson found the quandary so vexing that he finally handed the French a blank check. He appealed to French Foreign Minister Robert Schuman: "I believe that our policy in Germany, and the development of a German Government which can take its place in Western Europe, depends on the assumption by your country of leadership in Europe on these problems."[20]

The French seized on the offer to realize what has since been recognized as the single most decisive step in the creation of the European Community. The French proposed the creation of a European Coal and Steel Community that, in a manner that recalls the plan of the Comité des Forges before the war, placed the entire French and German outputs of coal and steel under a single European High Authority. It created a common market for coal and steel products but managed that market as a cartel. For the United States the ECSC meant that France now accepted the principle of German reunification. For France it meant secure access to the resources of the Ruhr, European markets for French firms, and the success of the Monnet Plan. Milward writes: "The market would be regulated more in the French than in the German interest, because the Federal Republic would have to make economic sacrifices in return for so dramatic an acknowledgement of its equal political status. And in those sacrifices France would achieve a better guarantee of access to German resources than by any other policy now conceivable. The Schuman Plan [which proposed the ECSC] was called into existence to save the Monnet Plan."[21]

Despite the fact that the ECSC included in its ranks the Benelux countries and Italy, it nevertheless came as close as France ever got to its second preference, that is, to a mercantilist arrangement that placed fetters on Germany's capacity to dispose of the resources of the Ruhr in a sovereign manner and awarded France privileged access to them. The next two decades—the formative decades of the European Community—would see the French try repeatedly to consolidate their hold on that second preference, sometimes with success, sometimes without.

This initial diplomatic success was almost immediately followed by a dismal failure. As the Cold War, the Chinese revolution, and the Korean War increased international tensions, the United States and Great Britain pressed for German rearmament. France resisted U.S. pressures but, inspired by the success of the Schuman Plan, produced in October 1950 their own proposal for German remilitarization, the European Defense Community. The French historian Jean-Pierre Rioux describes it as "the twin of the Schuman Plan (its elaboration was once again supervised by Jean Monnet), [applying] to the problem of arms the same principles being tried for coal and steel."[22]

The plan was presented to the French National Assembly as one that would avoid "the creation of a German army . . . the constitution of German divisions, and . . . of a German Ministry of Defense."[23] It created a European army under a European ministry of defense that was accountable to a European assembly. The military budget and arms programs were integrated, and the national forces were integrated from a low level of command upward. "The dual concern to limit German independence without making inroads too deeply into French sovereignty, notably where the use of troops overseas was concerned, was everywhere apparent [in the treaty]."[24] In geopolitical terms, the EDC promised to give the French a significant parcel of sovereign control over the use of the Ruhr's industrial power to generate military might.

The EDC turned out to be a fiasco, however. Although the Americans and the British accepted it grudgingly as the only workable way to rearm West Germany, their practical objections were such that the plan was gutted by amendments that left the French facing a German army of twelve divisions (compared with their own fourteen) that was much less integrated than the original plan called for. Meanwhile, neither the United States nor Great Britain offered any assurances regarding the future of their troops in Germany.

These revisions left the plan highly vulnerable to attack by domestic critics. It was denounced as a tool of American imperialism by the Communists and as an abdication of national sovereignty by the Gaullists. Successive French governments chose not to submit it for ratification for fear of being voted out of office. When the death of Stalin and the end of the Korean War deprived the proposal of its aura of urgency, Pierre Mendès France, who was critical of the proposal and wanted to clear the agenda of this divisive and cumbersome issue, submitted it for ratification in 1954. When the French assembly turned it down, Mendès France expressed no grief.

In conjunction with the ECSC and France's military presence on the upper Rhine, the EDC, even in its adulterated form, would have given France significant control over the military use of German resources. France's internal political weakness prevented French diplomacy from capitalizing on the success of the ECSC negotiations. France was obliged to pay the price of its weakness by admitting to an international arrangement in which the hegemonic role of the United States was far more visible and the solution to the geopolitics of the Rhine far more liberal and less exclusive than the French, in pursuit of their second preference, would have wanted.

After the rejection of the EDC by the French assembly, Germany was rapidly admitted to NATO. France received as indemnity the renewed and strengthened commitment by the United States to maintain troops on the continent and West Germany's explicit recognition of France's protectorate in the Saar. Moreover, it was agreed that all forces that were committed to the common defense of Western Europe would be placed under the authority of a Supreme Allied Command in Europe. As the entire German army was committed to the defense of Europe, the entire German army was thus subordinated to Allied authority.

The Paris accords that admitted Germany to NATO put an end to Germany's status as a legally occupied nation. Its territorial integrity was now more or less intact, though it remained a semisovereign state whose economic policy was constrained by the ECSC and whose military policy was constrained by NATO.[25] As a semisovereign nation Germany perceived an interest in spreading the "claims on its policy" as widely as possible and thus became a consistent and strong supporter of the most pro-Atlantic institutions and the most liberal forms of international integration. The more encompassing, the more liberal the international regime that defined the international institutional constraints that it had to obey, the more diluted those constraints became. For this reason, over the next twenty years Germany displayed a consistent interest in extending membership in European institutions to new members and in furthering the process of European economic and political integration, and it made clear its unflagging loyalty to NATO and to other Atlanticist institutions.[26]

France's hold on its second preference was threatened by this more liberal thrust of German policy. The French, however, did have a card: the Soviet occupation of East Germany. East Germany came between Germany and the other champions of liberalism, the United States and Great Britain, both of which, while supporting the Federal Republic's claim to the Soviet occupation zone, gravitated toward a modus vivendi with the Soviet Union that placed this issue on the farthest back burner. In the 1960s de Gaulle tried to exploit German frustration in a roundabout way. He courted the recognition of the Soviets as a credible go-between in East-West relations, a role that could be brokered to win international support of France's more exclusivist vision of Europe's future, one that offered a tighter grip on its second preference. This policy was not peculiar to Charles de Gaulle, however, and one finds elements of it being put together even before he assumed power in 1958.

French efforts to consolidate their hold on their second preference were complicated by their isolation in Europe after the EDC fiasco, and they knew that they had to spruce up their European credentials if they were to retain influence in Europe and influence over the future of Germany. France agreed in October 1956 to the return of the Saar to the Federal Republic (which corresponded to the desire of the inhabitants of that region) in exchange for continued control over the production of the coal mines of the Saar and 3 billion francs in compensation. Concomitantly, when Belgium and Luxemburg suggested in 1955 that the countries of the ECSC institute a limited tariff union among themselves, the French seized on the initiative with enthusiasm despite the fact that the idea of a Common Market—unlike the ECSC—went counter to French mercantilist efforts to force the pace of economic modernization. During the debates on the ratification of the Treaty of Rome, Pierre Mendès France was quite critical of the proposal because he thought it threatened France's agriculture, its overseas territories, and its industrial development. The treaty's supporters replied that the treaty was "a compromise between divers national interests, between economic liberalism and interventionism [*planisme*]. . . . The option is not between the Community and the *status quo*, but rather between the Community and isolation [*solitude*]."[27] Ratification of the Treaty of Rome created the conditions for negotiations with Germany "in the hope of forming some sort of continental front against the Anglo-American domination of the Alliance."[28] Negotiations began in November 1957, prior to de Gaulle's assumption of power in May 1958.

The compelling high political logic of France's attitude toward European integration is made plain by the continuity in policy between the Fourth Republic and the Fifth. Charles de Gaulle, who assumed power in the context of mutiny and revolt in Algeria, entertained an antipathy for European integration that is well known.[29] Nevertheless, he pledged to respect the Treaty of Rome and even acted to accelerate France's integration in the Common Market by freeing up protected sectors of the economy ahead of schedule, occasionally by shifting quotas to Great Britain and other non-EC countries. His new Europeanist credentials intact, he pursued efforts to form some sort of privileged relationship with the Germans. He met with German Chancellor Konrad Adenauer more than a dozen times between 1958 and 1963 and even succeeded in developing a warm, confidential relationship with him. In January 1963 the two leaders signed a Treaty of Reconciliation, establishing regular consultations between the two governments over most issues of common concern and requiring regular consultations to occur at different levels of government. It was agreed that the heads of government would meet at least twice a year and the ministers of foreign affairs at least three times a year. The principle of regular meetings between relevant authorities in the areas of defense, education, and youth was also established.[30]

The Franco-German treaty coincided with de Gaulle's veto of Great Britain's entry into the Common Market and his rejection of American proposals to participate in a multilateral nuclear force within NATO. The coincidence expressed France's ambition to retain its grasp on its second preference. That ambition, however, proved just beyond the reach of French diplomacy. There were clear indications that efforts to build a more exclusive European arrangement with Germany's cooperation were in vain. As the Bundestag debated ratification of the Franco-German Treaty, it voted unanimously to precede the treaty with a preamble stating that the Bundestag was

> determined to serve, by the application of this treaty, the great tasks that guide German policy and which the Federal Republic has advocated for years, in common with the other four allies. These tasks are: the maintenance and the consolidation of the entente between the free peoples—with a particularly close cooperation between Europe and the United States—the application of the German people's right of self-determination and the restoration of German unity, the common defense within the framework of NATO and the integration of the forces of countries belonging to this alliance, the unification of Europe in following the path defined by the creation of the European Communities and including England.[31]

For de Gaulle, the "unilateral preamble changed the entire meaning" of the treaty. When Adenauer retired in 1963, the government of Germany passed to the more liberal and staunchly pro-American Ludwig Erhart. When de Gaulle realized that Germany would not take part in the creation of a more exclusively European regional bloc, his relations with Germany turned exploitative. He took advantage of Germany's semisovereign status and its dependence on international institutions by resorting to brinkmanship that threatened the very existence of the Common Market. His efforts were repaid by the creation of the Common Agricultural Policy—according to which Germany was made to subsidize French agricultural policy—and the formal recognition of the "unit-veto" in community affairs.

This policy orientation isolated France and could not be sustained after de Gaulle's departure in 1969. His successor, Georges Pompidou, seized on the idea of European monetary union, advanced in 1969 by Pierre Werner, prime minister of Luxemburg, with much the same enthusiasm—and for the same reasons—as Edgar Faure had seized on the idea of a tariff union in 1955. Pompidou had to back France out of the dead-end in which events had left it. The need for fence-mending was great. De Gaulle's ambition to secure an exclusivist relationship with Germany had failed, leaving behind much ill will. His tilt toward the Soviet Union backfired when the Warsaw Pact intervened in 1968 to snuff out reformism in Czechoslovakia and was reduced to irrelevance when Willy Brandt and Richard Nixon, both of whom came to power in 1969, launched their own policies of rapprochement with the Soviets.[32] The French faced again the secular threat of being odd man out in a Europe ordered by German–Anglo-Saxon coaction.

The Third Period: French Internationalism, 1924–1931 and 1973–1992

In both the interwar period and the post–World War II period the French were compelled to relinquish their second preference and fall back on their third. In both cases the shove was financial, and in both cases the retreat to the third preference provoked a radical shift in the appearance of French policy. From unilateral it turned cooperative; from nationalist it turned internationalist. It is in the third period that one sees the development of Franco-German diplomacy's "famous couples," Aristide Briand and Gustav Stresemann, Valéry Giscard-d'Estaing and Helmut Schmidt.

In 1923 the occupation of the Ruhr by the French caused the United States to set aside its short-lived fantasy of recovering its prewar isolationism and induced it to assume leadership in finding a solution to the geopolitical puzzle of the Ruhr. United States intervention was seen by all as the sine qua non of extricating the belligerents from the mutually damaging embrace in which they were now caught. The U.S. ambassador to Germany, Alanson B. Houghton, wrote to Secretary of State Charles Hughes on February 27, 1923:

> Having destroyed any balance of power in Europe and left France for the moment all powerful, we have simply let loose a great elemental force which inevitably seeks to satisfy itself. . . . France must be met by force. One might as well attempt to reason with the law of gravitation. . . . I believe sincerely if it is to America's interest to save what is left of German capital and German industry . . . some positive action is required without too much delay."[33]

Poincaré initially welcomed involvement by American financiers, given the beleaguered position of the franc and the budget deficits that the occupation of the Ruhr had spawned. As for the Germans, they had been seeking to enlist American involvement since 1921. German Chancellor Gustav Stresemann recognized that the surest means of regaining sovereignty over the Rhine was to cleave to U.S. and British diplomacy and confided that an international loan, floated by the United States, "was the only means of alleviating the situation" in the Ruhr.[34] Early in 1924 the Auswärtiges Amt of the Weimar Republic reasoned that "if the United States could somehow be persuaded to invest large sums of idle and unproductive money in German industry, not only would Germany's capitalistic system benefit, but its economic recovery and the revision of the Versailles treaty would almost certainly be accelerated."[35]

American businessmen Charles Dawes, chairman of the board of directors of the Chicago Central Union Trust Company, and Owen D. Young, chairman of the board of General Electric, together tried to come up with a workable reparations payment scheme. They proposed a plan that provided for a temporary reduction in reparations payments pending the elaboration of a definitive payments schedule, the reorganization of Germany's financial structures, the requirement of unanimity among the Allies in the application of future sanctions, and the immediate military evacuation of the Ruhr. According to this plan the German government would issue 5 billion marks worth of bonds—chiefly to American financiers—the interest on which would be paid by the German railroads, and German industry would be used as collateral.

The London Conference was convened in July and August 1924 to negotiate the Dawes Plan. Édouard Herriot, who had succeeded Raymond Poincaré as French premier, made a final attempt to parlay France's military supremacy on the ground into a more exclusivist bilateral arrangement with Germany by offering to shorten the occupation if Germany agreed to armaments controls and entered into a trade treaty with France. The Germans, however, were clear on where their interests lay. They professed their allegiance to greater internationalism and greater liberalism and placed faith in American and British efforts to procure the withdrawal of French troops without German concessions. Meanwhile, the House of Morgan and the governor of the Bank of England made it clear to the French that they "could not advance sizable loans to Germany unless unilateral sanctions were banned in the future."[36] The French, financially strapped and hounded by the currency speculators, withdrew from the Ruhr in 1925 and agreed to withdraw all their occupation troops in 1929—five years ahead of the schedule established by the Treaty of Versailles.

The Dawes Plan signaled "the end of French predominance in Europe," as Stephen Schuker titles his book. France's foreign policy after 1924 differed radically from the realpolitik pursued by French governments since 1919—indeed since 1892 and the formation of the Russian alliance. Having officially relinquished their remaining unilateral claims on the Rhineland, they now invested heavily in efforts to internationalize it, that is, to contribute to the success of agreements and institutions that placed constraints on Germany's power to exploit the wealth of the Ruhr sovereignly. The French now looked to the League of Nations and the United States to secure respect of those articles of the Treaty of Versailles that regulated German activity in military matters and secured the partial transfer of German wealth to the allies through reparations. Because France was now more dependent on the success of the League and the new internationalist thrust of U.S. policy, the French became a willing and even activist supporter of U.S.-inspired reformism. Having lost its grip on its second preference, France now worked at assuring the success of its third.

French diplomacy's new look was first apparent at the Locarno conference of fall 1925. France agreed with Germany and Belgium to establish a demilitarized zone along the Rhine and to admit Germany to the League, thus renouncing the use of force to prosecute its rights as defined by the Treaty of Versailles. Aristide Briand, who throughout the period shuttled between the offices of prime minister and minister of foreign affairs, thought it was necessary to "show France's good will in order to favor 'moral disarmament' in Germany . . . to incite the German government to abandon any idea of an agreement with Soviet Russia and to admit to collaboration with the western powers; and finally . . . to pave the way toward some 'European organization in economic affairs.' "[37]

In September 1926 Stresemann and Briand met in informal discussions at Thoiry, where Stresemann offered to accelerate the reparations payments in exchange for an accelerated evacuation of the territories of the Rhine. The negotiations failed, not because of Briand's opposition but because the United States wanted to reserve certain technical aspects of Stresemann's offer for the definitive liquidation of the reparations problem.

In spring 1929, Owen D. Young made public the definitive reparations payment plan that was to bear his name. It scheduled annuities over a period of fifty-nine years at a reasonably manageable rate and created the Bank for International Settlements (BIS) to facilitate and supervise the operation. The BIS—the dean of contemporary "international organizations" and set symbolically in Basel on the banks of the Rhine—materialized the link between the competition for control of the Rhineland and the development of institutions that promoted international cooperation in economic affairs. The reparations themselves were, in French eyes, an integral part of this competition, and they opposed adamantly any suggestion that the reparations be abolished. This, claimed Pierre Laval, "would put German industry in such a favorable position compared with France, England, or America that we would all regret it."[38]

French internationalism was also apparent in France's relations with the United States. In June 1927 Briand proposed a bilateral agreement to the United States whereby both parties solemnly renounced war as an instrument of policy toward each other. The resultant Kellogg-Briand Pact has been interpreted as one of the foremost expressions of the ambient liberal reformism that marked international relations during the interwar period. For the French, however, it was a means to a more concrete end: that of improving relations with the United States. The United States shared this interpretation and responded through its Secretary of State Frank Kellogg that its "government could not enter into a treaty with France that it would not enter into with other powers"; it thus encouraged Briand to interest all the principal powers in signing on.[39] Briand nevertheless insisted that France and the United States sign first, to give at least the appearance of an alliance, while pressing the United States for reservations and amendments that would better accomplish French security objectives.[40]

France's internationalism was also apparent in its reaction to the announcement on March 21, 1931, that Austria and Germany had come together to form a customs union. Although France denounced the agreement as a violation of the Versailles Treaty, recalled short-term credits, and provoked a monetary crisis, André-François Poncet, France's ambassador to Germany, confided to his German counterpart that France did not object to the customs union per se but rather "wants to suggest the application of the same system to all of Europe, whereby the further pursuit of the Austro-German plan would become superfluous."[41]

France also adopted a more internationalist attitude toward the League of Nations. At the Geneva Disarmament Conference that convened late in 1932, the French proposed a disarmament plan that would have created under the auspices of the League of Nations a nonprofessional militia in Europe that effectively deprived nations of offensive capabilities. It also presented a more modest proposal whereby national forces would be placed under League command in order to develop a more believable and workable collective security arrangement.[42]

A similar turnabout in French diplomacy occurred after 1973, when French diplomacy once again turned almost aggressively supportive of integrationist institutions. Again it was financial weakness that forced the French to relinquish their claim to the second preference and reorient their foreign policy in order to assure their grip on the third. Following World War II the French had assigned a high priority to achieving economic equality with the great industrial powers of Europe and the United States. To do this, they implemented a mercantilistic and highly leveraged policy of industrial development and modernization, supported by diplomatic efforts to forge international arrangements, notably with regard to the Rhineland, that provided external support. This policy warped the structures of France's domestic political economy. It was a source of inflation, and financial interventionism blunted the monetary policy tools with which inflationary pressures could have been contained. The inflationary bias of their political economy caused the French to rely heavily on devaluation to achieve adjustment in prices and foreign trade. The franc was subjected to multiple devaluations in 1948–1949, 1958, and 1969. The government manipulated tariffs to produce a quasi-devaluation in 1954.

The monetary crisis of 1973 and the advent of the system of floating exchange rates robbed the French of this capacity to achieve adjustment in foreign payments through currency devaluation. France's growing dependence on foreign trade, coupled with its dependence on imported commodities such as oil that were purchased with dollars, denied currency depreciation the same effectiveness as devaluation under fixed rates. As late as 1969 the French saw currency devaluation as beneficial to trade. By 1974, however, the French had become preoccupied by the tendency of currency depreciation to feed inflation as higher import prices worked their way through the economy. Because currencies floated, moreover, domestic inflation provoked further depreciation in the currency, threatening the economy with destabilizing vicious circles of depreciation and inflation. The French took note of the success experienced by the Germans—who now reaped the reward of financial and monetary discipline—and the difficulties experienced by the Italians and the British, and in 1974 the French embraced the ambition to make the franc a strong currency. To this end the French joined the European currency float which pegged currencies to the deutsche mark.

France's strong currency ambition lay beyond the capacities of its economy. The policy of leveraged growth had burdened it with an industrial sector that was highly indebted to institutional lenders and a banking sector that sported an unusually high level of debt vis-à-vis the Banque de

France. Financial fragility rendered the French economy vulnerable to policies that pegged the franc to the ever-ascending German mark. Rising interest rates increased the debt service of industrial firms, while efforts to control lending at the source through administrative caps on bank lending threatened them with a liquidity crisis.[43]

Despite financial weakness, France under Valéry Giscard-d'Estaing stayed its strong currency course, enduring humiliation when the franc was twice forced to drop out of the joint European float. Minister of Finance Jean-Pierre Fourcade pressed for reforms of the joint float in 1974 that would have constrained the appreciation of the mark, allowed for greater flexibility in intra-EC exchange rate adjustments, and increased Community credit facilities. His proposals were rejected not only because the Germans saw virtue in currency appreciation as a means to contain inflation but because they feared that French proposals were meant to force Germany to absorb inflationary pressures generated by its less virtuous partners.

Fourcade's failure made it apparent that France now required Community and, therefore, German help to stabilize its economy. This situation deprived the French of the bargaining power they had once enjoyed vis-à-vis the Germans. During the Gaullist era, the Germans were dependent on the Community to regain a position of legitimacy among Western nations and international support for reunification. Following the monetary crisis of 1973 and the advent of floating rates, it was the French who were dependent on the Community, and notably on Germany, for economic help.

In 1978 the French were able to recapture some of that bargaining power by exploiting German exasperation with the policies of the Carter administration. The French used this lever to pry open the issue of reforming the European float and win concessions that facilitated participatión by the franc. The new float, baptized the European Monetary System, provided the support of a joint float in a manner that was more congenial to weak currencies. It made more multilateral aid available to deficit countries and placed greater constraints on German monetary policy by making currency realignment a multilateral affair. Despite this success, the EMS nevertheless reflected France's loss of power within the European Community. It catered to French interests in a much different way than, say, the ECSC. If the ECSC could be likened to a limousine, speeding the French political economy along the path of rapid industrial modernization, the EMS would have to be called a wheelchair. The ECSC facilitated the implementation of French policy preferences, whereas the EMS imposed the need for significant structural reforms within the French political economy and a humiliating policy U-turn when the French under the Socialists had to alter policy according to German recommendations in exchange for a revaluation of the mark. The ECSC consecrated France's leadership within the Community, whereas the EMS consecrated Germany's.

Greater dependence on European institutions deprived France of bargaining power to pursue the second preference and obliged it to alter its diplomatic course in order to consolidate its grasp on the third. This explains why France, which once expressed the greatest skepticism concerning the virtues of European integration, is in 1992 at the forefront of efforts to "deepen" the Community, that is, to increase the competence and power of Community institutions. It explains why France, once the most vociferous champion of national sovereignty, responded to German unification with a proposal to achieve the political integration of the Community. Nor is it foreign to France's surprising decision to engage its troops alongside American troops against its erstwhile partner, Iraq, in the Middle East.[44]

CONCLUSION:
WILL THERE BE A FOURTH PERIOD?

There is a geopolitical logic to European integration. Europe's statesmen have been able to solve the riddle of the Rhine only by discarding the realpolitik of the past and donning what in appearance is a modern-day and Europeanized version of Wilsonianism. It might be objected, however, that geopolitics, though relevant to the past, is hardly relevant to the present or the future. Indeed, one can argue that the very conceptualization of a geopolitically grounded "national interest"—as understood by a Clemenceau or a Brüning, a Briand or a Stresemann, a de Gaulle or an Adenauer—has been irrevocably altered if not rendered obsolete by the development of new structures, new processes, and new norms of interaction between the semisovereign states of the European Community. Political outcomes within the Community cannot be understood if these structures, processes, and norms—as analyzed in Chapter 4 by Peter Katzenstein—are ignored.

What does the riddle of the Rhine tell us about what is happening in 1992? First, it continues to explain French policy in Europe and, indeed, provides the best and simplest explanation of why Europe's most vocal champion of national sovereignty should have become one of its most vocal advocates of integration. Second, it explains as nothing else can the distinctive political geography of the European Community, a geography composed of concentric rings, with the Franco-German relationship at the center, the rest of the Rhenish fraternity grouped around that center, and the non-Rhenish countries relegated to the periphery. It is at the center that interest is greatest in "deepening" the Community—that is, endowing the Community with yet more of the attributes of national sovereignty. It is at the periphery that such interest is weakest and the willing-ness to see the EC as principally a "free trade zone" the greatest. However, peripheral countries display the greatest interest in "widening" the Com-munity, that is, in adding new members, while France, at the center, tends to look on that prospect with greater skepticism. Neither wealth nor se-niority in the Community explain such differences as well as geography.

Third, the riddle of the Rhine poses with particular acuity the question: Will there be a fourth period? In the interwar years, of course, there was a fourth period. The French were compelled to abandon their third prefer-ence and confront again their geopolitical nightmare: the return of the wealth of the Ruhr to unconstrained German sovereignty. The ideological conflict that rocked the Weimar Republic and that intensified after the fi-nancial crises of the early 1930s never allowed the international arrange-ments that resolved the interwar conflict over the Rhineland to achieve anything like legitimacy. On the contrary, on the radical right, the arrange-ment was thoroughly discredited by the *Dolchstoß* thesis according to which Germany had been stabbed in the back by German politicians and businessmen who had sold out to foreign interests. And when Hitler brought the radical right to power, international arrangements that had meted out claims to the wealth of the Ruhr became the first victims of Nazi diplomacy. The left bank was reoccupied, Germany rearmed in violation of the Treaty of Versailles, and reparations were renounced.

Germany recovered its territorial integrity again in 1990, but it did not recover the capacity to formulate policy within that territory unilaterally. The Ruhr is German, but the power to make policy that disposes of the re-sources of the Ruhr is shared with other nations within the EC and NATO. But the geopolitical anchor that once helped to bind Germany to its semisovereign status has rusted away. German statesmen since Adenauer cleaved to the concept of semisovereignty in part in reaction to the unfet-tered nationalism of the Nazi era but also in part to win international sup-port for their claims to the Soviet zone. Semisovereignty, as a tool of geo-political strategy, has since 1990 become irrelevant.[45]

In 1992 geopolitics drives French policy, not German policy. What is there to prevent German politicians from reclaiming the right to formulate policy unilaterally, in contravention to European Community rules and processes if need be? Given doubts concerning the motivations of its neighbor to the east, how solid is the geopolitical anchor that ties France to an EC that has imposed the need for such drastic reforms in its domestic political economy?

One might argue that both France and Germany are irreversibly at-tached to the European Community by new anchors that have effectively replaced the anchor of geopolitics. The new anchors are economic interde-pendence and the evolution of new norms of international—at least European—behavior. The factories of Germany and France produce more for the export market than for the home market, and the two countries are each other's best trade partners. Nationalism is effectively invalidated by economic interest. Meanwhile, the Community has favored the evolution of new standards of "normal" international behavior that, if infringed, would lose both the French and the German government support not only among their foreign political and economic partners but among their own domestic political actors and voters as well. Just as the Italian Communist party was obliged to swear allegiance to NATO in order to win acceptance as a viable party of government, no contender for power in Germany or France would be perceived as legitimate and viable if it advocated the wholesale rejection of their countries' European obligations.

Or would it? The weak link in the argument from interdependence and norms is in fact economic. European integration evolved as a solution to a problem of geopolitics. The riddle of the Rhine was solved by developing international institutions that bound the competing nations together in a constraining integrationist arrangement informed by the canons of economic liberalism. Liberalism as the foundation of economic policy and interaction was adopted out of geopolitical necessity—not because anyone really wanted it. There is in Europe a long history of people wanting protection from markets and getting it. The notion that people have a right to such protection is as entrenched in the norms and in the political economy of Europe as are the more recent norms of European intergovernmental collaboration. This dual assumption gives rise to a tension that in the best of cases will be creative but in the worst of cases disruptive.

Katzenstein suggests that Germany—along with the small nations of Europe—have learned to deal with this tension.[46] The French have not, nor does it appear that they are about to. Is it so inconceivable that a demagogue might arise in the heat of electoral competition in France—or even in Germany—and proclaim with success that the French or Germans are getting nothing out of the European Community but unemployment and runaway immigration? Or that German workers would be better off if they were not made to subsidize the rest of Western Europe? Or that French workers would be better off if Japanese goods were not allowed to make their way to French markets from Dutch ports? The success of the National Front in France has surprised all observers, even if it is far from assuming power. Parties of the extreme right have scored spectacular successes in Germany as well.

It can, of course, be argued that economic interdependence and the sanctions that come from violating international norms would eventually force the mavericks back. But how long does "eventually" last, and how much damage can be done in the interim? To raise these questions is not to advance predictions but rather to justify skepticism regarding the integrative power of economic interdependence and new, evolving standards or norms of legitimate state behavior. If the Europeans are to preserve the good that geopolitics—in a supreme irony of fate—has brought them, they will need more of that commodity that they enjoyed in such profusion in the years following the war: smart and creative statecraft.

6

TRANSFORMING RUSSIA

A Comparison of Reforms Under Alexander II and Mikhail Gorbachev

Imagine the following scenario. There is a huge country—which we shall call Rus—that is an empire bordering Europe and spanning Asia. This country is characterized by authoritarian politics, economic underdevelopment, and considerable power in the international system. A crisis eventually develops in Rus as a response to both foreign policy setbacks and growing economic difficulties. Eventually a new leader comes to power who perceives the growing imbalance between external power and internal resources and who decides that the only solution to the many problems facing Rus is selectively to copy political and economic arrangements in those European countries that are strong in both economic and political-military terms. As a result, this leader introduces radical reforms in economics, politics, and foreign policy.

These reforms have considerable if often unexpected effects. At home the reforms produce unprecedented liberalization of politics; growing tensions within the state, within the society, and between the regime and the society; and little in the way of needed structural changes in the economy. Abroad the reforms win support for Rus from powerful countries that were once adversaries, alienate former allies, encourage rebellion along the borders of Rus, and tempt one geopolitically important colony—Jagiellonia—to push for independence. Finally, the reforms facilitate the creation of a new state that becomes a major force in Europe—Volkland.

Reforming Rus, in short, has two important effects. One is to redistribute power at home and in the international system. The second is to bring domestic capabilities into closer alignment with international power, not through expansion of domestic capabilities but rather through their contraction. As a result, the state of Rus is weaker at home and abroad.

One may wonder why I have bothered to construct an imaginary scenario, when I could have simply presented a straightforward summary of

111

stagnation and reform in the Soviet Union—from the early 1970s, when Leonid Brezhnev was in power, to the second half of the 1980s, when Mikhail Gorbachev carried out his revolution from above in Soviet foreign and domestic policy. The reason I did not name names is that the story of Rus also happens to be the story of what happened in Russia and in the international system during the reigns of Tsars Nicholas I (1825–1855) and Alexander II (1855–1881).

The purpose of this chapter is to compare these two cycles of stagnation and major reform in Russia.[1] In the first half, I develop the many parallels between these two periods of Russian history by analyzing (1) the development of conjoined domestic and international economic and political crises during the reigns of Nicholas I and Brezhnev, (2) the similarities in both why and how Gorbachev and Alexander II launched major reforms from above, (3) the considerable impact these two reforms had not just on domestic but also on international affairs. In the second half of the chapter, I provide an explanation for these many surprising parallels and draw some implications for the study of both international relations in general and the Gorbachev period in particular.

THE ORIGINS OF MAJOR REFORM FROM ABOVE

Major reforms from above, such as those analyzed in this chapter,[2] occur under rather specific historical conditions.[3] In particular, one tends to see such virtual revolutions from above when two factors come together.[4] First, there must be a crisis severe enough to be perceived by many in important political and military positions to threaten—from within and from without—the very survival of the system. This crisis tends to be both economic and international.[5] Second, there must be a change in political leadership that produces not simply a new leader but a new leader who, because of the interaction among deepening systemic difficulties, succession dynamics, and more long-term changes in the nature of the elite stratum, has the opportunity and the desire to introduce radical reform.[6]

It is, therefore, hardly surprising that major reforms from above are quite rare historical events—except, it must be noted, in the Russian and Soviet cases.[7] Such reforms have what would appear to be contradictory requirements. For example, one would think that the very factors that led to the development of a crisis—for instance, increased state vulnerability (economic and/or political-military) in the international system or a type of state structure that discourages the system from making necessary adjustments to a changing international and domestic environment—would necessarily work against the development of a political leadership willing and able to respond in a forthright way to the crisis. Moreover, although a crisis might stimulate even secure leaders to action, there is no necessary reason for them to take radical measures. Such actions would mean that they would be turning on the very system and the very groups that had so "wisely" selected them to be leaders, and radical reform (as Mikhail Gorbachev might well be saying to himself) could very well stimulate, rather than impede, the development of revolutionary pressures from within the state and from below. Finally, the very fact of a crisis would seem to mean that even if leaders were reform-minded they would lack the resources needed to introduce, let alone implement, radical reforms.

Thus great reforms seem to require, oddly enough, a system that promotes stagnation and yet is well suited for innovation. But both tsarism and state socialism seemed to be such systems.[8] In order to understand why these two systems were prone to both stagnation and innovation, let us apply the two preconditions noted above to our four cases: Nicholas I and Alexander II in the nineteenth century and Leonid Brezhnev and Mikhail Gorbachev a century later.

STAGNATION UNDER NICHOLAS I AND BREZHNEV

The first precondition for major reform from above is the development of a system-threatening crisis, in this instance resulting from international and domestic developments in Russia during the rule of Nicholas I (1825–1855) and in the Soviet Union during the tenure of Leonid Brezhnev (1964–1982).[9] In the international realm, there are several parallel developments. First, through a military buildup and active engagement in the international system, both Nicholas I and Leonid Brezhnev oversaw a considerable expansion of Russian power in the international system. Earlier membership in the select club of great powers (as a consequence of the central role of Russia in defeating Napoleon and, more than a century later, the Nazis) was, as a result, sealed during these two administrations.

Second, these were periods of growing conflict between Russia and the reigning international hegemon of the time, that is, Britain in the first period and the United States in the second. These conflicts had to do with Russia's being on a clear upward international trajectory, with considerable differences in values as well as interests, with the degree to which an expansionist Russia had begun to upset the balance of power by moving into areas that were both quite unstable and very close to areas the hegemon considered its own, and with fears on the part of the hegemon that its dominant position within the international system was, for a variety of reasons aside from the Russian threat, in danger of eroding.[10]

However, there were factors that at the same time could be said to have moderated conflicts between Russia and the other great powers. One was the sense of the great powers that conflict with Russia was a dangerous proposition, given the military resources of the country and its geopolitical location next to an unstable East, which was, in turn, next to a rising Germany. As a result, mechanisms were developed to pacify Russia and constrain interstate conflict—for example, recognition and legitimation of Russian power through Russian membership in the Concert of Europe as constructed by the Congress of Vienna (1814–1815) and through the workings of détente in the 1970s.[11] Another factor moderating the possibility of direct conflict between Russia and the other great powers was the agreement that conflict between the great powers was to be avoided at all costs—hence, the "long peace" of the postwar era in Europe and, what is often forgotten, the unprecedented "long peace" of 1814–1854, wherein there were no wars between the great powers. Finally, there was the recognition on the part of the other great powers that Russia played a vital role in stabilizing what was considered a rather unstable part of Europe, east-central Europe and the Balkans. For example, one can point to Nicholas I's role in helping prop up the Ottomans, saving the Habsburgs in 1848–1849 by putting an end to the Hungarian revolution, controlling Poland (albeit with difficulty), and more generally, providing a bulwark against the dangerous ideologies of the French Revolution that had played havoc with Europe from Napoleonic times onward.

Leonid Brezhnev, of course, also functioned as the gendarme of Europe. Especially after the 1968 invasion of Czechoslovakia and the unusually long peace in Eastern Europe that followed until the rise of Solidarity in 1980, Brezhnev managed to stabilize the very same areas that Nicholas I did. And he, like his predecessors in office, provided one more benefit to the West in the bargain—that is, Soviet constraints on German power.

The final international parallel between these two periods was the sudden reversal in military fortunes at the end of both Nicholas I's and Brezhnev's terms in office. Just as the Crimean War (beginning in 1854—one year before Nicholas I died) put to rest the widespread assumption that Russia was invincible on the battlefield, so the war in Afghanistan, combined with a number of other international setbacks, advertised the limits of Soviet power in the international system. Thus the widespread feeling that Russia had finally arrived in the international system during the times of Nicholas I and Leonid Brezhnev was giving way, by the end of their terms in office, to increased awareness that the expansion of Russian presence in the international system might not mean expansion of Russian power in the international system.

In the domestic realm there are also a number of similar developments during the periods when Nicholas I was tsar and Leonid Brezhnev was general secretary. First, there are many similarities in the conditions under which these two leaders came into office and in how the leaders changed over time. Both of them followed liberalizers—Alexander I and Nikita Khrushchev, whose policies had generated significant domestic turmoil.

For example, Nicholas I faced a revolt by some reform-minded army officers—the Decembrist uprising—immediately after coming to power. Moreover, the successions in both cases were rather conflictual. Finally, although both Nicholas I and Brezhnev seemed to give early signals that they supported a liberalization of the system (for instance, with respect to censorship and with respect to looser policies in the colonies), they were relatively quick to become more conservative when confronted with domestic unrest in the empire and elsewhere—for example, the Polish uprisings and the revolutions in the 1830s in Belgium, Spain, and Greece and in much of Europe in 1848 in the case of Nicholas I, and in the case of Brezhnev, the Czechoslovak Spring of 1968.

Another parallel has to do with their very long tenure in office. Nicholas I was tsar for thirty years, and Brezhnev was general secretary for eighteen years. When this long tenure interacted with fears of domestic unrest and with a stance at home that sought "stability in cadres" along with stability in public policy and in the social structure, the results were predictable. These were both periods of economic stagnation, growing corruption among public officials and reduced central control over the bureaucracy, the military, and the intelligentsia. As a result, although the dominant message was conservative, there were nonetheless developing pockets of reform-minded people who began to congregate in preparation for the time when the political system might become more receptive to change.

Finally, the end of the rules of both Nicholas I and Leonid Brezhnev were marked by economic crises. These crises reflected the costs of having pursued a very ambitious foreign policy and the incapacity of a backward and quite rigid social and economic system to match what were during the 1830s and 1840s and again in the 1970s major economic and military innovations in the West.[12] Indeed, just as the economic crisis by the end of the 1970s reflected in part Soviet failures to undergo what in the West was a second industrial revolution, so the crisis 130 years before reflected Russian failures to match the Western experience of the first industrial revolution.[13]

Although all of these parallels are important, three need some elaboration because of the way in which they interacted to produce a systemic crisis. These three parallels are rapid upward international mobility, sudden military reversals, and the onset of an economic crisis.

Much has been written, of course, on these topics in the case of the Soviet Union under Brezhnev. I refer, for instance, to the work on Soviet achievement of both military parity with the United States and global power status during the Brezhnev era; the burdens on Soviet foreign policy imposed by an increasingly vigorous West, a prolonged and unsuccessful war in Afghanistan, an Eastern Europe that was increasingly unstable and indebted and at the same time less willing and able to share the regional defense burden, the acquisition of what could only be termed Fourth World client states, and the possibility of U.S. development of Star Wars technology; and the growing problems with the Soviet economy as a consequence of the size of the military burden, the size of the imperial burden, and the considerable and cumulative inefficiencies of an economy that is centrally planned, state owned, and isolated from the global economy.[14] The message in all this, of course, is clear. By the end of the Brezhnev era, the Soviet Union was facing a crisis in economics and a crisis in foreign policy, and the two were closely linked.

In the case of Nicholas I Russia came to be recognized in the period of the 1820s to the 1840s as a great power and as a state on an upwardly mobile trajectory. A number of factors contributed to this achievement—for example, the considerably greater size (and periodic modernization from Peter I onward) of the Russian army in comparison with the armies of the other major powers; the quite long run of important Russian military victories, beginning with Peter I's defeat of the Swedes at Poltava in 1709 and continuing through to Russian success in defeating Napoleon; and the rapid expansion of the Russian empire over the course of the eighteenth through the mid-nineteenth centuries. Added to this, of course, was the growing realization among the European powers that Russia's proximity to Prussia, Austria, the Ottoman Empire, and much of Asia translated into a superb geopolitical location. This advantage would only be enhanced, of course, once the West began to carve up Asia and step up competition for colonies, a vacuum began to develop in what came to be known much later as Eastern Europe, and Germany became a power in the international system.

Finally, there was the fact that Russia under Nicholas I demonstrated to the other great powers that it was not only insulated from the revolutionary upheavals that in the 1830s and in 1848 had hit virtually every continental European country but was also quite willing and able to put down its fair share of such revolts—in Poland, for instance, and later in Hungary. Indeed, in the revolutions of 1848, Russia stood alone fighting the revolutionary flood.[15] Thus Russia had become not just powerful but also a major contributor to stability in the European state system.

But in 1854 the Crimean War began, wherein Britain and France allied against Russia in order to stop Russian expansion. This war was, by the standards of the nineteenth and twentieth centuries, a very small war. However, the Crimean War was a turning point in the evolution of the international system in the nineteenth century.[16] It revealed that the Concert could no longer pretend a solidarity of values or interests among the great powers and that the Concert could no longer even structure the peace, let alone prevent war. Moreover, the collapse of the Concert laid the groundwork for a redistribution of power within Europe—a redistribution that could be cemented only, as is usually the case, by growing interstate conflicts. But the Crimean War also had powerful effects on Russia by ending the legitimacy of Russian claims to being an equal, let alone a possibly superior, member of the great powers' club.

Russia lost the Crimean War for several reasons. One was that Russia had not kept up with recent economic or military innovations in the West.[17] Although this was not a problem earlier in the reign of Nicholas I— as the technological determinants of success in war had stabilized for a time; the military impact of the industrial revolution was delayed; and the interdependence among political organization, economic development, and military power was only beginning to materialize—the failure to be like the West became a major problem in the 1850s.

The second reason Russia lost the Crimean War was socio-political. Russia had finally paid the price for lacking such important assets as literacy, an efficient administration, and regularized procedures for the mediation of political and social conflict.[18] The costs of being "a premodern actor on a modern political stage," as Alexander Yanov once put it, had finally (or once again) caught up with Russia. That the Russian elite and elites elsewhere in Europe had become used to thinking of Russia as a formidable military power, of course, merely exaggerated the impact of Russian defeat in the Crimean War.

If Nicholas I, like Brezhnev, presided over the rise and then the sudden fall of Russian power in the international system, then Nicholas I, also like Brezhnev, presided over a mounting crisis in the Russian economy. Although economic growth and structural change in the last years of Nicholas I's rule were not insignificant and although the backwardness of the Russian economy at the time has been exaggerated,[19] the fact remains that Russia had managed to miss out on all those changes in social structure, fiscal institutions, bureaucracy, and technology (military and civilian) that by the early nineteenth century had proven crucial in promoting agricultural efficiency, an industrial revolution, and military success in the West.[20] If the historically cumulative nature (to borrow from Crisp)[21] of Russian economic, social, and political backwardness were not enough of a problem, there were also some short-term economic setbacks coming into play by the mid-1850s—for example, a credit squeeze in European and American money markets that hit Russia very hard by 1858 and the financial burdens imposed by the Crimean War. When combined, these setbacks led to the collapse of the Russian Central Bank and not a small amount of domestic instability not long after the death of Nicholas I.[22]

What we see in both Brezhnev's Soviet Union and Nicholas I's Russia, then, is the development by the end of their rules of an interlocked domestic and international economic, political, and social crisis. Konstantin

Nikolayevich's observation about Russia after the Crimean War—that "we are both weaker and poorer than the first-class powers"[23]—was an observation that could very well have been made in 1982 as well.

Let us turn now to the second precondition for great reforms—the rise to power of new leaders with the commitment and the capacity to introduce radical reform.

THE DECISION TO REFORM:
ALEXANDER II AND GORBACHEV

Why did the successors to Nicholas I and Leonid Brezhnev—Alexander II and Mikhail Gorbachev—decide to introduce radical reforms of their systems? Part of the answer, of course, has already been presented. Their countries were in grave trouble. It was not just that Russia in 1855 and the Soviet Union in 1985 were facing downward mobility in the international system because of military weakness and economic deficiencies; it was also that the two were inextricably entwined. The severity of these crises and their interdependent character, of course, could be construed as forcing actions.

But this does not explain why Gorbachev and Alexander II did not, like their immediate predecessors, opt to fiddle while Moscow burned, or for that matter why they did not decide to follow a more moderate strategy of reform. After all, the changes required were intimidating—in economics, politics, social structure, and foreign policy—and they were historically unprecedented. Both leaders could reason that a serious overhaul of the system might produce not just few results but also less power for them and for the state, growing domestic political instability, and a virtual invitation to other states to capitalize on a Russia in turmoil. Moreover, both Alexander II and Gorbachev were very much products of their systems and were, because of their high positions and their long socialization, very much believers in their systems. Finally, both men were subject, of course, to the considerable ambivalence all Russian leaders have felt about the West since the beginnings of Western influence with the fur trade in the fifteenth century:

> Europe was perceived as both a source of progress and a threat. European culture, values, technology, organization and social structure were seen by some as a required set of preconditions for the development of Russia domestically and as the basis for competing with Europe internationally. The European threat was perceived both in terms of the conflict of national interests that expressed itself intermittently in the form of war and in terms of the colonial relationship that many Russians saw emerging in Russia's dealings with Europe.[24]

There are no definitive answers to the question of why Alexander II and Gorbachev were willing to go against their pasts and to take considerable personal and systemic risks in order to restructure their systems. Part of the answer to this question must necessarily be idiosyncratic, that is, located in the specifics of their personalities and experiences.[25] However, part of the reason they decided to let loose major reform from above must rest with more generalizable factors. After all, the structural context of reform in the two cases is quite similar, and Russian history features a number of cases of "big" reformers—for instance, not just Alexander II and Gorbachev, but also Ivan the Terrible, Peter I, Catherine, Stalin, and Khrushchev.[26]

One factor that seems to have played a role in both cases is the backgrounds of these two men. Both Alexander II and Mikhail Gorbachev were, given their education, their exposure to the West, and the significant mentoring provided by their predecessors, unusually well prepared for assuming the position of leading their country and engaging in significant, Western-oriented reforms. Moreover, both witnessed from their youth to their middle age radical changes in Russia that involved significant gains, especially on the international stage, and then sudden decline. Finally, both came to power after a leader who was long in office and through a succession that by Russian standards was unusually smooth. Their particular and similar experiences, therefore, could very well have given them a sense of urgency and a relatively well-specified agenda for change; an openness to new ideas, especially from the West; and considerable political power.

Another factor is the degree to which one finds in both periods a crucial role played by what W. Bruce Lincoln has called for the case of Alexander II "enlightened bureaucrats."[27] One consequence of the administrative reforms of Khrushchev and Brezhnev (in the early years) and in the nineteenth century case, the administrative reforms of Alexander I and Nicholas I (again, in the early years of his rule) was that the bureaucracy came to be populated more and more by a distinct group of people who were comparatively well educated, more professional, more aware and envious of trends in the West, and, more generally, shaped in significant ways by earlier rounds of reform. By the time Alexander II and Gorbachev came to power, this group of people had moved up through the ranks and established connections with each other and were quite frustrated by both the stagnation of the center and the constraints on their influence as a consequence of what was termed in the Brezhnev era the policy of "stability in cadres," that is, the absence of opportunities for both upward mobility and the circulation of new ideas. Once it was clear that the system was in dire straits and once the death of the leader liquified power and policy, these enlightened bureaucrats had the opportunity to make their ideas and their interests known.

There are two other factors, more systemic in nature, that seem to have encouraged Alexander II and Gorbachev to introduce major reform from above. One has to do with the nature of elite socialization in tsarism and in state socialism. It would seem logical to infer that elites in these two systems would have picked up certain values and attitudes that would, under the circumstances already noted, encourage receptivity to major reform. Such beliefs included (1) a strong commitment to the survival and prospering of the system, (2) considerable fears about becoming vulnerable in the international system, (3) the necessity for the state to regulate society (an idea that grew out of Peter's blending of absolutism and Muscovite culture), and (4) the central role of the leader as *the* source of change and stability in the system. Thus, elites in Russia carried a strong sense of personal responsibility for their fate and for the fate of the system. That both tsarism and state socialism created extraordinary degrees of dependence of elites on the leader and thereby encouraged subordinates to be yes-men merely reinforced this notion of the leader as *the* person responsible for the fate of individuals and the system.

The second factor is the nature of leadership succession in tsarism and state socialism. Succession rites in both cases feature a small "selectorate," nervous vested interests jockeying for position, pushy new interests, and finally, an eventual resolution of the crisis in which the new leader gains significant control over policy and personnel. What this means, particularly when combined with the beliefs inherent in elite socialization, is that succession can function as a mechanism of policy innovation by sensitizing the system and the new leader to problems confronting the system; by opening up the system to new ideas, new blood and new interests; by intertwining (rather than separating, as is the case in mass-based succession procedures) the struggle for power and the making of public policy; and by giving the leader the incentives (given the need to cement his powers) and the capacity (given centralization of the system, the importance of arbitrary authority, and the pressures on major interests to ally with the leader in order to survive) to enact major changes in the system. Thus, although the structure of the system, tsarist or Stalinist, can be said to encourage stagnation, the nature of succession in these systems can encourage innovation. What tsarism and state socialism lacked in capacity to make continual and small adjustments in response to changes in the environment, they gained in their capacity to make periodic and large adjustments. This trade-off is particularly the case, of course, when past reforms have left important traces and when the system is facing a crisis. Indeed, the process of succession, in interaction with the nature of the system, may very well explain what Alexander Yanov has termed the cycles of stagnation and innovation in Russian history.[28]

Thus the Great Reforms of Alexander II and the reforms of Mikhail Gorbachev (which we will discover were even greater) seem to have arisen as a result of three sets of factors. The first was the crisis, economic and political-military, that developed during the last years of Nicholas I's and Leonid Brezhnev's long tenure in office. The second set of factors was the background of Alexander II and of Gorbachev. Finally, there were some systemic factors at work—in particular, the values and attitudes fostered by the process of elite socialization in tsarism and state socialism and the pressures and possibilities for policy innovation arising from the process of leadership succession in highly centralized patrimonial dictatorships.

Let us now turn to the issue of comparing the reforms of Gorbachev with the reforms of Alexander II. As we will see, although there were important differences between the two reforms (as one would expect, as the world of the 1980s was, after all, not the world of the 1860s and 1870s), there were nonetheless some striking parallels between the two reform efforts. This is particularly the case with respect to the logic underlying these reforms.

GOALS, STRATEGIES, AND POLICIES: PERESTROIKA AND THE GREAT REFORMS

Perhaps the best way to summarize the approaches to reform taken by Alexander II and by Gorbachev is to focus on the ideas structuring these reforms and then to lay out the specifics of these two reform packages.[29] Both Alexander II and Gorbachev felt that their country was facing a severe crisis. If existing trends continued, in their views, their systems would face in the not-too-distant future the possibility of popular rebellion and the probability of rapid downward mobility in the international hierarchy of military power and economic might. That they would pay dearly on a personal level for such outcomes, of course, was not an insignificant consideration. However, although they were quite worried about the future of their country, they were not so worried as to rule out major reform as too risky a venture because they believed in the fundamental resilience of the system and their capacity to steer the system through the difficulties of reform. With this peculiar combination of fear and confidence, then, Alexander II and Gorbachev could opt for major reform from above.

Second, both leaders diagnosed the problem in a similar way. In particular, they saw the roots of the crisis as a function of three interrelated factors: inefficient government, a backward economy, and a foreign policy that had produced over time more and more costs but fewer and fewer gains. Thus the agenda of reform was clear: to make the government more efficient, to make the economy more efficient and productive, and to develop a foreign policy that would enhance national security.

Third, both Alexander II and Gorbachev sought reforms that were in some senses radical and in other respects moderate. The radical side of these reforms had to do with, first, their willingness to borrow from the West. After all, the West had demonstrated that its governments were more efficient, its economies more robust, and its capacity to influence outcomes in the international system far greater than seemed to be the case for Russia. But emulating the West, though a rational idea, was also a radical one, as Russians had long been divided between those who wanted to preserve the Russian past and those who wanted to emulate the West. But in the views of Alexander II and Gorbachev, there was little choice, as "Westernization was the price of survival."[30]

But these reforms were radical in two other ways. One was the degree to which many of the reforms of Alexander II and Gorbachev involved sharp breaks with the Russian and Soviet past—for example, the emancipation of the serfs, the judicial reform, and the creation of a form of representative government at the local level in the case of Alexander II and in Gorbachev's case, laying the base for the development of civil society, the breakup of the party's economic and political monopoly, decolonization of Eastern Europe, and the forging of a political-military alliance with the West.

The other aspect of these reforms that made them radical was that they took on so many parts of the system. Unlike some of the other cases of "big" reforms from above, such as the aptly named T'ung Chih Restoration in China or Roosevelt's so-called revolution in the United States,[31] the reforms of Alexander II and Gorbachev involved changing virtually every aspect of the system—the economy, the political system, the social structure, and foreign economic and political-military relations. Thus, although the changes introduced in any one of these areas could be seen as less than radical, especially if dilution during implementation is taken into account (a particularly compelling argument in the case of Alexander II), the fact that the reforms blanketed the system would seem to qualify them as instances of radical change.

But in other ways, the reforms of Gorbachev and Alexander II were moderate. After all, borrowing from the West was quite selective. Moreover, it was never their intention either to recreate the Western historical experience on Russian soil or, more importantly, to produce a great leap forward into capitalist liberal democracy.[32] The two leaders rejected such a radical turn in Russian and Soviet development because they were quite aware of the many historical and cultural differences between the East and the West; because the West was composed of small countries that had less to fear from the international system (there was, for instance, no equivalent to the Tartar Yoke); because Russia had no historical precedent for such a "passive" state; because development in the West tended to be organic in nature, whereas Russian development tended to be much more revolutionary in character; and because radical change might very well produce a collapse of the system but without a new system to take its place. Gorbachev and Alexander II also rejected radical reforms because both were reformers, that is, they accepted certain givens of the system. Thus the reforms could not go so far as to call into question either the boundaries of the state or the central role of the reformer within the political system. Tsarism would be amended tsarism, and state socialism would be converted into a "normal dictatorship."[33]

The final set of ideas that influenced these two reforms had to do with strategic considerations. Just as both Gorbachev and Alexander II assumed that these reforms might go too far in transforming their systems, so they assumed the reforms might not go far enough. Reform, in short, was a dangerous proposition, meaning that the strategies of reform were every bit as important as the reforms themselves. This assumption led Gorbachev and Alexander II at first to be quite sensitive to maintaining, if not expanding, their powers during the reform process. In part, this approach represented pure self-interest and in part a belief that the necessary reforms would not materialize unless they maintained control over the system and over the reform process. Thus, for instance, both used their appointment powers to the fullest, created commissions that would occupy opponents of reform and give them a sense of some influence over the process (while generating ideas and enhancing the prospects for implementation), restructured the political system in such a way as to guarantee their political centrality, and jumped all around the political spectrum in order to weaken enemies of reform and constrain overly liberal supporters of reform.

Second, both chose to ally with the intelligentsia during the early stages of reform. This association allowed them to inject the system with some new blood, co-opt the ideas and the support of the intelligentsia, provide a counterweight to those opposed to reform (who dominated important positions at the time of Gorbachev's and Alexander II's accession to office), and win some support abroad for their liberal stance. It also promised, at least in the short term, to provide some element of political stability, given the propensity of the Russian intelligentsia to function as a less than loyal opposition.

Third, both the tsar and the general secretary saw political reforms as crucial to the success of the reform process. For both, political reforms were valued because they would make the decisionmaking process more rational, enhance the powers of the reformer, and aid in the struggle for reforms in foreign policy and in the economy. Gorbachev, who went much farther down the path of liberalizing Russian politics than did Alexander

II, injected the Soviet system with competition, rationalized the political structure of the Soviet Union, created some of the foundations for representative government, and liberalized the role of the media. He did all this for a variety of reasons. In particular, he thought that these reforms were crucial to (1) making decisionmaking more informed, more efficient, and therefore more rational; (2) creating a new body of public officials with some stake in the reform process; (3) enhancing the possibility (rare in recent Soviet history) that policies made would actually be implemented; (4) obscuring all those moves that were in fact not just augmenting his political powers but also creating an institutionalized base for the exercise of those powers; (5) keeping his enemies divided; (6) giving the public and the intelligentsia a stake in the reform process; (7) kicking the state out of the economy by kicking the public into politics; (8) providing a cushion for the costs of economic reform by giving at least some segments of the public more political influence; and (9) mobilizing support in the West for the Soviet reform process in general and for Gorbachev in particular. Thus the political reforms of Gorbachev served a number of strategic functions.[34]

Finally, both Gorbachev and Alexander II introduced reforms in foreign policy that were strategic in nature, including such actions as courting Western elite opinion and making alliances in the international system that would, in effect, guard their security during the rigors of domestic reform. Thus just as Gorbachev reached out to the West, so Alexander II allied first with France and then with Prussia in order to stave off any territorial threats.[35] That the actions of both contributed (more directly in the case of Gorbachev) to the eventual unification of Germany will be addressed in the next section of this chapter.

We can now turn to a summary of the reforms enacted by Gorbachev and Alexander II. Because there were so many reforms in both cases and because the specifics of these reforms are elaborated elsewhere, I will present merely a general overview. This overview, it must be noted, stresses similarities in the two reforms and downplays their differences.[36] First, both Gorbachev and Alexander II introduced structural changes in the economy. These changes included, for instance, the beginning of capital markets in Russia, privatization of land ownership in the countryside, shifts in state investment priorities toward more "modern" sectors (for instance, railroads in the nineteenth century and computers in the 1980s), modernization of the fiscal system, encouragement of foreign capital investment, and more generally, encouragement of market transactions in the economy. Second, there were significant social reforms. There were, for instance, prison reform and educational reforms in both cases. Moreover, there was a reduction in state control over society and therefore an expansion of what could be termed civil society in Russia.

Finally, there were two types of significant political reforms in Gorbachev's and in Alexander's Russia. One type was what could be termed a liberalization of politics, that is, an expansion of citizen rights and citizen roles in politics. This liberalization involved, more specifically, release of political prisoners, expansion of civil liberties, judicial and legal reforms that enhanced the rights of citizens, and finally, creation and/or strengthening of representative political institutions—for example, the zemstvos in Alexander's time (the first formal representative institutions in Russia) and, in the Gorbachev case, the creation of a powerful and genuinely representative national legislature. But the most significant liberalization of politics came through the introduction of *glasnost* (publicity)—a term coined during Alexander II's time and picked up by Gorbachev.

The purpose of glasnost in the 1860s and 1870s was quite similar to that of Gorbachev's time. As Prince Petr Dolgorukov put it during the reign of Alexander II: "Without the broad development of 'glasnost' the government will never have the opportunity to recognize its abuses [in administration] and thus will never have the opportunity to eradicate them."[37] Glasnost, in short, was a device for encouraging people to speak out about failures of policy, corruption, and deficiencies of public officials. It was a device to promote feedback and enhance efficiency in a system that lacked the usual mechanisms for achieving these aims, that is, markets, political parties, interest groups, and more generally, political and economic competition. That glasnost went much further in Gorbachev's case and was combined, unlike the case in Alexander's time, with other reforms that greatly expanded political competition meant, of course, that "constructive feedback"—the goal in both cases—turned rapidly and easily into democratization of Soviet politics.[38]

But there was another side to the political reforms of Gorbachev and Alexander II—the commitment to creating orderly political procedures. In practice this meant, for instance, attempts to rationalize the bureaucracy and the ministerial system, calls for establishing rule of law and legality (*zakonnost*), reform of urban administration and budgeting, and changes in the judicial system that were to create something unknown in Russian history—an independent judiciary. These reforms, it must be noted, were not about placing constraints on the leader; they were about creating a more efficient state that would be not only stronger but also more responsive to political control exercised at the pinnacle of the system.[39] Moreover, there was substantial ambivalence about rule of law when that might mean infringing on *proizvol*, the arbitrary authority of the leader.[40] In the Soviet Union, as in Russia, even during reform the assumption was that "the Sovereign is the living law."[41]

Finally, there were significant reforms in foreign policy. Both Alexander II and Gorbachev forged new alliances in the international system, sought

Western support for their reforms, loosened the bonds of empire, and pared back on traditional Russian commitments to expansionism. These policies, in combination with the domestic reforms, led Russia to pursue a policy that was characterized during the Gorbachev period as "joining Europe." Moreover, both leaders engaged in significant reforms of their militaries. Finally, although both disengaged from active participation in the international system, their overriding and ultimate long-term concern was nonetheless to increase Russian power in international affairs.

As should be apparent from even this brief discussion, the reforms introduced by Gorbachev and Alexander II were many, extraordinary in their multifaceted character, and quite clear in their commitments to restructuring Russian domestic and foreign policy. The consequences of the reforms, moreover, were considerable, especially in the case of Gorbachev. It is to these that we now turn.

DOMESTIC AND INTERNATIONAL CONSEQUENCES OF THE REFORMS

There are many ways to think about the consequences of reform. One can evaluate consequences in terms of (1) the degree to which they met their stated goals; (2) their costs and benefits, irrespective of the goals of the reformers; and (3) their overall impact on domestic and foreign affairs. Rather than choosing among these various perspectives on impact, I will employ all three. However, I will be succinct—first, because a fair evaluation of the impact of these reforms would require a book-length treatment; second, because there are problems involved in comparing reforms with known consequences versus reforms, as in the Gorbachev case, whose repercussions are still not fully known.

There is no question that the Gorbachev and the Alexandrine reforms fell short of their objectives. The Russia that emerged from these two rounds of reform was not a Russia significantly more efficient in either economic or political terms or more stable or more powerful in the international system. For example, in the case of Alexander II, the structural changes necessary for producing an industrial revolution in Russia did not materialize in Alexander's time; Russian government continued to be plagued by arbitrary and overly centralized decisionmaking; and the military reforms—as the Balkan campaign demonstrated—did not make the Russian army equal to its main competitors in the West. Indeed, the areas that seemed to have been of greatest concern to Alexander—improving the efficiency of government and the international position of Russia— were the areas in which the reforms could be said to have had their most limited effects.

The Gorbachev reforms also fell far short of the mark. Rather than transforming the Communist party into an agent of enlightened change, Communist party hegemony collapsed in the Soviet Union. Rather than creating an efficient economy, the Gorbachev reforms (political as well as economic) led to the "de-planning" and then the collapse of the Soviet economy.[42] Finally, there is no question that domestic turmoil, economic collapse, and loss of empire together produced by 1990–1991 a Russia on a downward trajectory in the international system.

The Gorbachev and Alexandrine reforms, in short, failed to invigorate Russia. It is not surprising, therefore, that both men became targets of some scorn by the time they were forced out of their positions—Alexander through assassination and Gorbachev through a coup d'état, first by the military in August 1991 and then with greater success by the Russian president, Boris Yeltsin.

If we view these two reforms in terms of costs and benefits, however, we find a more complex picture. Let us turn first to the Alexandrine reforms. These were, of course, costly reforms. They revealed to the powers that be in the international system that Russia was far weaker than many had assumed; they encouraged domestic unrest and unrest in the empire; and they alienated many because they were too much for those who were powerful and too little for those who were not. Moreover, the reforms carried with them a very important lesson that was to shape Russian politics until the Bolshevik Revolution. The lesson was that there was an irreconcilable tension between maintaining tsarism and creating an efficient, just, and secure order in Russia. Amending tsarism, in short, could not work. Choices had to be made.

But there were, nonetheless, some significant benefits attached to these reforms. It can be argued that the Alexandrine reforms laid the base—particularly with respect to building railroads and beginning capital markets—for the rapid industrialization of Russia that followed in the reign of the next tsar.[43] The reforms also contributed greatly to the modernization of the Russian political and social system by liberating the serfs and introducing (albeit in limited form) such Western concepts and procedures as rule of law and representative government. Indeed, as Jerry Hough has argued,[44] Russia might have evolved in the direction of developing genuine liberal democracy (especially in view of the impact of political and economic developments during the reign of the last tsar, Nicholas II) had not the crisis of World War I and the Bolshevik Revolution intervened. In this sense, the reforms of Alexander II were important in opening up the possibility of a liberal developmental trajectory for Russia.

The costs and benefits of the Gorbachev reforms were similarly mixed and quite extreme. The costs are evident: the collapse of Communist party hegemony, the Soviet economy, the Soviet state, the Soviet empire and the world Communist movement; the end of the Soviet Union as the "other" superpower and as the leader of the world socialist movement; and the very real possibilities, particularly given the collapse of the Soviet Union and the explosive interaction between economic and political liberalization, of wars within and between the newly independent states that were once republics within the Soviet Union and that make up (minus the liberated Baltic republics) the Commonwealth of Independent States.[45]

But these many costs must be judged next to the considerable benefits gained from the reforms. We must keep in mind that the Gorbachev reforms are still in process insofar as their consequences are concerned. Although the Gorbachev era has ended, the revolution started by Gorbachev has not. Moreover, all revolutions, even those begun from above, tend to register many costs before their benefits can even begin to materialize. Radical change requires systemic collapse; otherwise, changes will be incremental in nature. What I am suggesting, then, is that we should place the many costs at the time of the Gorbachev reforms in the context of the past and, to the degree possible, in the context of the future.

Having said all this, what then are the benefits of these reforms? I see two major benefits. One is that Gorbachev created the necessary (albeit by themselves insufficient) conditions for the development of a liberal political and economic order in what is now called Russia. This he did by (1) introducing the foundations of a liberal order in Russia, and (2) destroying Stalinism. By the foundations of a liberal order, I refer to the beginnings from 1986 to 1991 of the development of capitalism—through, for instance, steps in the direction of marketization, privatization, and free trade and the development of liberal democracy through, for example, expansion of civil liberties, encouragement of political competition, and creation of representative government. But of equal importance—in itself and for the room it gave liberal reforms to survive and prosper—was the destruction of the Stalinist order. In particular, Gorbachev's reforms ended both the domestic side of Stalinism—that is, central planning, state ownership of the means of production, and dictatorship in the hands of a single, Leninist party—and the international side of Stalinism—that is, isolation from the global economy, the hierarchical regional system that tied Eastern Europe to the Soviet Union, and finally, economic and political-military competition with the West.

By introducing some of the elements of liberalism and by destroying Stalinism, then, Gorbachev made possible that which was impossible prior to these reforms—that Russia could evolve in the future into a liberal state. This is no small achievement. That the human costs of these revolutionary changes have been so small (as of 1992), moreover, makes this possible break with the authoritarian Russian past all the more impressive.

The second benefit is international. Although debates rage about whether the end of the Cold War is cause for relief or sorrow and whether the diffusion of liberalism will stabilize or destabilize the international order,[46] especially in the short term, the fact remains that Gorbachev has made significant contributions to international affairs. Again, the real issue is not what is going on today or yesterday, as these might very well be transition costs, but rather the possibilities that have been opened up as a consequence of the Gorbachev reforms. I refer to the possibilities that (1) the principles behind "new thinking" might serve as the basis for more just and more cooperative interactions among states; (2) the countries of Eastern Europe might evolve in the next few decades into liberal, stable, and prosperous systems; (3) a single Europe might emerge, connected through markets and liberal politics; and (4) the unusual long peace of the postwar era in Europe might become (once the transition costs work their way through the system) the rule rather than the exception. Thus the significance of the Gorbachev reforms abroad, as at home, is the addition of positive yet previously unthinkable scenarios for future developments—in Russia, in Europe, and in the international system. Although the costs of these reforms have been high (though hardly as high as one might imagine, given the collapse of the Soviet state, the Soviet economy, and the Soviet empire), the gains have been great as well. And in the long term, the gains might be even greater, once the detritus of the old order is cleared away. In this sense, the Gorbachev reforms are best understood as investments in the future of Russia, Europe, and the international system.

The final perspective on impact is the overall effects of the two reforms. Rather than repeat what has already been said, let me end with one point. Although it is clear that the Gorbachev reforms had far greater effects at home and abroad than the Alexandrine reforms, this difference should not detract from the fact that the two reforms had, nonetheless, some surprisingly similar consequences. One consequence is that both reforms laid the groundwork for revolutionary change—by mobilizing the public and by showing the bankruptcy of the ancien regime, tsarist or Stalinist. Another consequence is that the reforms succeeded far more in liberalizing politics than in liberalizing economics—the goals of the reformers notwithstanding. The final consequence is that the reforms contributed greatly to the redistribution of power on the European continent by laying the groundwork for the liberation of eastern Europe and for the formation of a unified Germany.

SUMMARY AND INTERPRETATIONS

What happened in the Soviet Union and in the international system from 1964 to 1991, then, seems to parallel in important ways what happened in

Russia and in the international system from 1825 to 1881. We find, first, similar trends at home and abroad during the tenure of the leaders who preceded Mikhail Gorbachev and Alexander II, that is, Leonid Brezhnev (1964–1982) and Nicholas I (1825–1855). These were times when relations among the dominant states in the international system were relatively peaceful and cooperative and when the Soviet Union and Russia were making stronger and stronger claims to power in the international system. There are domestic homologies as well—for instance, the brief stab at reform during the early days of the tenure of Gorbachev and Alexander II followed by quite conservative domestic policies, rising corruption, and finally, a gradual decline in the capacity of the state to control itself and society.

By the end of these two administrations, however, it is clear that Russia was confronting a number of interrelated difficulties. Tensions between the United States and the Soviet Union led to an unravelling of *razriadka* (détente), and the Soviet engagement in Afghanistan was going nowhere, just as in the nineteenth century, tensions among the members of the Concert weakened the capacity of these states to cooperate and eventually led some to wage war on Russia in the Crimea. However, what seemed to be political-military problems were actually much more. Russia, like the Soviet Union, was revealed to be a paper tiger. The economy and the social structure were backward, and the political system was inefficient and corrupt. Moreover, the future looked even grimmer, given the failure of Russia to participate in the trends overtaking the West at the time: an industrial revolution, considerable expansion of global trade, and the growing popularity of the ideas of the French Revolution. Thus the crisis that developed at the end of the reigns of Brezhnev and Nicholas I reflected not just the problems of the moment but also the likelihood that these problems would only worsen in the future, particularly given the trend in both periods in support of liberalizing politics and economics.

Immediately upon coming to power, Gorbachev and Alexander II pursued what Stephen Sestanovich has termed for the Gorbachev era a "diplomacy of decline" and both leaders launched major reforms. These reforms attempted to catch up with political and economic innovations in the West and therefore to create the necessary underpinnings for Soviet and Russian claims to being great powers in the international system. However, their desires both to maintain and to modernize the system, coupled with the sheer enormity of the task before them and the deleterious effects of the reforms on stability at home and in the empire, worked in both cases to compromise the gains of reform and the support at the top for the leader and the project of reform.

But the reforms in both cases had dramatic effects on the international system. The Soviet Union and Russia became shadows of their former selves, and the vacuum created by a Russia and a Soviet Union turned inward and a weakening of imperial control over Central and Eastern Europe together produced considerable domestic tensions in these regions and the rise of a new power in the international system—a unified Germany.

There is no question, then, that there are considerable parallels between these two periods. But there is also no question that these parallels are quite surprising. First, one would have expected there to be more traces left by the many things that happened over the course of the more than 100 years separating the times of Alexander II from the times of Mikhail Gorbachev. There were such "minor" developments, for instance, as Russian industrialization by the end of the nineteenth century, Russia's loss to Japan in the war of 1905, the 1905 Revolution, the reforms of Nicholas II, World War I, the Russian Revolution, the creation of a Stalinist state and a modern industrial society, World War II, the development of nuclear weapons, Soviet acquisition of an empire in Eastern Europe, and the rise of the Soviet Union as both a superpower and later a global power. Although these events meant, of course, that the specifics and the domestic and international consequences of perestroika could never be the same as those of the Great Reforms of Alexander II, the many changes in Russia and in the international system from the 1880s to the 1980s should nonetheless have rendered a story such as the one developed in this chapter virtually impossible.

The parallels are all the more puzzling because they cannot be explained by common understandings of the nature of Russian and Soviet historical evolution. On the one hand, if we treat state socialism as a very different kind of system from tsarism (as has been the wont of most political scientists, including myself), then how can we possibly explain the parallels uncovered in this chapter, particularly with respect to the nature of the state and the logic of the reform process? But on the other hand, if we agree with Alexander Yanov that Russian history is cyclical,[47] we are still left with the problem of having to account for the existence of cycles. Indeed, this is a particular problem because a weak Russia on the fringes of the West—as documented by historians and political scientists—should not have been able to have so much influence on international politics.

Finally, the comparison presented in this paper is puzzling from the perspective of theories in international relations. For instance, how can we explain the many parallels between these two periods in terms of Russian foreign policy and developments in international politics, when these two periods differed in those factors that are supposed to structure foreign policy and international behavior, that is, the structure of the international system and the power and place of Russia within the international hierarchy of power and privilege? Moreover, how are we to account for the powerful impact of these reforms on the international system, given, for instance, the realist view that domestic factors are unimportant, the common assumption that weak states have little international impact, and finally, the absence of any theory—despite the case of the French Revolution[48]—of a strong and combustible interaction between domestic and international transformation? Finally, how are we to reconcile the purportedly unique characteristics of the postwar long peace, the role of Gorbachev and his reforms, and the international consequences of those reforms[49] with what seem to be their many parallels with Russia and the international system from 1825 to 1881?

The many parallels between these two periods of Russian history and the history of the international system are not easy to explain. However, there is one factor that can help us begin to make sense of these domestic and international parallels. That factor is the geopolitical location of Russia. In particular, there are two aspects of geography that could be said to have shaped the evolution of the Russian state and the relationship of that state to the international system. The first aspect is the absence of natural borders, and the second is its location on the fringes of the West.

The absence of natural borders has meant that Russia has always been vulnerable to foreign invasion and at the same time repeatedly tempted, if not forced for reasons of security, to expand outward. National insecurity and international expansion, therefore, always went together in the historical evolution of Russia. This association had important consequences for the evolution of high politics in Russia. Elites in this state were quite insecure from within and from without, and military elites were political elites and vice versa. As a result, there developed in Russia a distinct elite culture. This culture defined expansion and security as the overriding goals of the Russian state and assumed that expansion of territories controlled by Russia would maximize the security of the state and vice versa. Moreover, this culture drew clear parallels between the fate of the state and the fate of those who functioned as elites within the state. Just as their security as wielders of political power was intimately connected with the security of the state in the international system, so the drive to expand their personal power was intimately connected to the drive to expand the territory of Russia outward. Thus as went expansion, so went security—at the level of the state and at the level of intraelite politics.

The vulnerability of Russia and the pressures to expand the reach of the state also shaped the character of the Russian state. This was a state in which the boundaries between civilian and military elites and between the civilian and military functions of the state were unusually blurred. This was also a state in which the boundaries between the bureaucracy and the nobility and between the state and the society were unusually blurred. It is no accident, then, that Russian tsars found it to be both very attractive and very easy to emulate—several centuries later and without the benefit of a feudal system in place—the absolutist principles of state structure in the West.[50]

But this absolutist state also faced tremendous difficulties in being genuinely absolutist. This was a state that always lacked control over its economy, its borders, and its population. After all, the constant pressures to defend and to expand had combined to produce a far-flung and ever-changing territory characterized by sparsely settled and ethnically diverse populations extraordinarily resistant to control from above. As a consequence, there were continual pressures on the Russian state to concentrate economic and political powers in order to meet the state's security needs and to compensate for all the costs to elite security and economic development that those needs necessarily generated. What this meant in practice was that the Russian state sought to compensate for its geographical vulnerability by being despotic at home, yet the very fact of that geographical vulnerability undermined the capacity of the state to be truly despotic. Thus the Russian state always seemed to be in the unenviable position of facing gaps—between its need to control its territory and its incapacity to do so and, therefore, between domestic capabilities, on the one hand, and international pressures and opportunities, on the other.

These contradictions also explain another characteristic of the Russian state—its peculiar administrative practices. Whereas in the West there were forces from the Middle Ages onward pushing in the direction of institutionalizing political authority, separating church and state, rationalizing the bureaucracy, establishing rule of law, and creating a system of ministries, cabinets, and legislatures that could advise the king, were responsible to the king, and were, finally, separated from the king, such pressures were absent in the Russian historical experience because of geographical constraints and possibilities. As a result, these many political developments in the direction of systematizing government (as Yaney has termed it)[51] did not evolve in Russia.[52]

This lack of institutional development meant that Russia was at the same time underadministered and overadministered. On the one hand, Russia was underadministered because the tsar had precious few means to extract compliance from either his state apparatus or from ordinary citizens and because he needed to protect his personal power by denying power to his lieutenants through, for instance, the exercise of purely arbitrary authority and through the sowing of divisions among departments in the bureaucracy and among his advisors. Thus despotism was joined, in this case, by limited penetration—a contradictory situation insofar as the power of the tsar and the state was concerned.[53] For example, whereas the ratio of public officials to population was 4.1 to 1,000 in Britain and 4.8 to 1,000 in France during the mid-nineteenth century, the ratio in Russia was only 1.3 to 1,000—and this in a state characterized by low population density and huge expanses of territory.[54]

On the other hand, Russia was overadministered. The need to fund an ambitious foreign policy, combined with the constant worries about national security, led the tsar continually to seek ways to establish more control over the economy and over public officials, the nobility, and the society. Thus despotism led to a constant search for more penetration. At the same time, with the tsar's arbitrary authority, with a state functioning as a political, economic, and religious monopoly, and with a public sector that was overworked, internally divided, and dependent in a personal sense (financially and in terms of job security and definition of functions) on the tsar, the system made it both very attractive and quite necessary for the tsar to attempt to micromanage the Russian system. Little could be done without the tsar, but then, little could be done with the tsar. The system was built for the maximization of power in the short term, not for the maximization of efficiency in either the short term or the longer term.

Of course, the constant tension between not enough administration and too much administration explains some of the patterns noted in this chapter. In particular, the administrative paradox of Russia—that is, its undergovernment and its overgovernment—worked to build up inefficiencies to the point of generating periodic crises; to make possible and necessary periodic reforms from above that through the exercise of the tsar's arbitrary authority sought to achieve the contradictory aims of rationalizing government and preserving, if not deepening, arbitrary authority; and to produce in the wake of reform the less than optimal outcome of more constraints on the power of the tsar and the general secretary with precious little in the way of a more efficient political system. The reforms, in short, reproduced the system.

If insecure borders had considerable effects on the development of the elite culture, the structure of the state, and the relationship between the state and the society in Russia, then so did the other fact of geographical life in Russia—its proximity to the West. First, it is important to note that Russia (and what we used to term Eastern Europe) developed as it did because Russia—more than the West—had to deal with countless migrations and countless invasions. As a result, Russia never had the luxury, as did the West, of relative security, relatively stable borders, and relatively stable populations.

Second, these disparate experiences meant in turn that the historical trajectories of Russia and the West were quite different. Absent in the Russian historical experience were not only the factors already mentioned (such as rule of law, rationalization of the bureaucracy, and the like); absent also were such developments as private property, feudalism, and an independent nobility. Therefore, the historical bases for the development of capitalism and a transition from dictatorship to democracy were never laid.

Third, with an insecure, very large, and potentially rich but economically backward Russia that could expand most easily for geographical reasons to the east and to the west and, at the same time, with a West next door in search of new areas for political and economic gain and tempted, given topography, to expand eastward, the result was predictable. Russia and the West were bound to confront each other in the international system. This confrontation, moreover, was bound to involve challenges that were international and domestic, economic, political, military, and social in nature because of the many differences between the East and the West and because of the power of the latter, given economic, political, and military developments in the West and given the increasing interdependence over time among military power, economic growth, the organizational capacity of the state, and technological innovation.[55]

The proximity to the West, then, meant that Russia had to fight the West and, moreover, to fight the West at a severe disadvantage—on the battlefield and at home. To increase Russia's competitive edge, innovations from the West had to be imported. But the other side of Russian geography—the impact of vulnerable borders on the evolution of the Russian state and Russian elite culture—ensured that the imports would always be delayed, simultaneous, from above, and quite selective. As V. O. Kliuchevskii, a prerevolutionary Russian historian, described the efforts of the first tsar who sought to save Russia by making it more like the West: "Peter took from the old Russia the absolute power, the law and the class structure; from the West he borrowed the technical knowledge required to organize the army, the navy, the economy and the government."[56]

Thus the absence of secure borders coupled with proximity to the West meant that, for Russia, geography structured development. This concept can be best understood by referring to the many contradictions created by Russian geography. Geography made this state at once vulnerable but powerful abroad. Geography made this state strong but weak at home. Geography made this state rich in resources but poorly endowed in capacity to mobilize those resources. Geography ensured that Russia could not develop like the West and would resist copying the West and would be very choosy about what it chose to import, but geography mandated that Russia would be under continual pressure to develop like the West and, as a consequence, to revise not only its foreign policy but also its domestic politics, economics, and social structure. Geography, then, encouraged this state to be a contradiction—stagnant but innovative. Finally, geography insured that the many contradictions inherent in Russia and the Soviet Union would play themselves out on the international stage.

CONCLUSION

To return to the subject of this chapter, then, I conclude, first, that it is a mistake to view Gorbachev and his reforms as events without historical precedent. Although it is true that these reforms had unusually strong domestic and international effects, it is also true that these reforms were in some sense a replay of what happened in Russia during the reigns of Nicholas I—the nineteenth century's version of the years of stagnation—and Alexander II—the author of the Great Reforms. The precedent is evident particularly if we focus on the issues of the development of a crisis in Russia, the origins of reform, the approach to reform, and the impact of reform on Central Europe and Russian power in the international system.

The many parallels between Russian evolution from 1825 to 1881 and developments in the Soviet Union from 1964 to 1991 can be explained by the one constant across these two spans of time: the geographical location of Russia. Moreover, geography—defined as both the absence of natural borders and the proximity to the West—also goes some way toward explaining the impact of stagnation and change in Russia on the structure and stability of the international system. Russia, then, was and is a state unusually well situated in a geographical sense to develop simultaneous and interdependent international and domestic crises. Moreover, geography, working through a number of other factors, has functioned to encourage Russia to launch revolutions from above in response to these crises. These reforms have combined innovations from the West with the givens of the Russian historical experience, thereby seeking to bring domestic capabilities into closer alignment with international needs and international ambitions. Finally, the geographical position of Russia has meant that these innovations worked significant changes in Russian foreign policy and in the very structure of the international system. Geography, then, helped make Russia strong and weak—at home and abroad.

7

EAST ASIA'S
AMERICA PROBLEM

The argument of this chapter is that American–East Asian relations are afflicted not just by the trade tensions that have grown since the early 1970s, to which we have become accustomed, but also by a new cultural and rhetorical divide that increases friction at the same time that it obscures the continuing realities of the relationship. This divide, in turn, is due to asymmetries of power that have been consistent in U.S.–East Asian relations for decades. Whereas the United States increasingly looks toward East Asia with apprehension, Asians look to the United States much as they have since 1945, as a bigger, stronger, even dominating nation that is nonetheless essential to their continuing growth.

I argue that certain aspects of this relationship are changing—the single-market dependency that has characterized Japan, Korea, and Taiwan, for example, and the security situation, which is considerably relaxed from the troubled years of the Cold War. East Asian moves toward diversifying markets—primarily in regard to Europe—signal a growing departure from the previous structure (going back to the World War II settlement) whereby the United States interacted bilaterally with Western Europe and Japan while Japan and Europe had little interaction. Additionally, the deepening of economic relations between Northeast and Southeast Asia heralds an interregional reorganization that will carve out more autonomy for all the Asian nations and perhaps lead to changes in the security structure.

I also argue that this attenuation of bilateral relations across the Pacific—perhaps we can call it constructive disengagement—is not necessarily bad and that it will afford the United States greater flexibility in its conduct of foreign economic policy.

While these changes occur, the deeper problem is the absence of an intellectual framework within which to understand the ongoing transition. I suggest that Japanese and East Asian economic success has provoked both admiration and deep worry in the United States, giving rise to a "new Orientalism" that both honors and shames Asians too much; quick to find fault and exaggerate differences, this tendency is also quick to patronize and praise, the excessiveness in both directions being the index of one's failure to understand the alien Other.

This chapter switches the optic in order to adopt the perspective of the Other, to see how it all looks from a different shore. It is then that one realizes there is a problem almost unmentioned in the contemporary East-West discourse: We might call it East Asia's America problem. I argue that the cultural constructs and contradictions by which Americans confront East Asian industrial prowess reflect not just an inability to apprehend a still-alien Other but also the antagonistic currents in American politics between protectionism and free trade and deep conflicts in the U.S. orientation to the world between expansionism and imperialism, or between what used to be called Asia-firsters and Europe-firsters.[1]

If East Asia has an America problem, of course, it is by no means only Americans who contribute to it. Indeed, the United States has been more tolerant and open than several European countries, particularly Italy and France. The well-known nationalism of the French, especially, increasingly has become the handmaiden of an appalling racism. The former prime minister, Edith Cresson, referred to "little yellow men" who stay up nights thinking about how to "screw" Europe. Japan is "another universe which wants to conquer," basing itself on a "hermetically sealed" system. "That's the way they are," she announced knowingly.[2]

THE NEW ORIENTALISM

Orientalism is a term used by Edward Said and others to connote a Western discourse about Asia that both projects Western hopes and fears onto Asia and fails to uncover the reality of Asia itself.[3] It is a species of prejudice so deeply rooted that its practitioners are generally unaware of it. American Orientalism in regard to East Asia today is Janus-faced and given to dramatic exaggeration: One face looks anxiously back to find in the past a prelude to a new yellow peril shaking the edifice of Western civilization or even to find analogues in the decade of fascist political economy in the 1930s, and the other looks forward euphorically to a Pacific Rim golden age in the next century, distinguished by "miracle" economies and budding East Asian postmodernity.

If Mark Twain's innocents abroad were non-Americans visiting America, one of the oddest cultural traits they might encounter would be America's mysterious liberal probity: Public utterance and private thoughts seem remarkably divorced, and voicing private thoughts is verboten. Yet racism appears to be on the rise on college campuses, on the far right, and elsewhere. We have heard much lately about a "politically correct" liberal

America in which ethnic jokes and racial stereotypes are forbidden in public discourse and for which a college student can be promptly expelled or a prominent person fired, unless the target is Asians in general and the Japanese in particular.

Some aspects of the problem are quite visible. It is still common on television, for example, to see crude stereotypes of rotund samurai made to masquerade as Japan's Everyman, with concomitant bellowing and swordplay. Even the stalwart critic of American education and popular culture, Allan Bloom, feels free to refer to Asians as "yellows" in his recent bestseller.[4] The business of "making strange" in regard to the Japanese and other "Asiatics" like them is still visible in spite of liberal probity, and it sells goods in the marketplace. Perhaps such stereotyping even acquires a patriotic halo in an age of perpetual trade deficits. But this realm of the visible is merely the tip of an iceberg.

If caricatures of East Asia in France are one aspect of its inveterate nationalism, we can argue that similar expressions in the United States are animated by the protectionist impulse of Middle America (or what Richard Nixon recently characterized as "mainstream," or "Newark factory gate").[5] Historically this current has been the repository of American nationalism and has conceived of East Asia as America's frontier to be conquered, organized, and civilized. The East Asian countries are perceived to be in but not of the world, free-riding on "defense" and predatory in economics—thus sapping American strength such that it fast becomes, in Joseph Chamberlain's words, "a weary Titan staggering under the too vast orb of its fate," or just an amicable fool, taken advantage of at every turn. The contemporary rancor of representatives of this view (Lee Iacocca, for example) indicates a frustration about Asians getting off the reservation and doing their own thing, so to speak.

The most influential book in the recent and growing genre of "Japan-bashing" literature is by Karel van Wolferen, a Dutch journalist stationed in Tokyo, who recently catapulted into the intellectual limelight in the United States when his book got rave reviews across the spectrum. *The Enigma of Japanese Power* both presents to us a cogent account of Japan's industrial growth and partakes of the new Orientalism. As does Chalmers Johnson's influential work, van Wolferen shows how a long pattern of state-led "developmentalism," combined with a typical pattern of followership in industrial development (copying more advanced technology and adapting previously successful management skills), lies behind Japan's successes. I agree with this analysis and have made similar arguments about South Korea. But if the best of authors cannot grasp that this industrial pattern can be understood apart from cultural and racial stereotypes, I make my point.

Van Wolferen indulges in harmful stereotyping by explaining Japanese success to Americans in terms that only multiply the misunderstanding by measuring Japanese deviance from what Westerners hold dear: The Japanese have no regard for "transcendental truths," are "less free than they should be," and are at odds with "one single command that has reverberated throughout Western intellectual development ever since the Greeks: 'Thou shalt not cherish contradictions.' "

The Japanese, the implication is, are not individuals; they are not rational, not logical, and perhaps not "enlightened"; there seems to be no Eastern equivalent of the great Western caesura termed the Enlightenment. Some Japanese, of course, cherish rationality and individualism—van Wolferen has even "met quite a few who want to be taken for distinct persons." But the Japanese remain, by and large, indistinct to him. In any case his generalizations are so blanketed and opaque that they make refutation difficult: that a people are "less free than they should be" can probably be said about any society in the world and rests on an unstated conception of freedom and morality.

When van Wolferen peered into the heart of the Japanese system of political economy, moreover, like Conrad he saw a horror staring back at him: not liberal pluralism but an all-encompassing and mysterious "System" with no exit, one "inescapable as the political system of the Soviet Union," only worse because it was more pervasive and culturally legitimate.[6]

To see Japan as enigmatic, impenetrable, not individualistic, and run by a mysterious system, of course, recalls stereotypes that go back to the first Western encounters with Asians, stereotypes that have popped in and out of the American consciousness since Perry's "black ships" first landed in Japan in 1852. What is more irresponsible, however, about the new Orientalism provoked by Japanese economic success is its dramatic exaggeration: not just indictment of Japan and its East Asian facsimiles—South Korea and Taiwan—as illiberal, run by subterranean "systems," and substituting strong states for the presumed natural workings of the market but also hints that this might really be a kind of fascism.

Van Wolferen thus exhorts Americans to deal harshly with "the Japan Problem," as Europe had to in the past with "the German Problem,"[7] and Ian Buruma, the peripatetic observer of all of Asia for *New York Review of Books*, compared the impressive Korean show during the opening ceremony of the Seoul Olympics to Hitler's Nuremberg extravaganza in 1936, which gave him the existential heebie-jeebies.[8] More recently he has argued for a "Pax Axis" between Japan and unified Germany, pacifist and quiescent in the wake of the Gulf War, but who knows what to expect from this "axis" in the future.[9] And the perhaps inevitable title has appeared: *The Coming War with Japan.*[10]

Akio Ishihara and Shintaro Morita do little more than reflect back to and play upon these dark fears in *The Japan That Can Say No*. In their idiosyncratic Japanese way they also proffer a postwar replay of the prewar repertoire. Their ethnocentric view asserts Yamato superiority in empire-building (as evidenced in the postcolonial performance of South Korea and Taiwan) over a slovenly Yankee imperialism (as seen in the Philippines). They indulge in a kind of epithet one-upmanship, seeing who can do best in previewing the contestation of the Pacific as a Japanese, and not an American, lake.[11] Perhaps Ishihara and Morita reveal more than they wish, however, because their book reads like the story of the battered schoolboy finding a way to get back at the playground bully; it reeks of insecurity.

The new Orientalism thus has counterparts on both sides of the Pacific, and it is contradictory and unsettled. For every dark worry about who the Japanese "really are," another American genre looks happily forward to a budding Pacific Rim century in the offing. An admixture of Saint-Simonism and genteel Darwinism, this prophetic culture—and its gurus, Alvin Toffler and the Naisbitts—privileges the denizens of the Pacific Rim as the mainstay of an international capitalist utopia in the next century.[12]

To these prophets the Confucian culture incapable of "transcendental truths" is swell, even if it is non-Western, and indeed constitutes what Roy Hofheinz and Kent Calder call the "East Asia Edge," traditional culture being the background and driving ethic of the "miracle" economies. The old shibboleth that Confucianism stifled the entrepreneurial spirit, so prevalent in the "modernization" literature of the 1950s, has been replaced by a new shibboleth that equates capitalist spirit with hyphenated Confucianism: Post-Confucianism, Aggressive-Confucianism, and even Samurai-Confucianism.[13] In other words, Confucianism is an all-purpose grab bag for both faulting and praising East Asia—but "as Confucius say," you can't have it both ways.

The cheerleaders for the Asia-Pacific capitalist utopia tout the internationalist line that nationalism is less important (or inconsequential) in an age of mobile capital and mobile labor. Pacific Asia is a manufacturing basin for consumer goods, while its wealthy class consumes Pacific America's high technology and agriculture: Cray supercomputers for the workaday world, California's mangoes for the dinner table. Meanwhile its poor labor for—anybody. America's competitive edge, so this argument goes, likewise is bolstered through free trade, including free movement of capital, commodities, and people—especially fresh infusions of skilled labor and brains that the new immigration law promises: 600,000 Koreans in the Los Angeles area show that you can bring the mountain to the prophet in the Pacific Rim era.

This is liberal imperialism at its finest, assuming that all are equal in the empyrean of free trade and ignoring the disparate power relations between the United States, the only remaining superpower, and Japan, South Korea, and Taiwan. From an objective point of view, Japan is an economic titan and a military wimp; South Korea is a rising economy but still just half of a divided country and has a semisovereign polity, its army still controlled by an American general; Taiwan is a rising economy, a political midget, and a diplomatic nonentity.

The futurologists and the Japan-bashers come together, however, in two ways: First, both have difficulty grasping an East Asia that is neither a miracle nor a menace but merely a few tens of millions of people working hard to better their lot, coming along "late" to the task of industrial development and trying to make the best of it, with a quite ordinary mixture of good and bad human traits. Second, both tend to soft-pedal the remaining power asymmetries between the United States and East Asia, which severely constrain either the best or the worst outcome and which predict that for the next several decades we will have neither fascist political economy nor capitalist Valhalla but a persisting structure in which East Asia will continue to play second fiddle. Thus both the futurologists and the Japan-bashers—and the periodic outbursts of Japan's leaders—conceal more than they reveal about the reality of power across the Pacific.

One would never know from the rhetoric of the new Orientalism that the Pacific is still an American lake, where a dominant United States holds sway with the Seventh Fleet, myriad military bases, and a panoply of high-tech and nuclear weapons, and also that the American presence in all its forms—cultural, political, economic—remains pervasive in East Asia. One would not know that Japan and the newly industrializing East Asian countries largely retain a single-market dependency that has influenced their political economies for several decades and that this market is the American one. Nor would one know that Japan and its East Asian neighbors still tend to interact with each other and with the rest of the world through a trilateral structure mediated by Washington.

The American lake has opened, of course, especially in the postwar years, a realm of opportunity for East Asia. But it has also been an albatross, denying the countries of the region their national agency and purpose. The American market has been both a realm of vast opportunity and a drag on the flexibility of East Asian economic policy. Both of these aspects of the relationship, however, are mostly concealed in the American discourse on East Asia, such that we end up either with the specter of authoritarian behemoth states chewing up American industries or the international capitalist utopia.

These fundamental limitations, however, are rarely voiced. America's East Asian counterparts tend to maintain silence about them, except for an occasional and predictably bigoted belch from the conservatives who rule Japan, people too often taken for all of Japan in the United States. The reason for this silence is that Japan, Korea, island China, and (increasingly) mainland China are "rule-takers" and not "rule-makers" in the international system. Perhaps more important, liberal free market discourse is *the* hegemonic discourse, with nothing else challenging it in the international realm.

No one stands for East Asia today and voices a distinctive regional perspective; rather its leaders tend to prefer a weak posture. (The last East Asian theorist of international politics was Mao Tse-tung, but both he and his thoughts are as dead as a doornail.) The East Asian response is reactive, usually a mark of insecurity—an occasional riposte that often partakes of the same visceral bias with which some Americans view newly risen Asian prowess.

Thus Japanese conservative leaders charge that America's problem is indolence, selfishness, greed, or racial diversity, almost always in the burp-like manner that reveals "what they really think," apart from surface politeness and diplomatic legerdemain. The liberals and internationalists of East Asia, in contrast, plead that their politics is no different from that in the West: democratic and open, a pluralist mirror image (after all, the ruling party is called Liberal Democratic in Japan and Democratic Liberal in South Korea). Their economies, too, are said to be open, with vast and impressive statistics on trade and investment deployed for the argument—and whatever trade barriers remain are on their way down, nothing more than a matter of time. This is a view of East Asia getting along and going along in the interstices of the international system, molding itself and being molded in the image of its Western creator.

Both the conservative belches and the liberal apologetics tend to obscure "private thoughts" that are increasingly strong, a growing nationalism in East Asia that lies behind a Japan trying to find a way to say "No" and a rising tide of self-assertion uniting right and left in South Korea, uniformly interpreted as anti-American by pundits and policymakers. The private thoughts cannot, however, gainsay the reality that the capitalist states of Northeast Asia are semisovereign in their politics and defense and barely sovereign in their mass culture—the epicenter of the latter still being firmly in Hollywood and New York. They are regionally bereft of anything akin to the European Economic Community (EEC), let alone a sense of Europeanness, or common adherence to the legitimacy of social democratic ideals. Japanese, Koreans, and Chinese barely talk to each other, if truth be known.

For all the talk about Japan as "Number One," Japan remains utterly unable to fashion an alternative hegemonic discourse, one that can leap across civilizational boundaries to create a universal appeal and turn Ja-

pan's solipsism into everyone else's universalism. There is little indigenous weight to offset overwhelming American influence, except the increasingly slim reed of "the East Asian tradition." Money can buy culture
and ideology, as Sony and Matsushita bought Columbia and MCA, but it
has not—as yet—created them; as one literary critic put it, Japan can produce "the signifiers, but not the signified."[14]

This poverty of philosophy, I argue, stems from the reality of postwar
American hegemony in East Asia, which has been overwhelming and unilateral, much more so than in Western Europe, and the reality of relations
today, where the American market remains the engine of the world economy and the talisman of East Asian export success. Starting with Douglas
MacArthur's suzerainty during the occupation of Japan, the United States
has had mostly unilateral sway in the region, symbolized by its frequent
apologetics for forgetting to "consult" with its East Asian allies—about
opening relations with China, withdrawing troops from Korea, or forgiv-
ing debts to the Poles (a recent brouhaha with Japan). And however penetrated its market may be by Asian imports, that market remains the basis
and lifeline of East Asian economic success, giving the United States a reverse influence that is rarely acknowledged.

THE POLITICAL ECONOMY OF AMERICAN EAST ASIA

Given all the heated rhetoric of recent years, it is useful to look at the basic
structure of the East Asian region. In the postwar years, America has prevailed over the capitalist countries of East Asia through two historic com-
pacts. One might be thought of as an international Brumairean compact[15]
between the victor in the last world war, on the one hand, and the defeated
and its colonial possessions, on the other. Just as the bourgeoisie of Louis-
Bonaparte's France, prostrate before the rifle butt, traded its political
rights for the right to make money, so did Japan—and in a curious working of the dialectic, its newly liberated colonies did so, too.

Through the "San Francisco framework" of postwar peacemaking, Japan essentially gave up its military power and its autonomy in foreign
policymaking. South Korea did the same at the time of the Korean War. El-
emental sovereignty over defense and security matters was and is mort-
gaged to the structure of American defense policy in Japan and Korea, and
the state's role in mediating the relationship between the domestic and the
international spheres is decidedly weak, at least where the United States is
concerned.

National defense, which would ordinarily be a primary task of any
state, Japan included, was passed on to Washington and to the American
bases in Japan and Korea. In the aftermath of the Korean War, moreover,
Washington created under its nuclear umbrella a modified apparition of

Japan's prewar military empire, with South Korea's massive military as a regional gendarme, not just to protect the Republic of Korea but to fight communist insurgents in Vietnam in the 1960s. Vietnam's seventeenth parallel was to have been another cordon sanitaire. Thus former colonies and dependencies, not to mention the GIs in the bases in the Pacific, were to do their bit in protecting the big enchilada, the Japanese archipelago. This was not a bad deal for Japan, of course, and the compact was justified by a weird formula that reverberates today: The Japanese really had be protected from themselves.

The result of this Brumairean compact was to place South Korea on the geopolitical fault line, with the Korean military as a backstop to Japan's defense—a political disaster for the Korean people. Korea's civil society came under the tight grip of the state, which was in turn thoroughly penetrated by the United States. Its formidable military force is one of the biggest and best in the world but under the operational control of the United States; South Korea is a semisovereign state. It has a vast military establishment it does not fully control and foreign policy that is essentially dictated from without. It was a great deal for the Korean military, which became the dominant force in political life, but it wasn't much of a deal for the South Korean people (not to mention the North Koreans). Even after the war, the Korean peninsula continued to be an armed-to-the-teeth tinderbox.

From 1948 to 1978 Taiwan had a similar "deal," with the Kuomintang mainlanders dealt the best hand, native Taiwanese excluded from power, another huge military organization devastating democracy, but all the islanders free to make money. In 1978, of course, the United States demonstrated its ultimate trump card by switching this China for the other one, leaving Taiwan to make the best of its very bad deal—the saving grace being that the Taiwanese were still free to make money, which they have done with a vengeance.

A virtual monopoly on the means of violence and the whip hand in important foreign policy decisions is one aspect of American hegemonic politics in East Asia. The other compact shaping the region is economic, and this compact was the maintenance of an American market open to the capitalist upstarts in East Asia. The history and the workings of this compact are complicated, but the upshot, I argue, was to deny the states of the region national agency in the conduct of domestic politics and economics. We can call this the compact of single-market dependence and seek to understand its political logic.

In 1988 the United States absorbed more than one-third of all of Japan's exports, about 40 percent of South Korea's exports, and 44 percent of Taiwan's exports. Even when Japan is excluded, U.S. imports from the four East Asian NICs (newly industrializing countries), ASEAN, and China totaled $90 billion in 1989. The three Northeast Asian capitalist economies are thus remarkably dependent on the American market. Canada and Mexico are the only other countries more singularly dependent on the U.S. market; no other West European, African, or Middle Eastern nation shows any comparable level of single-market dependence for their exports. It is a sobering thought that the only area in the world that is comparable in its trade pattern was the former East European bloc, with its single-market dependence on the Soviet Union.[16]

The political side of this economic coin is obvious. As Albert O. Hirschman once argued, a large economy that can accommodate a great portion of the exports of a small economy, with the latter having a relatively small fraction of import share, thus determines the relations of trade *and* political dependence for its trading partner.[17] Germany, for instance, cultivated this pattern vis-à-vis smaller East European nations in the interwar years. Hirschman's argument, one of the first to articulate the logic of international dependence, gave grist to the mill of the Latin American *dependencia* school but has been mostly overlooked by students of East Asia.

This situation is quite a reversal from the days of the Open Door policy toward East Asia at the turn of the century; in fact, one might with some license characterize the situation today as a Reverse Open Door. The Open Door was a model foreign policy for a rising power like the United States, say, from the 1870s to World War I, seeking to penetrate markets in East Asia and Latin America that were held or influenced by European powers. Once hegemony was achieved, however, in the post–World War I period, the door also opened on the home turf, threatening weak domestic industries.

This reversal did not happen without a struggle, of course. Some U.S. protectionist interests—mostly in declining industries and big business, which wished to invest behind the tariff barriers in the Third World—fought to encourage import substitution industrialization as the strategy for foreign economic development in the 1950s and not export-led growth as economic pundits would have us believe.[18] Even the economic reconstruction of Japan, which was deemed necessary for closing the postwar dollar gap, had been predicated on restoring for Japan its colonial markets and not on opening the American market.

Things worked out differently, however, in part because Japan's former colonies threw a monkey wrench into the plan for regional recovery. North Korea and China had their doors shut tight by 1949, recalcitrant South Korea all throughout the 1950s sabotaged U.S. attempts to recycle aid money by getting Koreans to procure goods from Japan, and even the Southeast market was difficult to penetrate because of competition from China and overseas Chinese. The only exception was Taiwan, which did welcome Japanese investment, but Japan did not want to touch it, looking nervously over its shoulder at China.[19] The major boost to the Japanese economy from the East Asian market—in fact, allowing Japan to take off— was the three years of the Korean War, "a gift of the gods," according to Prime Minister Yoshida Shigeru.[20]

With that boost Japan was able to sell in the American market, and the United States opened its market to Japanese products in a big way. In the 1950s, however, this was no problem. As John Foster Dulles put it to Yoshida Shigeru, "the Japanese [did] not make the things [the United States] likes." Taiwan and South Korea followed Japan into the American market, which remained open as an essential component of U.S.-sponsored models of export-led growth in the 1960s and as a trade-off to South Korea for its contribution to the U.S. war effort in Vietnam. The American market was also necessary to Korea and Taiwan because Japan remained mercantilist, closing its market to its former colonies. Even as of 1988 Japan, although the second largest export market after the United States for South Korea and Taiwan, took in only 18 percent of Korea's total exports and 13 percent of Taiwan's.

The deluge of commodities from East Asia to America since the 1960s did not occur without conflicts between the protectionist and internationalist camps, leading to periodic lifting and closing of the American gate. Japan and South Korea, for instance, are comparable in the speed and structure of industrial development, but they are by no means at the same level, with Korea remaining "behind" Japan by about fifteen years.[21] This has actually worked against the protectionists and has enabled the United States to play one East Asian ally off against another (and American protectionists and internationalists off against each other). That is, to appease its protectionists, the United States has often stiff-armed Japanese firms after they flood the U.S. market in a given commodity, only to have the Koreans supply the same goods even more cheaply, thus satisfying consumers but still doing harm to domestic industries. There has ordinarily been an interval of about fifteen years between the entry of a Japanese commodity and protectionist measures directed against it, followed by the entry of Korean goods into the space where the Japanese goods had been. This process has occurred in textiles, color television, steel, automobiles, VCRs, computers, and semiconductor chips.

Thus the United States has accommodated East Asian imports differentially and discriminately. But for all the East Asian economies, big and small, from the opposing shore the United States still looks like the only game in town, and this is where the United States has wielded unilateral influence, making and breaking the essential fabric of political economy in the region. The logic of these exchanges is rarely articulated, however, beyond lots of rhetoric about supporting free trade. In fact the logic has often been solipsistically American and not without contradictions governed by shifting American interests.

All throughout the 1950s, for instance, Americans urged the Japanese to reduce their trade barriers to conform to the General Agreement on Tariffs and Trade, only to turn around by the end of the decade and pressure Japan to curb its increasing exports of textiles, in violation of the spirit of GATT. Japan, to be sure, remained mercantilist despite the American urging. But this was acceptable because the United States came to see Japan as a designated defender, so to speak, of the dollar: Mercantilist Japan safely absorbed an immense quantity of America's exported dollars and by supporting the dollar helped to maintain the Bretton Woods order. In that sense it is possible to argue that Japanese neomercantilist practice happened in part because the United States specifically allowed it to happen.[22]

By 1971 all that had changed. Throughout the 1960s the United States had supported a regime of fixed exchange rates and convertible currencies. But with inflation on the rise and the dollar heading for a fall, Richard Nixon resorted to the New Economic Policy, a mercantilist revolution that suspended indefinitely the dollar's official convertibility into either gold or foreign currencies, leaving the Japanese and the Europeans holding the bag. Nixon also slapped a discriminatory 10 percent duty on Japanese imports. The hell with you, said Nixon and Treasury Secretary John B. Connally; and Europe and Japan took it because they had nowhere else to go.

The Japanese commitment to GATT was slow in coming, but it has grown systematically over time; the problem is that as it has done so, the American commitment to the same GATT system, though still strongly defended by free traders and the administration in power, has gotten more capricious as protectionists make inroads on U.S. trade policy.

What we might call "hegemonic irresponsibility" continued through the 1980s to the extent that the U.S. Treasury bill market came to be financed by Japan. The United States now combines selective closing of the American market ("voluntary restrictions") with mysterious codes— MOSS (market-oriented, sector-specific), SII (Structural Impediment Initiative) and Super 301—to restructure the way domestic politics and markets are organized in Japan. It has had more success than many observers realize.

Much the same can be said about American pressure on the smaller East Asian countries. But these countries lack reciprocal leverage even more than does Japan. Besides, their politics are much too brittle and their societies much too fragile to accommodate U.S. demands for liberalization, open markets, and democratized states without tidal waves of change. South Korea is one such country. With all its visceral animosity to-

ward Japan, it nonetheless fashioned its political economy after Japan's—
in part as a legacy of four decades of colonialism but mostly because Japanese neomercantilist alchemy had industrialized the country rapidly and
was there to be emulated. But the essential difference between South Korea and its much envied "mirror of the future" (that is, Japan) was that
South Korea was a bulwark of containment; thus instead of the "soft authoritarianism" of Japan, Korea ended up with hard-core military authoritarianism.

Another difference was that South Korea industrialized even later than
the "late" developing Japan and thus was allowed—by the United
States—a greater insularity in its conduct of political economy, so long as
it occupied an innocuous place in the pores of the international market.
The result was neomercantilism with a vengeance, a developmental economy that was rather more tightly sealed and orchestrated from above even
than Japan's.

In the 1980s when the United States began a frontal assault on South
Korea to liberalize its commodity and financial markets, leading from the
American comparative advantage in agribusiness, high technology, and
service industries, the authoritarian state went into a tailspin. Its power
had been predicated on its ubiquitous ability to control developmental resources, to mold the investment pattern by selectively allocating credit, to
supplant and supplement the market, and thus to create and control a
huge constellation of entrepreneurial forces. U.S. demands for economic
liberalization helped to shift power from the state to the society and from
the domestic to the international sphere. The military regime collapsed
like a house of cards in 1987, as Korea's haute bourgeoisie sat on the side,
silent spectators to a massive revolt begun by students and workers but
swelled by members of the middle class. This was an unexpected outcome
for a regime that had been so tightly embraced by the Reagan administration: It became a victim of the antinomies in U.S. foreign policy.[23]

The point here is not to argue the merits of this outcome, nor to say that
the Koreans were mere puppets of the United States, but merely to point
out its structural logic. The regime's demise came mainly because of widespread popular dissatisfaction, but American pressure was a factor that
helped shape the outcome. Hounding out a military dictator like Chun
Doo Hwan may be a good thing in itself, but a situation whereby a hegemonic power undermines and compromises the political economy underpinning another society is profoundly problematic. This situation is a dilemma for the East Asian semisovereign states, as they grapple with
American hegemony in the region, which still structures much of the political discourse by which we understand Asian politics.

The American policy of restructuring East Asian economies is generally
viewed as valid and enlightened, whereas Asian—especially Japanese—

obstruction is seen as devious and self-interested. From the East Asian perspective, however, it looks very different. Why this is so requires some discussion of how Asians think about the question of national agency and purpose and the role of the state in society. At bottom, as we will see, is a disparity over the purpose of politics and its agency, government.

THE STATE IN WEST AND EAST

Liberal political theory has always seen state power as problematic, if not dangerous. The state in America is an imagined vacuity, a space in which interest groups contend and conflict. According to pluralist theory the state is merely a referee that maintains rules and the political order and thus lubricates market and society. To the extent that the state is perceived to be autonomous of society, it has a negative image: a brooding presence that, as it grows, threatens to expropriate the market and civil society. These assumptions are so strong that it is often difficult even to discuss alternatives to the American political pattern; state intervention or state autonomy conjures in the liberal mind the European 1930s, and there discussion ceases and the shouting begins.

Alternative views of the state exist, however, apart from the extremes of fascism and Stalinism. The state, for instance, can be benevolent, protective, exemplary; it can be bountiful and generous, and it can be harsh and disciplinarian. Catholic cultures believed that, and so did Confucian cultures. State and society do not compete in an adversarial relation or expropriate each other. Instead the state was an exemplary and meritocratic order that guided and educated the society. The Anglo-Saxon tradition of the minimal state is the exception, not the rule (rather than the other way around, as the Orientalist discourse would have you believe).

It would be fair to say that the peoples of China, North Korea, South Korea, Japan, and other Confucian cultures deeply believe that the state ought to provide not only material wherewithal for its people but moral guidance, and in that sense, the distinction between state and society is not one that is sharply drawn. By and large, Westerners have no way to understand this point except to assert a series of absences: no individual rights, no civil society, no enlightenment, and thus a weak or absent liberalism. In so doing they are saying little more than that northern Europe and North America had a different historical pattern than did other parts of the world. But too often this particular pattern presents itself as universal.

The state conceived by the East Asian Other is, furthermore, a practical necessity of development. Karl Polanyi, who was a Catholic socialist of a sort, thought of the modern state (however tragically flawed it was at times) as a prophylactic to protect the society against the ravages of the world market. The resulting protected economy may have its inefficiencies—antique rice farmers and family store owners in East Asia, as well as the consumers who have to pay more for this "moral economy"—but who is to say, except the hegemonic power that believes in mammon and Adam Smith, that efficiency ought to reign as the only acceptable doctrine of political economy? And is it not true that the American state might have done more in recent years to protect its people—especially blue collar workers—against the vicissitudes of international competition?

Japan's habits of mercantilism are of long standing, of course. But from Japan's point of view this tried-and-true system has protected its domestic society from the ravages of the world market while Japan pursued "late" development, catch-up ball with the West. Viewed as narrow and irrational by liberal economists, this system has virtues that are rarely voiced in the United States.

For example, Japan is littered with small mom-and-pop stores of all types, with laws against major corporations absorbing them. Small business was a nineteenth-century ideal in the United States, too, but it has suffered dramatically as national and international franchises, fast-food chains, discount marts, and superstores have replaced family enterprises—late capitalism demolishing what some have called "moral economy." Japan's much-criticized protectionism also protects this valuable kind of business, and it now perceives that the United States will not be satisfied unless the whole world is turned into its mirror image of superstores and transnational economies of scale.

Simply to make this argument opens one to attack in the current climate in the United States, but American pressure on the Japanese domestic market is a counterpart to the interior desires of American Orientalists, who find the Japanese soul insular and unempathetic to the rest of the world and want to turn it inside out into a gleaming reflection of the American liberal Self: another triumph for "the end of history," the vanquishing of one more perceived nonliberal polity, after the demise of Stalinist systems in Eastern Europe.

EAST ASIAN SOLUTIONS FOR THE 1990s

If this analysis of growing tensions and misunderstanding in the East Asian–American relationship is correct, what ought to be done about it? It is important to call attention to the gross bias and exaggeration in recent American accounts of East Asia, but there is too much money and fame in Asia-bashing to think that it will go away soon. Similarly, the more deeply rooted and contrary ways that American and East Asians think about the state and politics are likely to persist. It does appear, however, that the East Asian states are moving slowly to attenuate the economic Gordian knot that ties the region to America's market, something that has been well known to policy makers in the region but about which little has been done until the late 1980s.

The single-market dependency that characterized previous economic relationships seems to have reached an impasse, partly because of American protectionism but also because, as I have argued, it leads to unwanted reciprocal pressures by the United States on Japan and Korea—in the first instance to "open markets" but in the last instance to give up domestic sovereignty and no longer protect the moral economy of small producers, that is, to give up national autonomy. Single-market dependency is something that policymakers can change, however, and they have recently begun to do so.

Recent figures suggest that Japanese dependence on the U.S. market has dropped from 33 percent of its total worldwide trade in 1986 to 27 percent in 1990 and is estimated to be 25 percent in 1991. Trade with Western and Eastern Europe is a particular target and has grown rapidly. Japan's imports from the United States climbed by 76 percent from 1986 to 1990, but they increased 300 percent from France and 133 percent from the EC countries in general. South Korea and Taiwan have followed suit, actively reducing their shares of exports to the United States and aggressively cultivating markets elsewhere.[24]

To the extent that this pattern continues, it means a move away from the previous structure whereby the United States interacted bilaterally with Western Europe and Japan while Japan and Europe had little interaction and a move toward a triangular structure, whose base would be created through growing investment and commodity trade between Europe and Japan. In the section that follows, I sketch out this scenario for East Asia, a revision of its position in the world system that continues moving toward a multiplicity of markets but away from trilateralism and toward a kind of triangulation and interregional reorganization. This move implies also that Japan would have more direct relations with the other East Asian economies, rather than relations mediated by and through the United States, and that the smaller East Asian economies would also have stronger ties with Europe.

This revised North-North articulation is likely to be accompanied by a reorganization of North-South relations within the region. This reorganization would be achieved by greater cohesion among the region's more prosperous Northeast Asian economies, looking eventually toward something like the EC in East Asia, and deepened links with Southeast Asia, a region that is increasingly a good bet for the next round of rapid industrialization.

Trilateralism, Bruce Cumings argues in Chapter 2, has characterized American global policy since the late 1940s. Western Europe and Japan were the legs of the triangle, with the United States spending Marshall

Plan and Agency for International Development (AID) money to get war-torn economies going in the 1940s, while maintaining for itself ultimate veto power over Allied behavior—especially that of Japan and Germany—maintained on an American defense dependency. The lineaments of the triangle, however, ran through Washington back to Tokyo or Bonn, with little contact on the East Asian–European "axis" (I use the term gingerly). Communication was frequently mediated by Washington, especially on issues of critical importance like the conflict with the Soviets or crises in Korea, Vietnam, or the Gulf.

Richard Nixon was the best symbol of this use of communication, somehow forgetting to consult Japan's leaders about dramatic departures like the New Economic Policy or dealing with Brezhnev over the heads of European leaders. It was all too apparent that communication flowed through Washington, on its terms. During the heyday of formal trilateralism in the Carter administration, however, everyone still assumed that the initiative remained in Washington's hands, and there was little Japanese-European bilateral contact. This structure is one of hegemonic power reigning over regional associates.

A shift toward triangulation in the 1990s is likely to entail increased Japanese investment in Europe (as a way to break into post-1992 fortress Europe), as well as the beginning of such investment by the East Asian NICs. The United States seeks to do the same thing, so it is likely to support such Asian initiatives. European firms may welcome such investments as a quid pro quo for technology transfer and for infiltrating into East and Southeast Asia, where returns on investment remain high. The announced collaboration of Daimler-Benz and Mitsubishi and of Kloeckner Werke and C. Itoh are moves in that direction.

To be sure, Japanese investment in Europe is still picayune in comparison to that by the United States: In 1990, Japanese direct investment in Germany remained, for instance, a paltry $1.1 billion against $32.5 billion made by the United States. Yet the Japanese figure for that year was double what it was a year before, and the trend is on the rise, as it has been for Taiwan and South Korea.

Japanese interaction with the territories of its former empire has been tightly controlled by the United States, more so than has the trilateral structure. This interaction is widely misunderstood and thus requires some explanation. Despite much talk about the atavistic return of the Greater East Asia Co-prosperity Sphere, the only area where ties were thick and thus easy to revive was in Northeast Asia. But even that development took two decades and a war in Vietnam to make into a reality; and when it happened, it did so under American auspices. Furthermore, the interaction between Japanese, Koreans, and Chinese was almost exclusively economic, rather than cultural or political, and it remains so nearly a half century after the Co-prosperity Sphere met its demise.

Containment of communism in the mid-1960s required, among other things, placing East Asian and Southeast Asian nations on a sound economic footing. Japan was thus reintroduced to the region in the 1960s as America's partner and surrogate in developmental efforts. The critical year 1965 saw the linking of the economies in the region, as America escalated its war efforts in Vietnam: the Normalization of the Japan-Korea Relationship that was, with its big package of loans and credits, in part responsible for the Korean economic takeoff. Also inaugurated was the Asian Development Bank, which, in addition to American and Japanese aid, transferred vast amounts of loans, with priority given to Taiwan and South Korea and secondary consideration to the Philippines, Thailand, and Malaysia.

This task of linking Japan to other Northeast Asian capitalist economies in the 1960s is slowly coming to fruition. If we accept the forecast that by the year 2000 Japan's living standard will rise by 50 percent and that of the East Asian NICs will almost double—and this increase is not so unrealistic—it would mean that the gap between the Japanese living standard and that of the other East Asian economies would have narrowed from 4.3 times to 3.3 times. That is comparable to the gap in living standards between the richest member of the EC (Germany) and the poorest (Portugal), which is currently about five times. Should North and South Korea and Taiwan and China reunify, the process of regional interpenetration in Northeast Asia would be expedited, and Japan's dominance in the region partly offset.

Southeast Asia is a different story. Japan had never left a colonial imprint from which the region could create a political economy resembling Japan's. Southeast Asia was really a classic wartime occupation territory, existing only to "contribute resources to Japan," as Hideki Tojo put it. Before Pearl Harbor there was no blueprint for administration and development of Southeast Asia, and Japan's information on the region derived from existing "enemy" sources, usually meaning British sources; often Japan simply reestablished the former colonial government, relying on local personnel who had worked for colonial regimes. Thus social systems in Southeast Asia remained, by and large, untouched.[25] Since the war Japan and the Southeast Asian countries have had a less intense and more distant interaction than Japan has had with Northeast Asia, and again, the interaction is mostly economic.

Change is underway, however, and we might think of it in terms of the East Asian product cycle extending to Southeast Asia. Whereas the northeast Asian economies represented an economic hierarchy created through transfer of labor-intensive industries from Japan to Taiwan and South Korea through the 1980s,[26] the same process is being reproduced vis-à-vis ASEAN, with Japan and the NICs busily bequeathing their obsolete industries. Combined investment in ASEAN, for instance, by four NICs—South Korea, Taiwan, Hong Kong, and Singapore—exceeded Japanese investment in the area in 1988.

Thus we have the creation of a more lateral economic structure between Japan and the NICs and a hierarchical structure stretching down from north to south in East Asia, from rich to poor countries. Economic activity within this dual structure has been bustling. Intraregional trade west of the Pacific is growing by more than 40 percent annually, amounting to $256 billion in 1989, representing a whopping 40 percent of its total worldwide trade. This ratio is anticipated to rise to 55 percent by 1999. As of 1992 Japan is investing upward of $10 billion a year in Asia, is engaging in $126 billion worth of trade, and has dispensed a total of $4.4 billion in aid to the area, overtaking the United States in the mid-1980s as the largest aid donor in the area. More importantly, however, a high proportion of Japanese investment in Asia is in manufacturing and thus is less sensitive to short-term factors. Whereas Japanese investment in the United States and Latin America is done primarily to defuse trade friction and thus tends to rise and fall with protectionist pressures, its investments in Asia tend to be driven by much longer-term objectives.

Another force propelling change in the area is geopolitical. Anticommunism and containment were the rationale for organizing Pacific Asia after 1947, but that rationale began to come apart with Nixon's opening to China and the fall of Saigon. Since the early 1970s economic development has replaced anticommunism as the defining trait in East Asia, with a sudden surge of euphoria about 1978 when the Chinese normalized relations with the United States and embarked on market-oriented reforms. Japan has moved into China in a big way, maintaining an embassy in Beijing that is second in size only to its Washington delegation. During the 1979–1989 decade of economic reform Japan invested some $2.2 billion in China, compared to $1.8 billion invested by the United States. The Chinese government, for its part, insists that Japan invest and manufacture in China, so as not to repeat the all-too-familiar agony of a nation hooked on perpetual trade deficits vis-à-vis Japan. Thus whereas China recorded $6 billion in trade deficit against Japan (36 percent of total Chinese imports) in 1985, it garnered $6 billion in trade surpluses from Japan, and imports from Japan were only a 15 percent share of total Chinese imports in 1990.[27] Taiwan, South Korea, Hong Kong, Singapore, and others have also been investing in China very heavily.

The late 1980s, moreover, saw a number of socialist countries linking up with the capitalist orbit in the region, and agencies of Japanese expansion abroad, the so-called General Trading Companies, have lost little time in opening offices in Mongolia, Laos, and Vietnam. The companies came armed with tried-and-true methods successfully tested elsewhere: feasibility studies, followed by enunciation of Japanese "strategic interest," then signing of official aid to pay for infrastructural development, which leads to a tapping of an inexpensive labor supply. Japan has been particularly quick to link Vietnam to its economy: Japan is now Vietnam's biggest oil customer and its second biggest trading partner, after the former Soviet Union, and business has been on the rise.

The East Asian NICs are also getting in on the act with alacrity. In the case of South Korea there is more than a little triumphalism in its desire to push the North Koreans up against the wall; South Korea normalized relations with the former Soviet Union amid much talk about billions of dollars in aid and of hastening the development of Siberia with South Korea's know-how in construction (and maybe North Korean labor). Meanwhile South Korea's conglomerates, known as the *chaebôl*, tried busily to supply the Russians with consumer goods, computers, and other high-technology equipment, in an unsuccessful bid to shore up Gorbachev's shaky rule. Taiwan's smaller firms have begun doing the same.

These trends harbinger an East Asia that wants to set itself free from the asymmetric and often smothering relations across the Pacific and to wrest greater autonomy from the world system. This development should be welcomed by the United States as it attempts to forge a New World Order because it also affords the United States an opportunity for disengagement from hegemonic burdens.

CONCLUSION

It would appear from the evidence that Japan and the East Asian NICs have made considerable progress in reducing their single-market dependence on the United States and that they increasingly are finding ways of interacting economically that are different from the rules of the game since 1945. Growing economic integration and interregional trade will establish more latitude for East Asians in determining their own fate, not necessarily separate from the United States but without the palpable American pressures of past years. Substantial changes in the economic realm, then, are slowly dissolving the Gordian knot that has created both economic opportunities and a political albatross for the nations in East Asia.

The security situation is likely also to continue relaxing, thus diminishing American leverage over the East Asian states. Tensions in East Asia have been significantly relaxed since 1985, the Soviets having withdrawn 200,000 troops from the Sino-Soviet border and the Chinese having demobilized 25 percent of their total military strength. And the preponderance of U.S. and Japanese conventional air and naval power over Soviet military power in the North Pacific—as part of a global strategy linked to the European situation—is an anachronism now that the Warsaw Pact does not even exist.

A relaxation of tensions, then, is clearly going on in East Asia. But unlike the economic realm, these changes have not begun to touch the basic security structure. As a result, it is much harder to project what will happen to the international Brumairean compact—what will be the role of the United States in Asian regional security in the future? The United States is slow to let go in East Asia and vice versa. Japan has thus far been content to keep the postwar security arrangement, and Japan's neighbors feel safer with American troops, certainly, than with Japanese. As one Chinese strategist noted, Japan has 300,000 troops, of whom 70 percent are officers and noncommissioned officers, and is thus capable of quickly increasing the number of troops. Japan also possesses the economic and technological potential to leap over several generations of weapons technology and develop intelligent, or "smart," weapons as it pleases—a choice it has not yet made and is unlikely to make in the near future.[28] For the neighbors of Japan this proposition is not one that they want to test. Regional security, then, is likely to remain in American hands for some time to come. It is likely that the United States will seek to hold on to the levers of security as a way of continuing its influence in the region.

The change that will be the slowest in coming (if at all) will be in regard to what one might call the hegemonic psychology in East Asia. The United States is still the world's greatest and most vibrant center of cultural and ideological production. Japan may slowly replace America's lead in finance, manufacturing, and technology, but it does not begin to articulate a posthegemonic ideology nor does its culture have a regional, let alone universal, appeal; at most, it exports Nintendo hardware (the signifier without the signified), maudlin songs, *karaoke* bars (where drunken males mimic pop hits), and the culture of sex tourism to East Asia.

Thus East Asia remains an area without an identity, a region incapable of imagining itself as a community. Former victims of Japanese aggression like Korea and China also partake of the either/or absolutes of the new Orientalism, projecting for the future either a dreaded neo–Co-prosperity Sphere or the capitalist utopia of the Pacific Rim. That Alvin Toffler is listened to as a prophet throughout the region, including the People's Republic of China, is merely a token of the utter absence of any regional self-definition.

East Asia lacks the language and psychology for self-assertion, a condition that is an artifact of its long domination by the West. This palpable absence is also testimony to the terrible difficulty of hegemonic transfer across a civilizational divide, something that has never before occurred. When England passed the hegemonic baton to the United States in the

1940s, it could do so in partnership with an ally sharing much of its culture and tradition. With Japan's meteoric rise another such transition perhaps beckons on the horizon, but all too many pundits can only greet it with thoughts of conflict, eternal difference, the dire absence of (our) "transcendental truths," and even "the coming war with Japan." Surely our imaginations ought to do more than merely project into the future a past everyone—the Japanese included—would rather forget.

Japan's neighbors can hardly bear to watch Japan again assert itself as a superior, homogeneous nation uniquely fit among Asians to the tasks of the modern world. But then it isn't particularly comforting, either, to see Americans also "going nationalist" over the past decade, with huge displays of flagwaving that perhaps began at the Los Angeles Olympics in 1984 and certainly continued through the national celebration of the humiliation of Iraq. The first display—Japan's—is thought to be pathological, and the second—America's—is accepted as normal. Yet both bespeak the attenuation of internationalism that occurred in the 1980s, caused both by Japan's competitiveness and by the unilateralism of Reagan's foreign policy.

Orientalism coupled with East Asian aphasia does not make for happy prognostication on the future of U.S.–East Asian relations. In the absence of a full airing of the issues that separate Americans and Japanese, public utterance becomes euphemistic, private thoughts run rampant, and slips of the tongue welling up from the viscera taint the relationship and poison the atmosphere.

It would be far better if we extrude antique conceptions of race and of Orient and Occident entirely from the ongoing debate and focus instead on what divides East and West, which is almost always some predictable and intelligible conflict of interest, and what unites East and West in a common endeavor of development.

Policies of "constructive disengagement" from the asymmetrical relations of the past not only can leave more room for Asian autonomy but also can aid the United States by reducing security burdens and promoting a salutary period of "looking inward" that could help domestic American industries revive and flourish—which, after all, is the best way to meet "the Asian challenge."

We need to think about a positive disengagement that prepares for truly equal and mutually beneficial relations in the future. We need to talk openly, if not "politically correctly," about what ties us together and what pushes us apart, what we really think about each other, how to build bridges of mutual understanding, and what American East Asia has truly been about.

8

PAX (NORTE) AMERICANA

Latin America
After the Cold War

The end of the Cold War marked the culmination of parallel economic trends that produced contrasting political effects in the peripheral states of the two superpowers. In both Latin America and Eastern Europe economic growth slowed noticeably in the late 1960s, declined further in the 1970s, and virtually ceased in the 1980s. In both regions economic stagnation fueled demands for fundamental political and economic change.

The authoritarian regimes of Latin America responded to adverse economic conditions and political unrest by ceding direct political power to elected governments.[1] Although the democratic regimes that took over in the 1980s failed to reverse the region's economic decline, they did prove effective, in their vulnerability to electoral defeats, in channeling popular protest away from revolutionary violence and toward electoral challenges to the governments in power.[2] The United States did not obstruct the democratic transitions in the region, despite the initial ambivalence of the Reagan government, because the preceding military rulers had largely succeeded in their efforts to liquidate revolutionary challenges.

In Eastern Europe the 1968 Warsaw Pact intervention in Czechoslovakia, the attendant suppression of dissent throughout eastern Europe, and the subsequent ossification of political regimes in the region foreclosed prospects for democratization, even within the framework of one-party rule.[3] Western attempts to meddle in the region had contradictory effects. Support for Romanian independence from Soviet pressures, for example, complemented Nicolae Ceausescu's efforts to insulate the country by extending his personal dictatorship. Rather than inducing liberalization, Western support tended to exacerbate the authoritarian features of the regime. In the case of Poland, with its huge debt to the West and particularly to West Germany, Western inaction at the imposition of martial law coincided with the Soviet interest in maintaining stability. Throughout the region political change came only after the Gorbachev regime renounced the Brezhnev Doctrine, began a process of reform at home, and exerted pressure on the East European states to do likewise.

Although the economic problems of the East European nations were no more acute (and in most cases, less serious) than those of Latin America, the Soviet liberalization produced pressures for change that could not be accommodated without explosive, even revolutionary, transformations. As the regimes themselves had so often insisted, politics and economics could not be separated; when political reform began, it could not be confined to the realm of politics. As it turned out, the East European leaderships had correctly assessed their positions. In stagnant economies, the failure to suppress reformism precipitated revolution. In Latin America, by contrast, the military suppression of both reformist and revolutionary movements during the two decades beginning with the 1964 coups facilitated democratic transitions that in the most notable cases, produced initial electoral victories for political coalitions far more conservative than those the military had ousted.[4]

The contrasting economic performance of the two superpowers played a key role in the process that led to political change or upheaval. In both cases economic difficulties at the beginning of the 1980s produced defensive reactions: the Brezhnev turn against dissent at home and abroad (particularly in Poland) and the Reagan move to improve relations with Latin America's military establishments (particularly in Argentina and to a lesser degree in Chile). The Reagan boom after 1983 (and the Malvinas, or Falklands, War) helped shift U.S. policy in South America toward modest and selective support for democratization (most notably in Chile), though the specific needs of the governing political coalition and the president's own whims made Central America an exception to the new policy. Soviet policy turned in a similar direction under fundamentally divergent circumstances. Liberal impulses in Washington coincided with the Reagan "boom." Those in Moscow stemmed in large part from growing economic difficulties.

Economic stagnation in Eastern Europe thus led to the political explosions of 1989 that eventually destroyed not only the political regimes but the economic systems on which they rested, along with Soviet dominance in the region. The parallel economic stagnation of Latin America also destroyed political regimes, but the dynamic of economic and strategic change differed. Like the new East European governments, the democratic regimes of the 1980s in Latin America moved to abandon state-directed, highly protectionist economic strategies, open their economies to greater external trade and capital flows, and privatize public enterprises. Unlike Eastern Europe, however, these changes took place in a juridical and institutional environment in which large-scale private enterprise already occupied a privileged position, subsidized and protected by public initiative. Moreover, although superpower dominance disappeared in Eastern Europe along with the regimes that conformed to it, in the case of Latin America the debt crisis that exploded in 1982 and the subsequent end of the Cold War actually strengthened Latin America's economic and political subordination to the United States.

The changes in Eastern Europe not only involved a more profound transformation of domestic political economies, they dramatically altered the strategic map of the globe. Although the full impact of the collapse of the Soviet Union has yet to be assimilated, the short-term effect has been to restore the United States to a position of military predominance in global affairs it has not enjoyed since the late 1950s. Unlike the immediate post–World War II decades, however, U.S. strategic predominance no longer rests on a foundation of unchallenged economic preeminence. To the contrary, the long-term relative economic decline of the United States, exacerbated by the 1991–1992 recession, has begun to generate consequential debate over issues of grand strategy and political economy within the country for the first time since the onset of the Cold War.

The reshuffling of security and economic positions among the great powers in the 1990s and the concurrent reordering of their peripheries has created an unusually complex international environment. The question addressed in this chapter is whether the history of Latin America's place in the global order during the Cold War Pax (Norte) Americana can help to clarify the options facing the region in the post–Cold War era. The answer, I think, is a qualified yes.

LATIN AMERICA: FROM THE END OF WORLD WAR II TO THE END OF THE COLD WAR

At the end of World War II, Latin America no less than Eastern Europe faced options constrained by the overwhelming military, political, and economic power of the nearest superpower. Postwar governments accepted, or were induced to accept, incorporation into military and political alliances dominated by the United States or the Soviet Union. In both regions this strategic and political subordination coincided with impressive programs of industrialization and rapid rates of economic growth. The achievements of the postwar regimes varied in accordance with previous levels of manufacturing development, the effectiveness of state policies to promote and protect new industries, and country (or market) size, but even the smaller and more backward regional clients of the two superpowers achieved high rates of economic advance.

In Eastern Europe the initial "forced" industrializations more or less followed the Stalinist model—state ownership of the means of production, central planning of most economic activity, administered prices for most outputs, full employment of labor, agrarian reform and/or collectivization of agriculture, and welfare floors on living standards and essential human services. Although carried out by repressive regimes under severe pressure to conform to the Soviet model, the East European transformations proved economically viable and achieved notable results. The relative decline in repressiveness that followed Stalin's death and accelerated after the Hungarian revolt in 1956 was in part related to the demonstrable modernization that the East European regimes cited as justification for the sacrifices imposed by the "revolutions" their populations had endured.

Latin America, by contrast, intensified its efforts toward industrialization along lines already established. During the depression and war years of 1930–1945 the Latin American countries found it impossible to maintain prior levels of imports of manufactured goods. During the depression the decline in imports stemmed largely from the sharp drop in foreign exchange earnings due to the fall in both the volume and the prices of the region's exports. By the time Latin America's exports recovered, shortly before or during World War II, the region's main foreign suppliers of manufactured goods were unable to respond to demand because of the diversion of their industrial capacity to war production. Between 1930 and 1945, then, domestic demand for manufactured goods in Latin America had to be met in large part by local industries. In the 1930s industrial recovery and growth occurred in those countries that, like Brazil and Mexico, stimulated demand by means of government spending. In others, like Argentina and Chile, industrial expansion did not take off until the wartime exports fueled rapidly rising income levels. Whatever the timing of this new wave of industrial growth, it involved more intense utilization of existing plants and equipment (operating around the clock and on weekends with additional labor) or, at best, an expansion of existing facilities at existing levels of technology. Manufacturing output rose, but productivity declined.[5]

The solution to the productivity problem, which laid the basis for the rapid growth of manufacturing in Latin America in the 1950s, had two parts. First, the Latin American governments, responding to increasingly vocal demands from industrialists and labor unions, began to develop explicit programs to promote industrial growth through higher levels of tariff (and nontariff) protection for national industry along with schemes to provide tax breaks, low-cost financing, infrastructure, and other incentives to stimulate industrial investment. Second, in response to these programs, foreign direct capital investment—initially flowing entirely from the United States—shifted from its pre-1930 concentration in mineral extraction and agriculture to manufacturing. Debt paper floated by Latin American governments for development purposes went increasingly to subsidized loans for industry and to improvements in infrastructure that benefited manufacturing enterprise. The new industries that developed in the 1950s, in contrast to those of the 1930s and 1940s, embodied technological advances that solved the productivity constraint. The larger Latin American economies moved from an industrial structure mainly characterized by a proliferation of light manufacturing enterprises to one that involved the production of consumer durables (automobiles, home appliances, and the like), steel, petroleum and chemical products, and even some capital goods.[6]

Nationalist industrialization policies—highly protectionist and increasingly state-financed and directed—produced impressive results. The policies that helped achieve these results did not, however, stem from domestic pressures alone. U.S. manufacturing firms, especially the larger enterprises that leapt over tariff walls to set up huge new industrial plants in many of the larger Latin American countries, also exerted powerful pressures on the Latin American governments to maintain and even to expand their protectionist policies. As James Nolt and Sylvia Maxwell have shown in the case of Argentina, the Philippines, and Turkey, U.S. policy consistently promoted import substitution industrialization (ISI) in the Third World in the first two decades after World War II. The United States also supported strategies for deepening ISI in the late 1950s, when it became clear in the larger economies that the potential for import substitution in light manufacturing had been exhausted.[7]

A turning point—or perhaps a series of turning points—occurred in the late 1960s and 1970s. In this period the newly emerging Asian NICs shifted from ISI to export-led industrialization (ELI). This new strategy followed the substantial liberalization of the international trade regime inspired by the Kennedy Round of trade negotiations, which helped to open markets in the United States and the rest of the developed world for Third World products, including manufactures. Gradually building on the productivity advances achieved in the first two postwar decades, the East Asian states began to change course by lowering tariff barriers to push their new industries toward greater efficiency. They also targeted extensive government aid and financing to those industries where business and government, working in close coordination, perceived opportunities for exporting manufactured goods. This new strategy proved to be highly successful. In Latin America, for reasons not yet studied in depth, moves toward ELI were either weaker or never even attempted. Instead, a number of major Latin American governments opted to further deepen ISI by maintaining or even increasing tariff and nontariff protection (to aid firms that faced growing threats from external competition). In some cases (Mexico was a notable example) governments began to take over failing local and foreign-owned firms (on terms generous to their owners) and in countries like Brazil, Mexico, and Venezuela to embark on costly projects to develop heavy industry through massive government-owned enterprises.[8]

The Latin American economic policy shifts in the late 1960s and 1970s tended to raise levels of state intervention in the economy but so did the changes introduced in the Asian cases. It was not the magnitude so much as the direction of state interventionism that distinguished the Asian cases from those of Latin America. Most of the Latin American countries drifted toward excessive protectionism and a policy of socializing the costs of inefficiency through state takeovers of bankrupt private firms at a time when the Asian NICs were shifting to more successful (but equally state-directed) export-led manufacturing growth.

Part of the reason for Latin America's uniquely inefficient response to changes in the external economic environment in the 1960s and 1970s can be found, ironically, in the region's closer economic, political, and security ties to the United States. Many of the great smokestack industries of the Latin American countries, which benefitted disproportionately from excessive protectionism, were (and still are) largely foreign owned. Foreign and particularly U.S. capital dominated a much larger proportion of Latin America's industries than in the East Asian cases. Pressures for protection from U.S.-owned companies received support from U.S. diplomats, whose influence and access in Latin America were often greater than in the Asian cases. This disproportionate influence stemmed, in part, from the greater need of the Latin American governments for U.S. aid in containing reformist, nationalist, and revolutionary threats to the existing order and the consequently deeper penetration of U.S. interests at all levels of government (including the armed forces). When direct pressures on behalf of foreign-owned industries played no role, it was usually because they were not needed. In addition to direct investment, the Latin American countries relied on foreign capital to finance a far larger proportion of public investment and expenditures than in East Asia. This reliance increased dramatically after the oil shock of 1973, when the region's public and private indebtedness skyrocketed. Most of this new debt was financed in the United States, often with funds deposited in U.S. commercial banks by the oil-exporting countries of the Middle East. Latin America's greater reliance on external resources to finance growth, most of which still came from the United States, created an environment in which economic policymakers in U.S.-backed conservative governments found it prudent, even necessary, to accommodate to U.S. and other foreign interests even without being asked to do so.

Differentially closer ties to the United States have also played an important role in perpetuating a uniquely Latin American pattern of inequality. In contrast both to Eastern Europe and East Asia (as well as the developed countries), income and wealth distribution in most of Latin America remained highly regressive; lagging social expenditures failed to achieve more than incremental improvements in health, education, housing, nutrition, and the like; and tax systems remained highly regressive. By contrast, social indicators in East Asia have tended to converge fairly rapidly toward the levels of the industrialized countries; and in Eastern Europe (until recently, at least) equality in income distribution exceeded Western levels, and most indicators of social welfare reached near parity with the West.[9]

It would be a mistake to blame U.S. influence alone for the exhausted overprotectionism and persistent inequality which afflicted the Latin American region in the waning decades of the Cold War. The United States did not have to search very long or very hard to find the kind of reliably anti-Communist elite allies whose desire to attract U.S. investment was exceeded only by their desire to avoid and evade social change. For much of the postwar era, U.S. official rhetoric explicitly opposed nationalist (or statist) economic experimentation as tantamount to embracing communism. Although promoted by U.S. aid programs and by pressures from U.S. corporations, particularly in areas like tariff protection and aid-subsidized finance for U.S. investment (which tended to reinforce profitable inefficiencies), "excessive" government intervention was often explicitly denounced by U.S. businessmen and policymakers.[10]

State-centered economic programs also drew encouragement beginning in the late 1960s from the reemergence of Japan and Europe as significant economic actors in the region. Latin American efforts to encourage extrahemispheric economic relations were often undertaken as a means of balancing against U.S. interests. The government of Luis Echeverría in Mexico (1970–1976), the signatories to the Andean Pact, and even the Brazilian and Argentine military regimes (at various times) all employed nationalist rhetoric, partly for domestic political reasons and partly because of actual policy differences with Washington. The more competitive international economic (and therefore political) environment of the 1970s, when European (especially German), Japanese, and even Soviet economic ties increased, served to enhance the autonomy of some Latin American governments in the face of specific U.S. pressures. The result, ironically, was even more protectionism and state intervention in the region. Latin America thus drifted into state-centered development programs and excessive protectionism under U.S. tutelage and continued on this course even when U.S. leverage diminished.

It is unlikely, moreover, that the opposition to U.S.-backed regimes in the region would have managed—especially in the face of inevitable U.S. hostility—to construct productive regimes capable of overcoming the kind of economic difficulties that led to the collapse of socialist regimes in

Eastern Europe and the Soviet Union. Not one of the powerful movements for social change that local military establishments allied to the United States managed to suppress in the 1960s and 1970s advocated the kind of economic model—export substitution through close coordination between government and private business—that the East Asian NICs were implementing at the time. Agrarian reform, nationalization of industry, nationalism in external economic policy, thoroughgoing redistribution of wealth and income, and massive social programs characterized opposition agendas in this era. Whatever other results such policies might have achieved, successful adjustment to trends in the world economy was not among them.

POST–COLD WAR SCENARIOS

At the August 1990 annual meeting of the American Political Science Association (APSA), Adam Przeworski placed a question mark in the title of his remarks to a session on the political transformations of Eastern Europe: "The 'East' Becomes the 'South'? The 'Autumn of the People' and the Future of Eastern Europe."[11] In the text of his paper, Przeworski compared the emerging postsocialist polities of Eastern Europe to the "poor capitalisms" of Latin America. "Forget for a moment the geographical location," he wrote,[12]

> and put Poland in the place of Argentina, Hungary in the place of Uruguay. You will see states [that are] weak as organizations, political parties and other associations that are ineffectual in representing and mobilizing, economies that are monopolistic, over-protected and over-regulated, agricultures that cannot feed their own people, public bureaucracies that are overgrown, welfare services that are fragmentary and rudimentary. And would you not conclude that such conditions breed governments vulnerable to pressures from large firms, populist movements of doubtful commitment to democratic institutions, armed forces that sit menacingly on the sidelines, church hierarchies torn between authoritarianism and social justice, nationalist sentiments vulnerable to xenophobia?

Przeworski tempered his pessimism, though only slightly, by referring to the southern European successes, notably Spain but also Greece and Portugal. Eastern Europe's future is not yet entirely fixed nor is Latin America utterly doomed in Przeworski's account. Nonetheless, his judgment on the prospects for the emergence of stable and prosperous capitalist democracies in these regions cannot be described as optimistic.

Przeworski is not alone in suggesting that Latin America's past may have some relevance for understanding Eastern Europe's future. The transformation from socialist client states into relatively backward, nominally independent neocolonies of the EEC (or in the case of the former German Democratic Republic, into a full-fledged colony)[13] places the new regimes of Eastern Europe in a political economic position similar to that occupied by the Latin American countries for nearly a century. Before embracing a new theory of "convergence," however, a number of key differences between the two regions need to be taken into account.

Internally, most East European societies (Romania is only a partial exception) can rely on the accumulated benefits of socialist investments in human resources and in public services. The populations of Eastern Europe enjoy better health, nutrition, housing, education, and public services than do those of most of Latin America. Many of these achievements are in danger of rapid deterioration as governments in the new market societies confront the same kinds of fiscal constraints that have beset Latin America for the past ten years. In Eastern Europe, however, the social capital built up since World War II together with popular resistance to cuts in essential government programs provide the region with a permanent edge over most of their Latin American counterparts, where social capital has developed more slowly and where demands for income redistribution and more extensive government services provoked a wave of military coups in the 1960s and 1970s.[14]

Externally, the new states of Eastern Europe face a more competitive international environment than do most of the Latin American republics. Although it is important to draw distinctions between the several countries and subregions of Latin America in respect to the degree of dominance exercised by the United States, all of the Latin American polities except Cuba form part of a political and military alliance in which the United States again exercises unchallenged preeminence. With few exceptions all have closer economic ties to the United States than to any other country or region. In the case of Eastern Europe a new post–Cold War pattern of international relations has only begun to emerge. Close economic ties to the EEC are to be expected, but competition within the West European community should provide the East European states with more room for maneuver than most Latin American nations will face. Moreover, the distracted successor states to the former Soviet Union will continue to play an important economic role, at least as important suppliers of energy and other raw materials and as potential consumers of East European manufactured and farm products. None of the new states of the former Soviet Union have even begun to define their long-term security and economic aims in Eastern Europe. For the next few years, their need for Western markets and external finance may bring them into competition with their East European neighbors. In the longer run, however, the relative poverty and dependence they share with the former satellites could lead to new patterns of coordination and even concert, though such an outcome would require consistent efforts to overcome historic animosities, divergent security needs, "free rider" problems, and the divisions induced by competition for Western resources. The extent to which the new East European governments will be able to play off the new East against the old West is thus still an open question.

Finally, Eastern Europe's primary external economic ties place the region in the orbit of one of the world's two most dynamic regional economies. The Western Hemisphere, in contrast, has failed to generate any net savings for nearly two decades. Latin America's economic fortunes remain tied to the United States, which has become a net importer of capital and thus competes with the region not only for European and Japanese investment but for the savings of Latin American investors as well. Geographic proximity to Western Europe may provide the East European states with yet another advantage not available to their Latin American counterparts. Eastern Europe's fortunes are now inextricably tied to West European models of capitalist development, in which highly centralized states assume the tasks of managing and orienting growth while simultaneously mitigating the inequities that attend it. The fortunes of the Latin American countries are once again, by contrast, more closely tied than at any time since the early 1960s to a North American model in which the central government cannot be made to assume these tasks consistently and is likely to continue to discourage its clients and dependents from doing so.

THE ROLE OF THE UNITED STATES

The relative decline of the U.S. economy and its increasing dependence on external finance produced a major shift in U.S. economic policy toward Latin America in the 1980s. In effect, the altered global economic position of the United States pushed U.S. policy into closer coordination with the free market rhetoric of its politicians and businessmen. The United States abandoned ISI, embraced ELI, and began forcefully to push Latin American governments to do the same. The circumstances of this shift do not, however, augur well for a successful transition to ELI in most of Latin America. Delayed first by a convergence of U.S. policy and the interests of most of the region's governments and then by the debt crisis of the 1980s, the transition will now be carried out by governments that lack the resources and regulatory leverage to manage the process as successfully as they might have done two decades ago.

Latin America's economic stagnation in the 1980s struck hardest at the industries dominated by U.S. firms in the region. As domestic markets in the region collapsed, U.S. firms quickly discovered a need to export to more dynamic markets. To do so, they had to become as efficient as competing producers in other countries. Tariff protection lost its value. Meanwhile, existing trade barriers in Latin America invited retaliation from governments in the markets they now sought to penetrate. In the United States itself, *maquiladora*-type operations became commonplace, as U.S.-based manufacturers sought to lower costs by moving production or assembling processes offshore. In this sense the competitiveness of U.S. industry, and thus the U.S. economy's capacity to generate earnings for debt service and profit remittances, came to depend to a greater extent on free trade policies both at home and in the low-wage countries of Latin America and elsewhere. These changes gave rise to a new and more consistent internationalism in U.S. foreign economic policy and led to the Reagan Caribbean Basin Initiative, among other measures, and to subsequently intensified pressures and incentives for the dismantling of ISI throughout Latin America.

As applied to both Latin America and Eastern Europe, unfortunately, the new ELI model has come to imply a radical diminution in the role of the state both in the economy and in its social and redistributive functions. In Eastern Europe as in the former Soviet republics, however, the main thrust of the new policies has gone to removing the state from tasks that, in Latin America, it never assumed or took up late and only partially: central planning and administration of prices, ownership of productive enterprise, and the elaborate networks of cradle-to-grave social service institutions. Moreover, at least in spirit if not yet in accomplishment, most of the new East European governments have committed themselves to sweeping reform of the state apparatus. In Latin America, by contrast, the downsizing of the state has gone closer to the bone. Every country in the region has experienced prolonged depression and a mounting social deficit compounded by deteriorating infrastructure and public services of all kinds. In some cases[15] public order and state capacities have declined at times to near extinction. In others the privatization of public services and enterprises in response to fiscal crises has deprived even stable governments of political and regulatory resources once manipulated, albeit with great inefficiencies, to maintain employment levels and cushion economies against external shocks. None of the Latin American countries has yet announced a thoroughgoing program to reform the state.

Despite the continuing relative decline of the U.S. economy and the transformation of the country into a debtor nation, the power of the United States in Latin America increased dramatically during the 1980s. As Mexican President Carlos Salinas de Gortari found on his trip to Western Europe in 1990, potential competitors now show much more interest in their new East European hinterlands than in Latin America.[16] Japan has not leapt at new opportunities in Latin America, confining its investments to Brazil, Mexico, and more recently, Chile.[17] As the Sandinista government of Nicaragua learned to its dismay, the West European interest in pursuing policies independent of the United States in the region had severe limits, even before the collapse of communism in Eastern Europe. In the 1980s Latin American presidents and finance ministers flocked to Washington and New York with greater frequency than ever before. Even Argentina, once the self-proclaimed regional competitor of the United States, found it convenient to dispatch two ships to the Gulf War, and its ambassador to the United States, proclaiming a new and more "serious" foreign policy, stated in early 1990 that Argentina would no longer be expressing "gratuitous" hostility to U.S. policy in the region. "You can invade Panama any time you want," he said. "In fact, you can invade one Central American country a year if you like. We won't say anything. What we want is to discuss matters of substance, such as your prohibition on the importation of ladies' pants."[18]

Just as in Eastern Europe, substantial regional variation will be evident in the post–Cold War configuration of Latin America. The next decade will see Mexico's increasing economic integration into the United States economy, whether or not the hotly debated North American Free Trade Agreement (NAFTA) is negotiated between the two countries. Central America will complete its transition back to the volatile clientelism that characterized its relations with the United States prior to the Sandinista revolution of 1979, whether or not the Sandinista National Liberation Front (FSLN) returns to power in the general elections of 1995. The island states of the Caribbean, chastened by the economic turmoil of the 1980s and by the U.S. invasion of Grenada, will do likewise. Most of South America will reap neither the fruits of economic integration nor the costs of clientelism. Brazil, which had begun to shift from ISI to ELI by the early 1980s, has lost a decade of growth but remains unique in retaining an industrial establishment with independent ambition and capacity. The rest of the continent, with the exception of oil-rich Venezuela, faces an international environment in which U.S. dominance is now greater than at any time since the 1960s. Pressures for systemic change, like those of the 1960s, are likely to reappear or to be strengthened in most countries as political failures multiply, restructuring fails to attract sufficient external resources, and economic performance remains well below that of the pre-1970 era.

Mexico began its historic shift away from Latin America and toward the United States long ago. This shift was obscured by nationalist rhetoric, by high levels of protection coupled with close regulation (and exclusion from some sectors) of foreign investment, and by an independent foreign policy in Central America. Official rhetoric has now changed, protection and regulation have all but disappeared, and a business-like foreign policy has earned the Salinas government high marks in Washington. These changes are not yet entirely irreversible, but even the left-wing opposition does not oppose economic integration with the United States on principle and would be likely to accommodate to it in the event of an unexpected opposition victory in the 1994 presidential elections.

The economic impact of a free trade pact between Mexico and the United States in the short run would be small in both countries because both have already reduced barriers to trade substantially over the past decade. The addition of Canada, with its minimal interests in Mexico, to a North American Free Trade Agreement would not change the outcome. Although opponents of the agreement have elected to mobilize on economic grounds, the NAFTA proposal is seen by both the Mexican and the U.S. government as a primarily political agreement. Its purpose on the Mexican side is to consolidate and make irreversible the economic policies of the Salinas administration. The NAFTA would make broad areas of economic policymaking subject to an international agreement that could be abrogated but only at great cost to Mexico. Because it would represent a major achievement for the current administration, it would also have the effect of strengthening the policymakers who negotiated it, particularly President Salinas, vis-à-vis rivals within as well as outside Mexico's governing party. By assuring U.S. businessmen and political leaders that Mexico's economic policies—the rules of the game—are not likely to change, even with a more open political system, and by simultaneously strengthening the official party and its current leadership against domestic challenges, the NAFTA is expected to increase investor confidence and thus position Mexico to attract capital that would otherwise go elsewhere.[19]

With the NAFTA (and probably without it) Mexico will become the only Latin American country likely to be successful in competing for external resources in the near to medium term. The tangible benefits of the Salinas strategy in terms of capital flows to Mexico will be balanced, however, by the multiple constraints and uncertainties that will attend still closer ties to the United States. Mexican officials recognize that for a successful NAFTA negotiation to take place and for Mexico to capture the long-term benefits the NAFTA promises, the country will have to accommodate limits on its domestic and foreign policymaking narrower than the Mexican public has been willing historically to accept. The Salinas strategy already embodies a far greater sensitivity to U.S. public opinion (and particularly to elite business views), to U.S. congressional good will, and to the whims of the U.S. administration than Mexican governments have ever contemplated in the past. Given the virtually irreducible asymmetries in this relationship, Mexico's strategy amounts to conceding a portion of its once jealously guarded (albeit already attenuated) sovereignty in exchange for economic growth.

Mexico's economic integration with the United States has raised concern about the formation of a trading bloc with exclusivist ambitions. The

Enterprise Initiative for the Americas, announced by President Bush on the eve of his trip to Latin America in June 1990, contemplates free trade pacts not only with Mexico and Canada but with all the countries of the hemisphere. Several countries, including Argentina and Chile, have already announced their interest in negotiating such accords. As Larry Sjaastad has observed in relation to the Mexican case, such free trade pacts amount to a new form of trade discrimination.[20] Parties to such agreements with the United States will not be prevented from negotiation, but do not contemplate and have not been offered, similar pacts with other major economies. Thus Mexico and the United States (together with Canada and possibly others) will eliminate tariffs on each other's products without reducing barriers on products imported from other countries such as Japan and the EEC economies. As Sjaastad observes, this is precisely the kind of discriminatory trade practice that led to trade wars as well as military conflicts in the past.

Nonetheless, the prospects for commercial warfare are diminished by the discipline of the GATT and by the widespread rejection in Latin America of any commercial arrangements that would diminish the region's attractiveness to the EEC and Japan. Although most of the Latin American countries have supported U.S. initiatives in the Uruguay Round (though with reservations about U.S. insistence on agreements in the area of services and the protection of patents and copyrights), few beyond the client states of the Caribbean and Central America would be willing to follow a U.S. strategy of exclusion and open confrontation. For Mexico as well as others, freer trade with the United States is intended to make Mexico more attractive to investors in Western Europe and Japan, an objective that could be jeopardized by any move to organize an exclusive regional trading bloc.

The continuing dependence of the United States on substantial net flows of capital from the EEC and Japan and the internationalization of or even outright transfer of control over U.S. firms with interests in Latin America not only reduce the prospects for outright commercial warfare but also serve to tie the interests of potential competitors to the success of U.S. policies in the region. Western Europe and Japan are thus likely to become more rather than less supportive of U.S. economic aims in Latin America than in the past.[21] Conversely, U.S. leaders will be likely to consult with the Japanese and West Europeans and to adopt and adapt their policy suggestions (as in the case of the Brady plan) more than ever before. They may also be more willing to accommodate some of their policy preferences to attract private and government capital from outside the hemisphere. Thus, although cooperation among the leading economic powers will diminish prospects for commercial warfare to Latin America's benefit, this same cooperation will also reduce the region's bargaining power by further centralizing economic leverage in the hands of U.S. policymakers.[22]

THE COLD WAR CONTINUES

Because Mexico alone stands to benefit substantially from free trade with the United States in the near to medium term, the question arises whether a reassertion of U.S. preeminence in the Western Hemisphere is likely to be stable and long lasting. The arguments in favor of such a view are largely negative. The assumption of U.S. economic preeminence rests largely on the prospect that Western Europe and Japan will be distracted by investment and trade opportunities in their proximate hinterlands (and each other's economies) for some time to come. Latin Americans will accept a reassertion of U.S. leadership because they have nowhere else to turn. This assumption may be true, but if the benefits to be derived from dependence on the United States prove to be too small or too volatile or to require too many concessions of actual sovereignty or national sentiment, then the governments that tie their fate to U.S. resources and good will could face serious internal opposition. The outlines of a counterstrategy have yet to emerge from the political ferment of newly restored democracies. In most cases socialist and social democratic movements have made their peace for the time being with neoliberalism as an economic strategy and based their objections on the magnitude of the inevitable social and human costs entailed or on the splendors of the national ambitions thus sacrificed.

Indeed, a certain optimism has begun to emerge on the Latin American left. The end of the Cold War, Jorge Castañeda has argued, has removed or diluted the security concerns that led U.S. policymakers to intervene in Latin America's political and social conflicts over the past forty years.[23] Absent the overriding fear of Soviet expansion, U.S. policymakers may find it possible to tolerate a degree of social and economic "experimentation" they have acted to suppress in the past. The strength of this argument lies mainly in its perception of the constraints on U.S. policy induced by the Vietnam syndrome, according to which U.S. public opinion expressed in polling results and through the ballot box prevents policymakers from using military force abroad. Absent a credible Soviet threat, policymakers may be unable to deploy military force (or use the CIA) to intervene in Third World conflicts. During the Reagan years, for example, public opposition to the administration's Central American policies acted as a brake on policies that might otherwise have culminated in direct U.S. military intervention in Nicaragua. As the Sandinistas gave up power after losing the 1990 elections in Nicaragua and the Salvadoran rebels did not manage to defeat the national army, the United States has thus far managed to achieve its objectives without resort to military force. And in both of these cases, as elsewhere, U.S. policy remained consistently hostile to unorthodox regimes and movements and backed this hostility with immense resources.

The end of the Cold War is thus likely to alter the rhetoric of U.S. interventionism in Latin America without changing its aims or altering its frequency. In fact, the Cold War in Latin America began earlier than it did elsewhere and is likely to outlive the fall of the Berlin Wall by many decades. When U.S. troops returned to Nicaragua after a brief absence in late 1925 and early 1926 to help suppress a liberal revolt eventually headed by César Augusto Sandino, Secretary of State Frank Kellogg submitted a memorandum to the Senate Foreign Relations Committee entitled "Bolshevik Aims and Policies in Mexico and Latin America."[24] The memorandum cited Comintern and other documents to show that the United States faced an organized effort, orchestrated from Moscow and aided by the government of Plutarco Elías Callas in Mexico, to oppose the United States in the region. Although U.S. official attitudes moderated during the Roosevelt government, U.S. opposition to "Communist" influence after World War II extended well beyond efforts to limit direct Soviet influence in the region. For many years U.S. policymakers routinely identified any opposition to U.S. strategic, economic, or political aims as either Communist, Communist-inspired, or helpful to Communists. The analytical issue is therefore twofold. First, will U.S. policymakers redefine U.S. aims in the region in such a way as to reduce U.S. opposition to experiments once deemed helpful to "communism" or to the Soviet Union? Second, if the United States does not redefine its aims and policies, will public opinion in the United States prevent policymakers from aggressively expressing their opposition to future experiments anyway?

The answer to both of these questions is probably no. Probably, because the political leadership of the United States itself may be subject to change in the near to medium term as the end of the Cold War and continuing economic difficulties impact domestic political alignments. No, because the United States will nonetheless continue to assert its economic interests in the region and has enhanced its conventional military capacity and credibility as a result of the Gulf War.

Nevertheless, it would be surprising if the momentous changes in the world during the past two years were to have no effect at all on U.S. political life. The world is a far less frightening place than it once was and the North American public knows it. The preemptive cuts in military spending adopted by the Bush administration before the Gulf War, the mounting fiscal deficit, and the virtual disappearance of demands for a substantial peace dividend since Iraq invaded Kuwait may have succeeded for the moment in dimming the prospects for a transition to a European-style social-market economy. The pressures to move in that direction will re-emerge in coming electoral contests, even if the persistent racism of a portion of the electorate revives as new waves of immigrants, documented and undocumented, arrive in the country. Such a transition could have important consequences for Latin America but would be unlikely to lead to a repetition of the Good Neighbor Policy's tolerance of leftward shifts in social and economic policy in the region. The foreign policy implications of a shift to social engineering in U.S. domestic policy, if there were any at all, could produce a repeat of the anti-Communist interventionism of the Alliance for Progress in the 1960s and lead, amid equally uplifting sloganeering from Washington, to a new round of repressive authoritarianism in the least stable of the Latin American states.

Until Saddam Hussein provided the Bush administration with a battleground ideally suited to the deployment of the U.S. air power and tank formations rendered obsolete by the changes in Europe, opponents of reductions in the U.S. defense budget were devoting much of their time and attention to new opportunities for deployments within the Western Hemisphere. The first major post–Cold War military operation took place not in the Gulf but in Panama. Other suggestions for reducing the supply of illegal drugs involved naval operations off the Colombian coast, more and larger deployments to Bolivia, and the construction of a major "training" base in the Upper Huallaga valley of Peru, deep into the territory held by the Sendero Luminoso guerrillas.

The unilateral Soviet withdrawal from political and military competition with the United States has lowered the costs and reduced the risks of U.S. military intervention throughout the Third World. In the absence of a coherent grand strategy and a foreign policy doctrine that might specify the conditions under which the United States would mount military campaigns or, more to the point, the conditions under which it would not dispatch troops to Latin America or other Third World regions, the end of the Cold War has radically diminished the security of states throughout the South. Although the U.S. role in the Gulf War developed in close consultation with a "coalition" of powers and conformed punctiliously to the terms of U.N. resolutions on the subject, U.S. policymakers have never subjected themselves to comparable self-discipline in the Caribbean and Central America. The Organization of American States specifically opposed the invasion of Panama, for example. Having demonstrated its capacity to carry out major military operations as far away as the Gulf with great success, the United States may be unable to resist temptations closer to home in the coming years. Cuba, of course, lies well within the traditional theater of such interventions; one or another of the Andean countries could become the first South American destination for U.S. forces.

CONCLUSION

At the end of World War II the Latin American nations had little choice but to accommodate their interests to the constraints imposed by their unequal strategic and economic alliance with the United States. At the end of the Cold War they are faced with a similar fate. The United States remains, as it has been for half a century, the only great power with the capacity to project effective military power throughout the hemisphere. In economic terms the U.S. economy has been expanding at a slower rate than most other industrial nations and no longer generates savings and investment sufficient to maintain its own modest growth, but its economic preeminence in Latin America remains largely unchallenged and its ability to shape economic policymaking in the region is greater now than at any time since the 1950s.

Latin America's position in the New World Order does not compare favorably with that of the new states of Eastern Europe. The international environment facing Latin American governments is less competitive in security, economic, and political terms. Its external economic ties link it to the least dynamic of the industrial economies whose domestic political economies rank among the least open to needed social change and reform. Latin America's social deficit is greater than Eastern Europe's and its human capital substantially less developed.

In the post–World War II era the Latin American states increased in size and capacity. The model favored by the United States helped to induce a rapid development in the states' capacity to finance, protect, subsidize, and otherwise promote rapid industrialization. It also included, in most cases, a substantial increase in repressive powers. In its later stages the model induced some of the Latin American states to nationalize failing industries and even to create vast public-sector enterprises as they sought to evade pressures to internationalize through "deepening" ISI. The model did not involve a commensurate strengthening of state capacities to levy direct taxes, redistribute income, invest in human capital, or attend to social needs. In the post–Cold War era, the new internationalist free market model envisions reducing or eliminating many of the state capacities that grew up during the period from 1945 to 1980 and generated inefficiency but does not contemplate strengthening state capacities in the fields of public sector activity that were relatively neglected in this era. The new model may generate economic growth, but it is also likely to produce social and political instability, just as its predecessor did.

The shape of the domestic challenges to the reigning political-economic model in Latin America cannot be predicted with any precision, but it does seem likely that the response of governing elites both in the United States and in the region will parallel those of the 1960s and 1970s, when

Latin America fell victim to a wave of military takeovers. Three related developments could, it seems to me, make it possible to avoid such a repetition. First, it is conceivable that political change in the United States could induce an unexpectedly high measure of tolerance for social change in Latin America, though the extent and limits of that tolerance would be difficult to foresee. Second, the new model could begin to generate more rapid economic growth than now seems likely and thus provide reformist governments in the region with the resources to respond to popular agendas without sacrificing external finance and investment. Finally, one might even envision the evolution of EEC-like regulatory, legislative, and juridical institutions, initially as an outgrowth of a free trade pact between the United States, Canada, and Mexico, that might in time succeed in generating and making effective the kinds of social and ecological standards that have evolved in the EEC region. For the moment, however, Latin America seems more likely to repeat than to escape its history.

9

AFTER DESERT STORM

Interest, Ideology, and History in American Foreign Policy

The contributors to this volume have collectively asked how history can be used to shed light on the future of world politics after the Cold War. In this chapter I ask how history can inform speculation about the place of the United States in the world of the future. History has meant different things to different people, and so the scholar must first be clear on what he or she understands by the term. History in the first instance was the story of the state. Early histories were stories deriving from public memories of great conquerors, rulers, battles, ambitions, creations and destructions, dramas and infamies. History was a conservative force. The shapers of the stories were in or close to the ruling group. It was the consciousness of the conquerors, not the conquered, that determined the "plots" of the stories.

With the Enlightenment, however, a new view of history came into being. History began to be seen not just as the unending, unchanging, cyclical flow of great actions but as a flow that on occasion underwent radical changes of course. Humans, for the first time, felt a God-like power to control nature. The river of history could be dammed and its course changed by an act of intelligence and will. Marx, breathing with the new spirit, exhorted people to reconstruct their history. Written history, Marx argued, was all lies. Real history is social and economic. This vision inspired orthodoxy in the Stalinist regimes of Eastern Europe and Asia, and it is intriguing to note that, as socialism comes crashing down all over the world, the stories that people are listening to again with rapt attention are the old legends of states and battles. Those stories deal with kings and queens and fierce foes—not with the efforts of farmers to meet their production quotas.

179

HISTORY AS THE STORY OF THE STATE

For me, history belongs in the realm of the state, not in the realm of society. Societies and cultures, of course, change and evolve and so have a story to tell. But states change in ways that are quite different and unique. There is an arbitrariness, impermanence, wildness about the state one does not generally find in societies and cultures. The latter have a common-sense quality to them—they never seem entirely strange or alien. States, on the other hand, just as legends and histories indicate, are subject to the creative or destructive action of more fanciful individuals, endowed with ambitions, vanities, genius, the penchant for doing good or evil, dreams, and nightmares. It is in the realm of the state, far more than in the realm of society, that human freedom flourishes, just as Hegel recognized. And it is no accident that social evolution in modern societies has seen an enormous enlargement of the public realm at the expense of civil society. In the modern world anyone who is educated spends much of his or her life in the realm of the state. We are all mainly public figures, however private we may seem to our spouses and children. In the world, states play enormous roles. What they do affects our personal lives in almost everything we do. Much of what is called social science is an examination of our relationship with the state. Virtually all of economics in the end deals with the state; so too, clearly, does political science. Even sociology has come to deal more with the public than with the private world. And a glance at what historians do shows that much of history, as in past centuries, remains political history: what kings, queens, presidents, and their operatives did.

Most scholars now recognize that "the state" is a valid concept, worth examination and observation in its own right, and goes well beyond the Anglo-American notion of a government produced through some Lockean social contract. Tosun Aricanli, a Harvard economist, taking cues from Samuel Bowles and Herbert Gintis, argues that one must adopt the eyeglasses of the anthropologist and examine human interactions as they occur in particular "sites" of activity: where people live, work, and think together.[1] The state is one such site, though one that is endowed with a uniqueness of its own that issues principally from its monopoly of legitimate violence. My own idea of the state as a public realm—a very large one in modern societies—is similar to Aricanli's idea of a "state site."

Modern histories say a lot about where those state sites come from. But they do so in different ways. Official histories, on the one hand, seek to serve the interest of the state and so tend to downplay the importance of frictions that occur within the confines of the state site. They tell us little about the conflicts, weaknesses, evils, corruptions, and vanities that affect the evolution of states. Dissident histories, on the other hand, highlight just those features. They reflect the fact that the state is the realm of freedom and individuality. Vanities and ambition are everywhere. Interests clash, leaders emerge in the struggle, the vanquished go underground or are eliminated. Until the 1960s much of written American history was loyal to the "great experiment." Although never as hagiographic as official history in the Soviet Union or China, American historians by and large shared the pride felt by much of the population over the great achievements of their country. But from the early 1970s on, dissident histories became more common. And indeed radical and left-wing historians who were regarded on the outermost brink of acceptability suddenly found themselves on center stage.

There is a third kind of history, more cosmopolitan in scope. It studies states as particular emanations and manifestations of broader historical forces. One finds it first in the works of Rashîd-ud-Dîn, a high official of the fourteenth-century Mongol Ilkhanid Empire in what is now Iran. Rashîd-ud-Dîn compiled histories of all the major civilizations of the world, including China and Europe. This more cosmopolitan conceptualization of history is also found in Europe in the work of Gianbattista Vico, Gottfried Herder, and the nineteenth-century German historians, taking a leap forward with Marxism. It appears in America in the writings of Harvard's Barrington Moore and has continued to inspire younger writers in various disciplines in the 1970s and 1980s. "Comparative studies," which appeared in the late 1950s at the instigation of young social scientists who tended to have leftist but non-Communist pasts, also contributed to the success of this perspective. This third school in the United States has served to undermine earlier notions of "American exceptionalism."[2]

In the 1970s and 1980s the sense of history in the United States in particular underwent major changes. Revisionist, radical, and reductionist history swept away much of the official history of earlier days. Much of that history now seems quaint, and a lot of it is dismissed as racist, biased, and outmoded. Marxism, on the other hand, entered the American social science arena just as it was falling from fashion in much of the rest of the world. In the 1970s dissident historians were attacking the state from within the public arena, whereas those who had adopted a more cosmopolitan perspective brought society in as a proper subject of historical inquiry to counterbalance the state-centeredness of much conventional history.

My view of history is quite old-fashioned. History is in the end mainly—and perhaps only—the story of the state. This view of history explains this chapter. I have not written it either as a loyal client of this state nor as a broad-brush comparative historian or political analyst. I focus uniquely on the realm of the state and write as a dissident who was once involved in ideological struggle against certain interest groups active within the "state site."

The argument is couched in terms of clashing interests and clashing ideologies. The difference between the two categories is defined essentially
by the conceptualizations of time that they embody. In the case of interests
the future is discounted. Material gain is pursued in the here and now, and
interests are defined in terms of the rewards that are sought. In the case of
ideology the future is not discounted, but the present is. Future reward
justifies present sacrifice. Ideology implies more than material reward,
however. It implies the idea of betterment, of political improvement
through reform or revolution. Improvement thus manifests itself not only
in the acquisition of material goods but in that of the more intangible
good, justice. In this chapter I focus principally on the economic interests
of the international business class and the electoral and political interests
of the presidency and examine how they inform the definition of attitudes
and policies toward the Gulf region. As for ideologies, I focus on three: nationalism, internationalism, and universalism. I examine how they inter-
fere and combine with interests, how they interact with the more traditional ideologies of societal improvement of the left and the right, and how
they manifest themselves in temporally and geographically more specific
avatars, such as anticommunism or nearly unconditional support for Israel.[3]

This chapter assumes three main domains: state, society, and history.
The analysis deals with the relationship of the first to the other two. The
state's relationship to society is couched in economic terms and deals with
an interdependent world economy that affects everyone through consumer capitalism. The state's relationship to history is shaped by recurring
patterns of diplomacy and politics. As in a river, strong swimmers can exercise much free will, but at the same time they are carried along by a current that comes from what was upriver, that is, in the past.

The chapter is divided into three parts. I begin with what is essentially a
factional-political analysis of how U.S. goals were defined in the Gulf War.
I follow this with a look at deeper and recurrent patterns that are revealed
by the politics of the Gulf War. The last part offers a broader analysis of
these patterns.

In the entire chapter particular attention is given to the unique and significant role of the chief executive, the American president. In my book,
The Foreign Politics of Richard Nixon, I highlighted Nixon's autonomous
role in shaping the relations of the United States with the world but offered no explanation. In this chapter I suggest that that executive role is related to the emergence of a new configuration in world history, that is, an
elusive yet real linkage between the major powers of the North: Japan,
China, the (former) Soviet Union, Western Europe, and the United States.[4]
These powers are not only at peace with each other as they have never
been in history, but despite instabilities, frictions, and obvious incompati-

bilities the ties between them are growing stronger. This evolving club or league of the North is founded on the interests of the international business class, on the one hand, and on the other, on the de facto collusion of state leaders to exploit their strategic role as mediators between the nation and the international community to enhance their domestic political power.

Finally, the chapter singles out two major factions in the power game at the White House level. One is "internationalist," concerned with furthering a world system in which the interdependent world economy is a key component. The other is "nationalist" and reflects an older political reality: the United States as a sovereign nation-state that places the effort to promote national identity, cohesion, sovereignty, and independence ahead of efforts to address global challenges. Both factions played a key role during the Gulf crisis.[5]

BEFORE THE STORM:
INTERESTS, IDEOLOGIES, AND SADDAM HUSSEIN

President Bush scored a smashing victory in the Gulf War. The victory came at a time when doomsayers were prophesying that the United States was losing its capacity to lead the industrialized democracies. New challengers, Japan and Germany, had been waxing more powerful. After the war, however, European Community President Jacques Delors was bemoaning "the sick man of Europe," and an Arab writer, Ibrahim Salama, was noting how the power of Germany and Japan had suddenly been deflated because of their impotence in the Gulf crisis. He wondered whether "the United States could carry the responsibility for the world all by itself." Prime Minister John Major reveled in Britain's status as loyal servitor, and France's proud and aloof President François Mitterrand publicized his role as a lesser but still brilliant light in the new collaboration with the United States, while the French press extolled the "George and François" relationship.

It is true that the decline of the Soviet Union as a superpower had rekindled faith in the international role of the United States. Some months before the Iraqi invasion of Kuwait, General Colin Powell, chairman of the Joint Chiefs of Staff, claimed that the United States should hang out a new shingle: "Solo-superpower lives here." President Bush, during the five months leading up to the war, said repeatedly that there would be no new Vietnam because he was going to give the generals and admirals a free hand to win. Subsequently, not unlike the Mongols who destroyed Baghdad in 1258, U.S. warriors planned a massive high-tech bombing of Iraq's armed forces that, to the astonishment of most observers, produced a quick battlefield victory and reestablished the U.S. position as the world's new Rome, its only imperial power.

As late as August 2, 1990, however, the road that led to this reaffirmation of imperial grandeur was still hardly visible. Iraq had just invaded Kuwait under circumstances that still remain obscure. It took President Bush four days to decide to send troops to protect Saudi Arabia against a possible Iraqi attack. And unlike the comparable situation that obtained in Korea in 1950, in which U.S. intervention meant war right away, it was unclear what would happen once American troops reached Saudi soil.

Opinion in the United States was divided. Ever since Truman decided to recognize the new State of Israel in 1948, U.S. policy in the Middle East had been buffeted by severe factional splits. The splits dealt with one main question: Should the Arabs or Israel have priority in American foreign policy? The split has remained largely unchanged since its first appearance during the Truman administration. At that time "Arabists" in the State Department defended the international interests of the United States in the Gulf—mainly oil. An opposing faction, in which Clark Clifford played a key role, favored immediate recognition of Israel. Although Clifford claims that this group was motivated by humanitarian considerations, they were in fact responding to strong pressure from within the Democratic party to embrace the new Jewish state. And Truman, seeing a very difficult election campaign ahead, needed all the political support he could get.

Until 1980 the main split over Middle East policy within the political class remained one of "Israel versus Oil." That year, however, a third faction arose that was engendered by the Islamic revolution in Iran. The Arabists, centered in the generally aloof State Department, were very hostile to Iran. They saw in the pulsating waves of Islamic fundamentalism a mortal threat to American interests in the Gulf.[6] They feared that an Iranian victory in the Iran-Iraq War would unleash a fundamentalist Islamic wave that could engulf the Middle East's most important oil fields. With the onset of the hostage crisis the Arabists enjoyed great popular support. There was more to their fears, however, than this vision of a fundamentalist Islamic wave. The Arabists feared for the future of a fragile diplomatic edifice that they had painstakingly erected over the past twenty years. During the Nixon and Kissinger period, they developed a stratagem to build a new diplomatic bloc in the Middle East called the "twin pillars" policy. According to this policy, American power in the Gulf would rest on two pillars—Iran, ruled by America's friend the Shah, and Saudi Arabia, ruled by a royal family in intimate oil-mediated alliance with the United States. When Nixon and Kissinger succeeded in weaning Egypt away from its pro-Soviet alignment after the October 1973 war, Egypt joined Iran and Saudi Arabia to form a de facto triple alliance.

Iran's fall in 1978 forced the Arabists to look for a replacement, which they soon found in Iraq.[7] Iraq was Arab, fiercely nationalistic and secular, and seemed intent on modernizing and industrializing its economy rather than on expanding its territory or influence. As an Arab writer put it, a "love-hate" relationship developed between the United States and the Saddam regime. During the factional controversies surrounding the Iran-Contra issue, Secretary of State George Shultz, whose background at Bechtel and economic philosophy made him sympathetic to international business (especially oil), vehemently opposed the idea of resuming ties with Iran. During his six years in office, U.S. policy moved closer and closer to Baghdad. This helps explain the context surrounding Ambassador April Glaspie's controversial discussions with Saddam Hussein on the eve of the Iraqi invasion of Kuwait.

The revolution in Iran gave rise to another faction, however, that tilted toward Iran. It included the now notorious figures of Colonel Oliver North; former director of the National Security Council (NSC), Robert ("Bud") McFarlane; and his successor at NSC, Admiral John Poindexter.[8] This faction also included the shadowy figure of CIA director William Casey, who died—conveniently for some—at the height of the Iran-Contra scandal. I have called this faction the "Ollie North" faction, not only because of North's flamboyance but because of its clear, right-wing ideological flair. We know from revelations during the Iran-Contra scandals that this faction received strong support from the Israelis and some elements in the Israeli lobby. The Israelis made no secret of their preference for Iran over Iraq in the eight-year war between the two powers. We also know that this faction was supported by members of the national security bureaucracy who distrusted any policy that provided support for a regime that had been armed by the Soviets and that still kept up strong ties with Moscow. A pro-Iraqi policy smelled to them too much of the illusion that the United States and the Soviet Union might become partners in peace. The anti-Iraq faction thus reached into the far corners of the American right, which continued deeply to distrust and fear the Soviet Union right up to the collapse of Soviet communism in August 1991.

Although North, Poindexter, and McFarlane were tried and convicted for the Iran-Contra crimes, the factional split that gave rise to those crimes hardly vanished from the corridors of power when Bush assumed the presidency. These factional splits were driven by deeper political currents that had been flowing through the American political class since the end of World War II. The State Department (as any ordinary American traveler knows who has often vainly sought consular help abroad while business travelers get preferential attention) has long been close to American business. Its chief mandate has been to defend American interests abroad, and it turns out that this has meant mainly business interests. It defends those interests with pragmatism and a deep commitment to reason and reason-ableness. The State Department has never shown much patience for ideo-logical conflict or with regimes (or American administrations) that were driven by ideological concerns. In my earlier writings I made a distinction between a "realm of interests" and a "realm of ideology" in U.S. foreign affairs.[9]

The State Department unequivocally belongs in the former realm. This is also true of U.S. oil interests. The great Anglo-American oil companies are mainly interested in extracting, processing, and marketing oil in what-ever way guarantees them secure profits. In American diplomatic history, as a rule, reasonable and pragmatic foreign policies have been designed to serve the interests of American business.

U.S. foreign policy, however, especially since World War II, has also been marked by strong ideological thrusts, coming mainly but not exclu-sively from the political right. The most powerful thrust has been anticom-munism. Anticommunism has been particularly visible in our policies to-ward East Asia. In the Middle East, however, anticommunism has generally not been a major force behind U.S. policy. Until Desert Storm the U.S. military presence was negligible, and there were no right-wing mili-tary regimes in the region—such as those in Pakistan, Thailand, South Vietnam, Taiwan, and South Korea—to fan the flames of American ideo-logical militancy against the "Red menace."

Ideology per se has not been absent from U.S. policy in the Middle East. But unlike U.S. policy in East Asia where the ideological thrust was anti-Communist and came from the right, U.S. policy in the Middle East was informed by an ideology that was centered on Israel and that had its source mainly in the liberal left. It is true that American Jews and many Christians support Israel for personal reasons that cannot be called ideo-logical. But the most passionate defense of Israel has come from social democratic and (especially) labor circles, as well as from intellectuals who in the beginning believed Israel showed how socialism and democracy could be successfully wed, a stark contrast to the "great Soviet experi-ment." In a sense one can say that Israel was to the American left what Tai-wan was to the American right. Until the 1980s, the defense of Israel was as sacred to liberals as the defense of Taiwan was to conservatives.

Whenever ideologies and interests clash, deep passions are stirred, and of course this is the case with issues surrounding Israel and the Arabs. Those antagonisms were—and are—reflected in the corridors of the American foreign policy establishment. The interest-oriented approach to Middle Eastern affairs suggested that main interest in the region was oil. Other concerns, including the welfare of Israel, had to come second. Pro-Israeli liberals, emboldened by their dislike of big business, detested the idea that the U.S. government would be the handmaiden of the big oil companies. Assigning Israel top priority was a way of demanding a decent and democratic policy in the Middle East, as opposed to propping up archaic and corrupt monarchies just to keep the oil flowing.

Enter the Arabists; Exit the Ollie North Faction

The split over policy toward Iraq and Iran during the Reagan era was not directly the product of the older split between pro-Israeli and pro-Arab factions. It was a split between pragmatic Arabists on the one hand and right-wing cold warriors on the other. To the latter, common sense suggested that the Soviet Union was still the main threat to American interests in the region. This assumption meant that Iran rather than Iraq was our natural ally in the Middle East. The Iranians had broken with the Soviets, and Ruhollah Khomeini, after receiving the support of Tudeh Communists, turned around and executed many of their leaders. Saddam, on the other hand, even though he was moving closer to the West, kept up his connections—especially his military and intelligence connections—with the Soviet Union.

The Arabists gained a decisive advantage in the factional struggle over foreign and security policy in June 1982 when Secretary of State Alexander Haig was suddenly fired because of his support of the Israeli invasion of Lebanon. George Shultz, who replaced Haig at State, was the perfect figure for the job. He was highly trusted in Washington circles, and personally he was very pro-Israeli and pro-Jewish. He was also a good and honest man. Yet he gradually tilted American foreign policy away from its close identification with Israel and worked hard to consolidate the Middle Eastern triple alliance. It was Shultz who ordered the beginning of a dialogue between the United States and the Palestine Liberation Organization (PLO).

The State Department's Middle East policy, especially after 1985, was also informed by new efforts to normalize relations with the Soviet Union. One of the conditions for normalization that the Reagan administration imposed on the Soviet Union was the settlement of regional conflicts. While the Cambodian, Afghan, Ethiopian, Angolan, and Central American conflicts were major points of friction between the United States and the Soviet Union, none was potentially as dangerous as the three conflicts in the Middle East: the Iran-Iraq War, the civil war in Lebanon, and the Israeli-Palestinian conflict. Soviet cooperation in settling these regional conflicts, especially in the Middle East, would be seen as strong evidence that the Cold War was indeed over and that a new U.S.-Soviet relationship could begin.

The Soviets made good on U.S. demands. They agreed to withdraw from Afghanistan, they became tacit partners with the United States in containing Iranian expansion by propping up Iraq's resistance, and they did not press their client, Syria, to take advantage of the withdrawal of U.S. Marines from Beirut in October 1983. Indeed, new threads were being spun between Washington and Damascus, which culminated in Syria's joining the coalition against Iraq in 1990. But the most persuasive evidence of Soviet cooperation came in the Israeli-Palestinian dispute. When tens of thousands of Soviet Jews started pouring into Israel—to the consternation of Palestinians and other Arabs—Washington knew that Moscow had made the one gesture that the Israelis and their supporters in the U.S. Congress most appreciated, one that allowed a big buildup of the Jewish population of Israel (particularly of European origin).

When the Iran-Contra scandal erupted, right-wing anti-Communist conservatives rallied to North's support. Israel, however, emerged as a key player on the Casey-Poindexter-North team. In other words, it proved to be an ally of the Cold War right, leaving its social democratic supporters in an uneasy position.[10] In the end, the Ollie North faction, which one might have expected Reagan to support out of ideological preference, lost out. If it had won, the great Reagan-led rapprochement between the United States and the Soviet Union, which was very visible by the time of the November 1985 Geneva summit, might not have taken place. Instead it was the State Department's policy of covertly backing Iraq in the Iran-Iraq War that won out, in part because it helped grease the wheels of U.S.-Soviet rapprochement.

By the mid-1980s it was apparent to many people (though not generally in the United States) that Washington favored arming Iraq to prevent an Iranian victory. The fact that the United States allowed the sale of $8 billion worth of grain to Iraq while turning a blind eye to huge arms shipments to Iraq by countries with close ties to the United States should have made it clear that Iraq had become part of the post-1979 triple alliance in the Middle East along with Egypt and Saudi Arabia. During the eight-year Iran-Iraq War, Saudi money and Egyptian manpower were of great importance to the Iraqi war effort.

August 1990: Exit the Arabists and Reenter the Ollie North Faction

The publicity generated by Ambassador April Glaspie's dealings with Iraq prior to the August 2 invasion made it clear that Saddam's grab of Kuwait was a heavy blow to the State Department. Suddenly the Israeli argument according to which Saddam was a dangerous regional hegemon made a lot of sense. He allegedly had the fourth most powerful army in the world, and his amassing of high-tech weaponry, his launching of an earth-orbiting satellite, his determination to acquire nuclear weapons, and his stockpiling and use of chemical weapons made him a fearsome antagonist who had to be eliminated.

When Arab efforts to convince Saddam Hussein to withdraw from Kuwait failed, the Arabist faction suffered a precipitate loss of power in Washington. U.S.-Soviet relations also suffered as a consequence of the Iraqi invasion of Kuwait. A Bush-Gorbachev summit was postponed, and arms control treaties that were supposed to be signed were not. Although there is no evidence that Washington was suspicious of a Soviet role in Saddam's decision to invade, there was nevertheless plenty of fear in Washington that Saddam could at any time slide back into a closer Soviet embrace. If that were to happen, Iraq's possession of Kuwait could give a Soviet client a grip on Gulf oil that would prove dangerous to American interests. There was also suspicion that Iran and Iraq might be getting together again themselves, despite their bloody war. Saddam agreed to vacate Iranian territory still held by his troops. The Arab press reported Iraqi proposals for an Iran-Iraq alliance to exercise joint control over the Gulf. The apprehensions of the anti-Arabist faction were worsened by fears of a military or hard-liner coup in the Soviet Union and the prospect of a rapprochement between a new anti-Western Soviet Union and a new Iran-Iraq alliance.

As the anti-Arabist faction rang the alarm bell, the Arabists made a serious miscalculation in the days preceding the invasion of August 2, 1990.[11] A "palace coup" took place in Washington in August, the victim of which was Secretary of State James Baker III. At the time of the invasion Baker was in southern Mongolia, preparing to go on a hunting expedition. Learning of the invasion, he hurried back to Moscow and the United States. But then, rather than assume a position of leadership, as the circumstances dictated, he repaired in apparent disgrace to his rural retreat in Woods Hole, Wyoming. In Washington, Baker was eclipsed by newer, more military figures like Richard Cheney, Colin Powell, and of course, the commander in chief himself.

Did this mean that the Ollie North faction had made a comeback? In a sense, it did. The militants in the military and intelligence services who wanted to deal a serious blow to a dangerous regional hegemon and Soviet client assumed leadership roles. The Israeli perspective was also heard in debates regarding American policy goals in the Gulf. And though the world welcomed the revitalization of the United Nations as it confronted a dangerous provocation to world peace and stability, a storm cloud began gathering force in the White House inner circle that made war a virtual certainty. It is in the debates and the confusion that reigned within the U.S. political class in the weeks preceding the outbreak of war that one can discern a number of fundamental patterns of United States foreign policy formation that go back to the earliest years of the post–World War II period.

Ambivalence and Indecision in the White House

During the five months that separated the invasion of Kuwait and the out-break of war on January 16, 1991, President Bush could be heard defending three different and not entirely compatible U.S. policy goals. The first was the clearest and the one most in harmony with international sentiment: the complete annulment of the Iraqi takeover of Kuwait. The status quo ante had to be reestablished. But when heavy reinforcements were sent to bolster the U.S. military presence in Saudi Arabia after the elections of November 1990, Bush announced a second goal. He began to talk about overthrowing Saddam Hussein and destroying Iraq's offensive military capabilities labelling Saddam a would-be regional hegemon, a "Hitler" who had to be checked before he gobbled up other countries. Subsequently Bush advanced a third rationale for U.S. action in the Gulf when he introduced his Wilsonian theme of a New World Order. Although he never spelled out concretely what he meant, he did reawaken memories of the postwar era when the United Nations was created and a new international order under American leadership (or rather, hegemony) was established.

All three goals were informed by broader political and factional currents. Liberating Kuwait and getting oil production going again seemed to be what the global oil community and its friends at State wanted most. The behavior of the markets—prices jumping with news of war and falling with news of peace—seemed to indicate that big oil wanted no war or, at worst, a short one that minimized damage to all sides. Appeasement, which would have left Iraq in control of Kuwait, was out of the question, but some kind of deal that would let Saddam save face yet restore the status quo ante appeared to be the solution most favored by Secretary of State James Baker (who, like George Shultz, has a long record of ties to the oil industry). When Baker and Soviet Foreign Minister Eduard Shevarnadze met later in 1990 and indicated that some concessions might be made to entice Iraq to evacuate Kuwait, it was apparent that Baker and the State Department wanted to deal rather than fight.

Were the Arabists still seeking to preserve Iraq for the triple alliance, hoping that the Kuwait flurry could be settled and Saddam convinced that his best bet was to begin serious reconstruction in his own country and solicit whatever international support he could for that purpose? That seems indeed to have been the case. It was the hope not only of the Arabist faction in the United States but that of the international business community in general. This same attitude was apparent in the positions taken by the Germans and the Japanese, as well as by the Chinese and, in the end, by the Soviets, too.[12]

How the ejection of the Iraqis from Kuwait could be achieved without military force was never made clear. Yet the Arabists believed that more could be accomplished ultimately by dealing than by fighting. But the war mood was growing, fed by the British, French, and American media and encouraged by the war faction in the White House inner circle. The demonization of Saddam Hussein reached dramatic proportions. The West had witnessed such demonization in the past, most notably in the case of the Communist leadership of the People's Republic of China. In the 1950s, however, demonization was the work of the right. This time it came from the left. In France the newspaper *Libération*, the voice of the angry 1960s, called for war to put an end to the new Hitler. In the Soviet Union liberals (democrats in the new political parlance) cheered the Americans on to smash Saddam. In the United States, National Public Radio, despite its style of bland detachment, nourished the war mood. The once mighty peace movement in the United States and Western Europe disintegrated as many of its intellectuals deserted it for the war camp. In Israel the left disintegrated when Palestinians rallied to Saddam, and many leftists rallied around the war party in much the same way as in Europe and the United States.

Given this mood, it is hardly surprising that Bush escalated his demands, calling no longer for the mere liberation of Kuwait but rather for Saddam Hussein's unconditional surrender. These currents could not be satisfied with the mere liberation of Kuwait. Saddam had to be toppled and his armies destroyed so that, it was hoped, democracy could be brought to Iraq as it had been brought to occupied Germany and Japan after World War II. The liberal left was particularly sensitive to this message. Fear of what Saddam might do in the Middle East, especially to Israel, accounted for a good part of the left's hawkishness. The liberal and left-wing demonization of Saddam Hussein provided an unexpected ally for a U.S. military facing deep budget cuts and redefinitions of mission in the aftermath of the Cold War.[13]

Reinforcement by the left was welcomed by the Ollie North faction, and the coaction of these two ideological forces helped to create the unprecedented national mood of patriotism that swept the political class and the population as a whole. Factional cooperation, however, did not mean that a new identity of views obtained between them. The Ollie North faction marched to a different drummer. Despite the new closeness between the United States and the Soviet Union and despite the growing consensus between the anti-Communist right and the liberal and social democratic left, many in military and in intelligence circles still felt deep suspicion about the Soviet Union. The Soviet army, despite its retreat from Afghanistan and its withdrawal from Eastern Europe, remained a powerful fighting force armed with nuclear weapons. Saddam's armed forces were outfitted with Soviet weapons and there were many Soviet advisers in Iraq. A decisive defeat of Iraq would be an indirect defeat of the Soviet Union by the

United States. The opportunity to strike a blow at the waning superpower was too good to be missed.

The victory of the war party was not immediate, however. Many military commanders were wary about going to war, and many liberals in Congress—including at least half the Jewish contingent—voted against giving the president authorization to do so. The latter hated Saddam and were sympathetic to Israel. Other ideological values, however, including antimilitarism, still inclined them to vote no. As for the military, many commanders were worried not only about high American casualties but whether it was actually worth it to shed "blood for oil," in the words of what was perhaps the most effective slogan of the peace movement, such as it was.

The war party did not carry the day until a new factor—fear—entered the picture and brought interests and values together to shape foreign policy attitudes in a decisive way. Liberals and the military skeptics alike were gradually overcome by the argument that Saddam was potentially as dangerous to world peace as Hitler when he grabbed Austria. War was, inescapably, the only option left. The anti-Saddam press, national and international, undoubtedly played an important role in swaying the American political class. Liberal and military skeptics, once they agreed that war was inevitable, also agreed that the liberation of Kuwait was too limited a goal. Saddam's military capabilities had to be destroyed, even if this meant going all the way to Baghdad or subjecting Iraq to saturation bombing. In factional terms, therefore, support for Bush's second goal (destroying Saddam's military power) came—in the end—both from the military and a coalition of liberal and conservative forces in Congress.

The New World Order

Although one can trace the factional politics that drove Bush to intervene in the Gulf and to escalate his stated war aims, there is no readily apparent factional explanation for Bush's third goal, the institution of a New World Order. Bush's decision to seek United Nations sanction for his Gulf policy recalls a similar move by President Truman in 1950 after North Korea invaded South Korea. It is possible that Bush was moved to do so by remembering Reagan's difficulties with his Contra policy. Bush could not be sure that Congress would support him in the Gulf and needed a vote of confidence from a body such as the United Nations that, though not exactly beloved of Congress, could not simply be ignored by it, either. The votes in the Security Council did succeed in impressing Congress and American public opinion. For the first time since its founding, the five permanent members of the United Nations voted together to support what was, in effect, a risky American thrust into the Gulf. And although the Chinese abstained on the crucial Resolution 660 authorizing the use of force to com-

pel the Iraqis to get out of Kuwait, the overall sense was that the United
States had gained support not only from the other four of the United Nations' Big Five, but also from two of the world's great powers that were not
permanent members of the Security Council: Japan and Germany. They,
too, offered support, if only by agreeing to write big checks.

But it is too simple to see Bush's appeal to the United Nations as nothing more than a political ploy. If Bush's first two goals were designed to
win support from the multinational business community, the military, and
key elements of the American political class, the goal of building a New
World Order appealed to few people in the United States, and those to
whom it appealed were mostly marginal academics and armchair
Wilsonians. It was a nice turn of phrase, papers noted, but it did not seem
to have much serious content. The proposal, however, was not directed at
domestic opinion at all but rather was directed at the swath of nations that
extend across the northern half of the globe, the great powers of the industrialized North—Japan, China, the (former) Soviet Union, the countries of
Western Europe, and the United States—which are at peace with each
other and working together in a way that they never have been at any time
in history.

In going to the United Nations, Bush was appealing less to the American audience than to the nations of the North. He was appealing in particular to the Soviet Union and to China to go along with the United States
and thereby to help lay a foundation for the future development and prosperity of the Northern partnership. Bush made it particularly clear to the
Soviets that some modicum of support was necessary if the new Soviet-
American relationship was to continue. The Soviets were well aware that
opposing the United States could cost them not only American sympathy
but could adversely affect their rapidly developing relations with the new
unified Germany and the European Community as well. As for the Chinese, it was made clear to them that support for the United States would
help to mitigate the adverse effects of the Tiananmen massacre on U.S.-
Chinese relations. The Bush administration also pressured Japan, Germany, and France to give support. Despite serious public controversy in
Japan, the Kaifu government agreed to write a very large check for the
Gulf expedition, as did Germany. France, after the sacking of Chevènement, also joined the war enthusiastically.

Whatever concrete results come out of the New World Order approach,
especially in the Middle East, the content of that order is becoming clear. It
is Wilsonian. The five permanent members of the Security Council plus
the two great economic powers, Japan and Germany, are to become the
global Big Seven who, under the leadership of the United States as primus
inter pares, will assume responsibility for the defense of the global status
quo and the interests of the Northern tier. Wilson had always assumed

that the big powers would work together for the general good of the world, an idea that was not fully worked out, however, until the Dumbarton Oaks conference of 1944 created a bicameral United Nations that gave the Big Five a predominant say in UN decisions. Under Bush, it would appear, the Wilsonian idea became a reality, or at least more of a reality than it had ever been before.

IN THE EYE OF THE STORM:
SHIFTING COALITIONS AND CHANGING FORTUNES

U.S. foreign policymakers have the reputation of operating by the seat of their pants. Kissinger, for example, describes the Nixon Doctrine as a basket of ideas thrown together rather quickly on the island of Guam in July 1969. Just as no psychologist disputes the importance of the genetic roots in the psychological makeup of any individual human being, one cannot dispute the importance of the historical roots of U.S. foreign policy.

The Universalism of the Presidency

The actions of the United States in the Korean crisis of 1950 show some remarkable similarities to those in the 1990 Gulf crisis. In the Korean crisis, Truman faced pressures coming from the State Department and, acting behind the State Department, the British government. Both agreed that the United States had to respond firmly to the North Korean provocation, but they also wanted to avoid at all cost a war with China and the Soviet Union. The British government came under fire from the American right wing for seeking only to protect their own extensive economic interests in East Asia. At the same time Truman faced countervailing pressures from the military and their Far Eastern chieftain, General Douglas MacArthur, as well as from the rapidly growing anti-Communist right wing. His initial decision to go into Korea satisfied both factions. The military and the right welcomed a war that gave them a chance to strike at the new Communist enemy. The Seventh Fleet, however, was placed in the Taiwan Straits to prevent the People's Republic and Taiwan from going to war with each other. This action satisfied the concerns of the State Department and the British. Truman, like Bush, also made the Wilsonian move of seeking authorization from the United Nations to intervene militarily. Given the fortuitous absence of the Soviet Union from the Security Council, the United States was able to win overwhelming support from the other members. What came to be called the Free World arose largely out of that vote.

Factional crosscurrents and ideological cleavages can be found as well in the policies of presidents who followed Truman. In the Vietnam War, Lyndon Johnson, like Truman, also had to maneuver between hawks and doves, all the more so as the war began to go badly. Unlike Truman and

Bush, however, he did not make any Wilsonian moves. He did try to keep U.S.-Soviet relations on a firm footing, but his incompetence in the foreign field prevented him from moving successfully in a more Wilsonian direction. Nixon was the opposite of Johnson. He played an extraordinary game in an effort to draw the United States closer to the big foreign powers. Not only did he build bridges to China and the Soviet Union, but he strengthened ties with West European powers and even Japan, despite the fact that they were reeling from a series of economic shocks that were largely the effect of his own policies. In this sense one might call Nixon a closet Wilsonian—though the analogy needs some stretching. It was on the domestic front that Nixon failed. Unlike Johnson, who sought the support of liberal and conservative factions alike, Nixon alienated both by trying to manipulate them. Factional politics were apparent during the Reagan administration, as well. Reagan, however, never quite managed to work his way through the factional thicket. When the Iran-Contra scandal exploded, he was barely able to avoid impeachment.

Since World War II the presidency has been both close to and distant from the factions seeking to sway it. Although there are myriads of different interests and even many different kinds of ideologies, general ideological and factional lines tend to form when it comes to persistent and important issues. These lines take on their most general form when they fall into some dualism, like the hawks and doves of the Vietnam period. The factions have dealings with Congress, with members of the political class including journalists, and with the public as a whole. Many, of course, also have extensive dealings with foreigners. For the presidency factions are both a resource that can be exploited and a threat to presidential sovereignty.

We have very few good studies of what actually goes on in the president's inner circle. The White House is the emperor's palace, imposing and mysterious. The late Reinhard Bendix, a lifelong student of Max Weber, argued that there always was a fundamental irrationality at the top of all legal and rational authority. In the United States that irrationality takes the form of a presidency endowed with awesome powers. Yet it is often impossible to pinpoint where that power is exactly or even what it is. A substantial proportion of the real power of the president comes from three sources. First, in domestic affairs the president has power over the means of communication. He can use them to reach down to the people and impress—or frighten—the politicians by invoking foreign threats or the people's collective sentiments. Second, he is the commander in chief of the armed forces and in more modern terms, the head of the national security establishment. He has the ability to order the armed forces into war, as he did in the Gulf, and gain an enormous accretion of power as a result. Third, he has the capacity to deal with other leaders throughout the world and thus derive power from the fact that in a highly interdependent world the president can seek and win favors from foreign leaders that can favorably affect the lives of millions of American citizens. It is not hard to understand why so many are lured to seek the supreme position in any nation—it confers immense powers, even in tiny countries.

The executive office has assumed particular importance in recent times because it has become one of the principal agents of universalism. Universalism means maintaining peace and partnership with the world's major powers. Universalism is promoted not only by the American presidency but by other chief executives as well. It is often noted that in many poorer developing countries, the chief executive, if he is not a tyrant, functions mainly as an intermediary between his own government and foreign powers who are a source of needed financial, military, and diplomatic support for his impoverished nation. The chief executive of any nation occupies a key strategic locus between the aspirations of his or her people and the rewards that the outside world can shower on them (or vice versa).

Similarly for Bush, foreign policy is exploited as a source of domestic power. The opportunity to use foreign policy in this way accounts for Bush's universalism—his search for a New World Order. Peace is popular, and the magic that the chief executive can wield to bring peace about can be a significant source of strength and power for his office. For Nixon, summitry with the heads of other states was the main source of presidential power and influence. In Reagan's case his discovery that the Soviet Union had virtues and was not just an "evil empire," a discovery that he had made by the time of the November 1985 Geneva summit, helped him weather the storm of Iran-Contra. The political class realized that if he were toppled, as Nixon had been, the peace process that most representatives in Congress favored would be placed in jeopardy.[14]

At the time of the Gulf crisis, it was in Bush's presidential interest to keep the growing cooperative relationship with the Soviet Union alive. The factional pressures, particularly those emanating from the realm of interests (concerned mainly with oil, the world economy, and the entire nexus of relations with various foreign countries), were not hostile to the Soviet Union. But they did not hold the U.S.-Soviet relationship as central as did the president. During the entire Gulf crisis, from the Iraqi seizure of Kuwait to the cease-fire, U.S.-Soviet ties were jolted repeatedly. Because of the domestic weakness of the Soviet Union, advocates of a solo superpower role for the United States even suggested that ties with the Soviet Union be downgraded. Yet there was never any hint from the Oval Office that the president shared this view. Indeed, the surprise proclamation of a cease-fire at the moment that the road to Baghdad seemed open can be read in part as a gesture to the Soviet Union, where some circles had become alarmed by what looked like a precipitate expansion of the American zone of influence in the Middle East.

Pragmatists Versus Ideologues

Turning from the presidency itself to look at factional struggles over policy that occur within the president's inner circle, a different picture emerges. Ever since the National Security Council and what was supposed to be its intelligence arm, the Central Intelligence Agency, were created in the late 1940s, tugs-of-war have marked their relationship with the State Department. By law, State is the exclusive instrument for foreign affairs in the U.S. federal structure. Yet, when the Cold War gave rise to a situation in which both peace and war prevailed at the same time, security matters became as important in the day-to-day routine of foreign affairs as the promotion of U.S. interests under peacetime conditions, that is, they became the normal prerogative of the State Department. Because of their rationalism and pragmatism, State Department personnel are hostile to ideology. Any country in the grip of ideological fervor is radically distrusted. If that country emerges from a state of ideological madness, however, then dealings with it become feasible again.

This attitude produced friction between State and not only ideologically driven factions in the United States, but between State and the presidency as well. During the 1960s Secretary of State Dean Rusk entertained highly negative views about the People's Republic of China, then in the grip of the Cultural Revolution. Nixon, however, who knew full well how ideological the politics of the right wing were, and Kissinger, who came out of a hard-headed national security tradition that prevailed in Nelson Rockefeller's circle, had no trouble dealing directly with the chief madman himself, Mao Tse-tung, in pursuit of their more presidential—and Wilsonian—strategy. To do this, the Nixon administration had to demote the State Department into a more managerial role.[15]

During the Carter administration Secretary of State Cyrus Vance and Zbigniew Brzezinski, director of the National Security Council, became involved in a highly visible State-NSC tug-of-war that by that time had become a quasi-permanent feature of the American political scene. In the early Reagan administration State was headed by a general, Alexander Haig, who had a national security as well as a military background, and so was well armed to repress State's more characteristically pragmatic bureaucratic culture.

With George Shultz, however, State came into its own. Shultz was an economist, a man with a long record in government but none of it in security or military affairs. It was the political-military side of the executive branch that was demoted with his appointment. When thereafter the Iran-Contra scandal broke, the NSC suffered its worst defeat in its forty-year history. State and its pragmatic interest-oriented philosophy triumphed, a triumph that was consolidated when Bush named his close friend James Baker III as secretary of state. Pragmatism seemed to have become institutionalized. With the changing of the guard, political and especially economic issues rose in importance while military issues declined in importance, especially after the fall of communism in Eastern Europe.

Summitry, Oil, the Navy, and RAND

The Iran-Contra scandal created the conditions for the rapprochement between the pragmatic State Department and the universalist presidency that continues to characterize U.S. foreign policy in 1992. State was particularly interested in the political-economic domain, which it conceptualized on a world scale. The rise of summitry among the advanced industrialized democracies enhanced the importance of this conceptualization. In 1975 the first meeting of the world's seven largest free market powers (the Group of Seven, or G-7) took place in Rambouillet, France. French President Valéry Giscard d'Estaing, who shared the outlook of the conservative banking establishment of his country, was delighted by President Gerald Ford's new openness to his kind of elite internationalism. It not only signified American recognition of the importance of France in the Western world, it also marked the first step in a process that, Western leaders hoped, would unite Western governments in a kind of informal governing body of the Western world. The world economy had become so big and complex that some sort of political-economic governance was needed.

Trilateralism also arose about this time, providing a parallel, informal networking that brought Western and Japanese leaders together at a subsummit level. The G-7 summits and trilateralism were a recognition that no single power, not even the United States, could dominate the world economy. Governance was needed, and it required collaboration and cooperation among all the major industrial powers. The G-7 summits and trilateralism also embodied the new awareness that national economies were giving way to transnational and global economies—at least in the West. As capital flowed back and forth across national boundaries in massive amounts, it became evident that national economic interests were becoming very blurred. Like Bush's New World Order, the global economic order (and environmental order—in the 1989 Paris summit, the leaders spoke of their "debt to nature") was to be based on a partnership. The United States was assigned at most the role of primus inter pares.

This conceptualization, however, requires one important qualification. In one key sector of the world economy—oil—the United States remained more than primus inter pares. Oil was vital to the world economy not only as a source of energy. Change in the price of oil, because it was one of the principal sources of inflation, could make or break national economies. It was in the interest of all national economies, even those of the socialist countries, to keep the economics of oil orderly and stable. This required active U.S. involvement. Despite the rise of major non–Anglo-American oil companies, oil was still mainly an Anglo-American affair. OPEC, a cartel of oil-producing countries that did not include the United States, nevertheless operated in close collaboration with the giant Anglo-American oil companies and subsequently with the American and British governments.

Between 1950 and 1970, when the market was firmly under the control of the Anglo-American firms, the price of oil was stable in nominal terms. Price stability was made possible by the power of the Anglo-American oil monopoly to control the market. That monopoly came under attack, however, in the late 1960s. When, during the Yom Kippur War of October 1973, the Arab oil-producing countries came to the support of Egypt with the threat of an oil boycott on Western countries that supported Israel, a major offensive by the producing states seemed in the offing. By the end of the year the price of oil had quadrupled. Nevertheless, the Organization of Petroleum Exporting Countries dominated by the Saudis and the Iranians, close friends of the United States, quickly restored order to the market. The price of oil, which many feared would hit $20 a barrel, stabilized at about $12.

The U.S. role in stabilizing the oil market fed into factional rivalry over foreign policy in an intriguing manner, notably in the way it nourished interservice rivalries within the defense establishment. The State Department's view of the world has traditionally been dominated by values and concerns that are Eurocentric. Its values and concerns reflected those of eastern big business. The navy, which like other branches of the armed forces pursues particular interests within the Department of Defense, had an aristocratic tradition that was more southern than anything else (its persistent racism was in good part due to this southern tradition). But the navy also drew on the tradition of the expanding frontier, as expressed in the writings of Frederick Jackson Turner.[16] The navy's frontier was not California, however, but East Asia, the Caribbean, and Central and South America. Although it was an army general who became shogun of Japan in 1945, the spirit and substance of the new American postwar empire in East Asia was naval.

It is oil that brought the navy and the State Department together. Both Europe and Japan are vitally dependent on the Middle East for oil. When President Nixon opened the door to massive oil imports into the United States, the navy redefined and expanded its mission. Protection of the sea lanes leading to areas of the world vital to the U.S. national interest had always been one of the navy's chief responsibilities. Growing concern over the supply of Middle East oil to the advanced industrialized democracies prompted the navy to assert its power in a geographic area that it had historically ignored: the Indian Ocean. In 1971 the carrier *Enterprise* of the Seventh Fleet entered the Bay of Bengal, thus marking the addition of the Indian Ocean to its theater of operations, hitherto confined to the Pacific. Bit by bit the navy's presence in the Indian Ocean was extended—a ship in Bahrain, port calls in Mombasa, naval exercises in the Arabian Sea. For the navy, the protection of sea lanes that provided access to oil was second in importance only to the overall strategic defense against Soviet attack. As the Pacific Seventh Fleet moved into the Indian Ocean, however, it also moved into the Middle East. It is there that its concerns encountered those of the State Department.

The navy's new mission confirmed the centrality of the United States despite the fact that the world was evolving toward a more collegial form of governance dominated by the G-7 countries. Because the United States (with its close ally Britain) still controlled world oil, it remained the linchpin of the world economy.[17] The Japanese and the Germans may have the money and the productive capacity, but the United States has the military power with which to safeguard the flow of oil. The importance of the navy in ensuring the economic welfare of the industrialized West caused the navy to grow closer both to the business-oriented State Department and the universalist presidency. The growing alliance between Navy and State first became apparent in an incident that occurred during the Nixon administration, when James Schlesinger, secretary of defense and Kissinger's archrival in the White House inner circle, was trying to cut back the navy's budget as well as its defensive role. It was Henry Kissinger, secretary of state and one of the principal artisans of Nixon's universalist policy orientation, who sprang to the defense of the admirals and saved their allocations and their attributions.

The incident becomes more meaningful if we recall that Schlesinger came to government from the RAND Corporation. RAND, which was bankrolled by the U.S. Air Force, was founded in the late 1940s to do research on targets in the Soviet Union and became the principal think tank for strategic affairs. Schlesinger's view that the Soviet Union was the chief threat to the United States reflected similar views at RAND and in the air force, which at the time was the only service arm capable of striking at Soviet targets.[18] The air force thus saw its primary role as one of deterring Soviet expansionism, whereas the navy saw its primary role as one of asserting American influence in the world.[19] Although the concept of solo superpower would not mean much to the navy, it would mean a great deal to the air force. The term has the ring of technological competitiveness that characterizes the spirit of the air force. The navy, befitting its conservative traditions, displays greater interest in and sensitivity to issues of international politics and diplomacy. The navy operates within the "realm of interests," whereas the air force is much more at home in the "realm of ideology." Anticommunism and nuclear competition are ideologies that have meaning for the air force. They do not have the same resonance for the navy.[20]

After the ouster of the Ollie North faction from the White House inner circle, the alliance between State and Navy became particularly strong. When the U.S. frigate *Starke* was struck by an Iraqi Exocet missile in 1987, State worked hard to brush off the incident because it threatened the rapprochement between the United States and the Saddam regime. Navy obliged by sending a naval court of inquiry to Baghdad and allowing it to return after a week or so of investigations during which nothing much had been learned. It was a remarkable cover-up.

The Iraqi invasion of Kuwait was a hard blow for both the State Department and the navy.[21] A decade after Iran's Islamic revolution had wrecked the complex efforts of Nixon and Kissinger to build alliances in the Gulf region, another wrecking operation was launched—this time by Iraq. The crisis in 1990, like the Iranian revolution of 1980, had serious implications for the economy and for the electoral hopes of the party in power. In 1980 Jimmy Carter was defeated not only by the hostage crisis but by a surge of inflation that his economists had not predicted. In 1990 the invasion of Kuwait again sent oil prices skyrocketing, just at a time when serious recessionary signs were appearing in the American economy.

When Bush intervened in Saudi Arabia, he sent in the army and the air force. It took the navy a while to get on the scene, and it is illustrative of factional rivalries and dissensions in Washington that the marines saw little action in the ground war. The laurels of victory went overwhelmingly to the air force, and the award for best supporting role went to the army, which put on a wonderful show of being a citizens' militia in which mobilized reservists worked alongside regular army men and women. The army, in the Gulf War, sided with the air force. General Powell, in embracing the notion of a solo superpower, expressed the conviction that the United States should not be content to restore stability in the Middle East but should make a show of its strength to warn the other but now waning superpower that the end of the Cold War did not mean that the United States was disarming and returning home, as Soviet forces had done.

Cease Fire: The New World Order

The first of President Bush's goals, the liberation of Kuwait, won the support of much of the world, which hoped that the world economy would not be shattered by events in the Gulf. Realities are realities, it was understood, and the world economy was, like it or not, controlled by the G-7 countries with the United States in the key position. This reality did not mean, however, that the world supported the idea of war with Iraq. Japan, China, the Soviet Union, Western Europe, and broad segments of the

American political class wanted Iraq to pull out of Kuwait in the same way it pulled out in 1961. This action would make it possible to deal with Iraq's grievances and, bit by bit, stabilize politics in the Middle East in the interest of all the interests, of which those of the big oil companies and the world economy were paramount. The initial recourse to the United Nations by the United States did not explicitly involve any concern for a New World Order. What was wanted was a rollback, an annulment of the Iraqi move. Such an acquiescence by the Iraqis would have strengthened the efforts of the G-7 countries and the Soviet Union to bring about a kind of collegial New World Order in a natural and spontaneous way.

The Europeans, in particular, placed their hopes in a peaceful outcome. The EC bureaucracy certainly wanted nothing better than a world governed by people who thought in terms of interests rather than in terms of ideologies or fears. But at the time of the invasion of Kuwait, the EC was reeling from another shock that had preceded the invasion. German reunification had suddenly altered the subtle balance of power within the EC according to which, it was believed, no single European power was dominant. Germany was not regarded as the European primus inter pares, but merely as a partner that was just a bit stronger and wealthier than the others. European unification was predicated on a balance between France and Germany, with other EC members acting as a kind of third force coming down sometimes on the side of one or the other if there was disagreement. With reunification and growing evidence of weakness in Britain, France, and Italy, Germany became what many had suspected it was all along: a regional superpower. Matters were made worse when German reunification was followed by the crisis in the Soviet Union. Dissension and repression tarnished the comforting image of a Soviet Union moving to institute social, economic, and political systems similar to those of Western Europe and the corresponding hope that a House of Europe could be built that would stretch from the Atlantic to the Urals.

With the Gulf War things changed. Both the Germans and the Japanese experienced a deflation of their power, and in many ways both seemed relieved that they had been cut down a notch. Neither, as the Gulf crisis showed, was prepared to assume any major international responsibility beyond its borders. The smashing triumph of the United States reaffirmed the reality of a powerful world-spanning economic and military power, a reaffirmation that had a lot to do with oil. The Gulf crisis revealed the centrality of the United States. Its bold actions had the effect of assuring continued European access to Middle East oil, an access that cannot be replaced by new access to Soviet oil.

It was a new and temporary alliance between the presidency, which remained universalist, the ideological anti-Communist right, and the pro-Israeli left that had propelled the country into war, sidelining the interest-oriented faction surrounding State and Navy. That alliance was not a durable one, however. It was, indeed, an unnatural alliance, which was doomed to break up and give way to the more harmonious configuration of interests that linked the presidency to international business and State.

This matter of interests explains why the war was not fought "to the finish." On the contrary, once Iraqi troops were expelled from Kuwait, the president proclaimed a cease-fire, apparently over the objections of his commander of operations, General Norman Schwarzkopf, who preferred to press on to Baghdad. After Bush proclaimed the cease-fire, the Baker faction reclaimed much of the power it had lost. The White House had decided, in conformity with its own "Wilsonian" universalist interests, that it did not want to jeopardize its success in the United Nations or to see the disintegration of Iraq, even if that meant allowing the "demon" Saddam to remain in power. The alternative was a Shi'i regime coming to power in Baghdad that would benefit the Iranians. Although this turnabout disappointed the Israelis, who had long seen in Arab disunity their best hope for longer-term security in the Middle East, it did meet the wishes of the Arab members of the coalition. The turnabout strengthened the hand of the Arabists who now capitalized on the victory to force a settlement of the Israeli-Palestinian dispute on the stubborn Yitzhak Shamir. The Arabists had snatched victory from the jaws of defeat.

After the cease-fire, economic indicators suggested that the recession was waning. This development heartened the administration and American big business, which was elated moreover by the astonishingly rapid drop in oil prices and the stability of the dollar on world currency markets. The Ollie North faction was robbed of the victory laurels it had won in the low-casualty blitzkrieg. By summer 1991 it was clear that both Congress and the administration were keen on cashing in on the peace dividend. The military budget fell to its lowest share of GNP since World War II. The collapse of communism augured an even greater demilitarization in the United States as Washington's policies shifted increasingly from a political-military orientation to a political-economic one. Yet ironically, this shift was predicated on the preeminence of the United States as the leader of the industrialized democracies. After the Gulf War the prospect that Germany and Japan would emerge as major world and regional powers alongside the United States had diminished considerably.

PRAGMATISM, SUMMITRY, AND THE PENTAGONAL WORLD

In 1991 the world witnessed a remarkable crumble of the left generally almost everywhere in the world. In the Soviet Union the democrats of the "left" triumphed over the Communists of the "right." After Tiananmen,

Chinese leaders who not so long ago were placed at the vanguard of progressive (that is, leftist) political movements were now being called "reactionary." In Mexico the entire left collapsed in the face of a ruling party that practices the new authoritarianism. In Nicaragua left and right share power in uneasy cooperation. The Shining Path (*Sendero Luminoso*) in Peru flourishes but in ways so mysterious that they cannot be explained in the usual leftist terms. In South Africa the African National Congress (ANC) shed its Marxist-Leninist legacy even though, as in Robert Mugabe's one-party state of Zimbabwe, the rhetoric and jargon of the left remains. In the Islamic world and in India the torch of rebellion, radicalism, and revolution is no longer carried by the left but rather by religious movements.

In the United States we find a similar though less dramatic evolution. Ideology is declining in American political life. The pragmatism that is apparent in the new leadership and policy orientations of erstwhile revolutionary states is equally apparent in the United States. The Baker faction reflects the interests of an American business class that has by now become so enmeshed with the global economy that it is no longer even recognizably American. In the terms I used in *The Logic of World Power*, this faction is "internationalist." The Ollie North faction, on the other hand, espouses an ideology that is "nationalist." It reflects the aspirations of an era when the United States, like most other countries in the world, sought to make itself into a nation-state, built by and for a "nation" that was culturally and linguistically (though not racially) unified.

Many scholars have claimed that the nation-state, which triumphed at the time of the American and French revolutions as the most successful, dynamic, and powerful form of political organization the world had seen, is now suffering an irreversible decline. If this is so, then one must expect its factional representation to decline. In addition to a worldwide decline of the left, therefore, we also see a decline of its counterpart—nationalism—on the right. This decline means that forms of political organization and political concepts that have been predominant since the end of the eighteenth century are waning as the world approaches not just a new century and millennium, but a turning point in its political history.

This observation brings us back to summitry, the New World Order, and the embedded Wilsonianism of the American presidency. Franklin Roosevelt inaugurated the practice of summitry through his frequent meetings with Winston Churchill during World War II. Summitry could not have arisen earlier because of the inadequacy of premodern modes of transportation. Now only a dozen hours or so are needed to get to most diplomatically significant places on the globe. Summitry can flourish. And just as Roosevelt's and Churchill's initial experiments in summitry gave rise to a "special relationship" between the two countries they represented, summitry since that time has created a multiplicity of "special relationships." By 1990 the United States enjoyed summit-mediated special relationships with Britain, France, Japan, the Soviet Union, China, Canada, and Mexico.[22]

Since the early 1970s there has been a distinct evolution toward an international politics of the North, mediated by the more informal relationships between chief executives brought together by the benefits that summitry confers on their office, in spite of whatever competitive relationship might characterize the dealings between the states that they represent. This evolution, however, has not been an entirely smooth one. The idea of some kind of broader, more collective kind of cooperation between the great powers of the Northern tier originally surfaced during the Nixon administration. The idea was made explicit in Nixon's July 1971 Kansas City speech in which he spoke of a new "pentagonal world." When Nixon visited China in February 1972 and Moscow in May 1972, it seemed as if the gates were open to a Northern entente stretching from Japan across northern Asia to Europe and North America.

The gates slammed shut, however, when a left-wing version of the old China lobby leapt onto the political scene. This new lobby—a pro-Israeli lobby—was led by the late Senator Henry Jackson, who was close to American labor where pro-Israeli sentiment arguably had its strongest bastion. This new lobby was against normalizing relations with the Soviet Union without prior commitment by the Soviets to allow free emigration of Soviet Jews to Israel. Its demands were contained in the Jackson-Vanik amendment to the Senate motion ratifying the Strategic Arms Limitation Treaty (SALT). This amendment, along with the Watergate scandal, effectively torpedoed Nixon's grand design for a world order governed collectively by the major powers of the Northern tier. U.S.-Soviet relations subsequently suffered, reaching their nadir during the first years of the Reagan administration. But in 1985 the pendulum began to swing in the other direction again. During the last years of the Reagan administration the world watched with astonishment as the most anti-Communist of American presidents entered quite willingly into a new summit relationship with his Soviet counterpart, Mikhail Gorbachev. Reagan's attitude was a major factor in convincing Gorbachev that he could let go of the Soviet Union's costly and inefficient empire in Eastern Europe.

Why did this turnabout occur? Did it come from State Department lobbying? The State Department, in fact, took a very hard-nosed approach toward Gorbachev. It wanted to see real progress made in the settlement of regional conflicts before it took seriously the notion that relations with the Soviet Union could be normalized. Deng Xiaoping and his cronies in China took the same hard-nosed approach. Both State and Zhongnanhai (where the Chinese leadership lives) wanted to see real changes in Soviet behavior before acquiescing in the notion that relations with the Soviet

Union had assumed a radically new and far more cooperative orientation. It was only when Gorbachev provided convincing proof of change in Soviet policy—Soviet withdrawal from Afghanistan, the pullback of troops from the Sino-Soviet frontier, pressure on Vietnam to withdraw from Cambodia, promotion of a cooperative settlement to the civil war in Angola, pressure on the Syrians to develop a new and more cooperative relationship with the United States, key concessions on the Israeli-Palestinian issue (notably regarding Jewish emigration), and it can be inferred, covert cooperation with the United States in supporting Iraq against Iran—that State was willing to admit that Gorbachev was for real.

The turnabout in Reagan's attitude toward the Soviet Union was not the work of any internationalist faction either in or out of government but rather the consequence of Reagan's own discovery that the president's position—at the strategic nexus of political relations with other states—conferred power on the presidency qua political office. Summitry, by reinforcing the presidency's personal occupation of that strategic nexus, enhances the presidency's power. The recent history of the presidency can largely be understood as a process of gradual discovery of that power.

Harry Truman did not engage in summitry. For Truman foreign policy was not divorced from the need to court domestic groups for political support. His decision to give full backing to the new Jewish state of Israel in 1948, for example, was part and parcel of his efforts to piece together an electoral coalition that allowed him to win the 1948 election by a hair. Dwight Eisenhower, however, because he had no partisan political past, badly needed the power that summitry conferred. His efforts to improve relations with both the Soviet Union and the People's Republic of China infuriated his ideologically driven anti-Communist supporters in the Republican party. But the treaty that ended the occupation of Austria and the withdrawal of Soviet troops from that country, along with growing evidence that Khrushchev was moving decisively away from Stalinism, strengthened Eisenhower's position. Diplomatic success in Europe gave Eisenhower a freer hand to make policy in Asia without consulting the powerful China lobby. He pressured Chiang Kai-shek to surrender a small chain of islands south of Shanghai and he initiated the Geneva talks with the Chinese Communists.

Richard Nixon's power was based almost entirely on his capacity to deliver the goods in international affairs, and so summitry played a key role during his presidency. As one walked into regional Republican campaign headquarters around the country in 1972, one was generally greeted by a picture of Nixon shaking hands with Chinese Premier Chou En-lai. The party pros perceived that Nixon's summitry was popular with the voters, and they made use of it to ensure his second presidential term.

Gerald Ford's economic summitry with the G-7 marked a leap forward in the globalization of the American economy. He hoped that economic summitry could succeed in rekindling economic prosperity in the wake of the oil and monetary shocks of 1973, but his hopes were dashed by the 1976 elections. His successor, Jimmy Carter, perhaps because of his provincial origins, never showed any real understanding of summitry. Nor did Ronald Reagan understand it when he took office, but he did finally come to understand its importance and to take full advantage of the power it confers (he may have been coached in this direction by Nixon). Summitry, as stated earlier in this chapter, helped him escape impeachment when the Iran-Contra scandal erupted, and his principal historical legacy may turn out to be the dramatic turnabout in U.S.-Soviet relations that occurred during his administration.

George Bush, of course, has played the role of consummate summiteer to the hilt. When he first sounded the theme of a New World Order, he was in the most precarious power-political position that he had been in since becoming president. Having reneged on his pledge not to call for higher taxes, he faced the prospect of calling for new taxes at precisely the moment that the United States economy began to slide into recession.

If we return to the Gulf War and try to place it within the context of this evolution, we see that the decision to intervene was a tremendous gamble by the presidency. It promised enormous benefits in the form of enhanced presidential power and prestige, but it also harbored the threat of immense losses: the alienation of the internationalist faction—the natural ally of a summiteering president—as well as the alienation of other great powers whose collusion in the game of summitry is indispensable. Bush could in no way be sure in August that the operation would end in triumph. Another Vietnam seemed a more likely possibility. It was apparent to the Soviets, moreover, that the Baker faction had been dislodged in a kind of coup by factions hostile to the Soviet Union. Moscow knew that many in Washington questioned whether the Cold War was really over and that the skeptics included people who were suddenly playing very prominent roles, such as Dick Cheney and Colin Powell.

When the stock markets revealed the concerns of the business class, Bush must have realized how immense was the chance that he had taken when he decided to intervene. He turned to the United Nations to assure the cohesion and solidarity of the league of the North. Truman had of course chosen a similar path when he sought the support of the United Nations in 1950 for his intervention in Korea. But Bush wanted the support of the Soviets and the Chinese as well as that of the Japanese and the Europeans. His call for a New World Order encompassed both Communist powers. This strategy was made apparent by U.S. actions in the Security Council that were clearly aimed at avoiding a veto.

Just as Reagan may have taken his cue from Nixon, Bush may have taken his cue from Gorbachev, whose own power depended disproportionately on summitry. Gorbachev relied so much on foreign links to shore up his own domestic power that he came to resemble a Third World leader. But there is more to summitry than domestic political strategy. As a strategy it would be worthless if it did not draw on the emergence of a Northern tier of advanced industrialized countries with enough commonalities to collaborate in the governance of world politics. This Northern tier is, in fact, the pentagonal world prophesied by Nixon in 1971.

THE UNITED STATES AT THE CROSSROADS

As the twentieth century comes to a close, the United States approaches a historic turning point. From the time of its birth 200 years ago, U.S. growth and expansion were informed by ideology even more than by interests. Since Thomas Jefferson inaugurated the course of westward expansion, the United States has been ideologically expansionist but not imperialist in the way either France or Great Britain was imperialist. For Americans expansionism meant progress. Territories and peoples were not subjected to American rule but were absorbed into the great experiment. Territories became states, that is, full-fledged participants in the national project. Even Puerto Rico became a virtual state, and Cuba, the Philippines, and Panama were regarded basically as inalienable provinces.

A page was turned in the history of the United States in 1947, however, when the Truman administration took over imperial responsibilities from a Great Britain too enfeebled by war to assume them any longer. The United States chose the imperial path that it had earlier spurned. It became the steward of the world, a new Rome-like imperium, spreading its wings over a vast territory marked increasingly by a common way of life, that of American-style consumer capitalism. This new global role was nevertheless supported by a broad spectrum of opinion in the United States: nonisolationist but nationalist right-wingers, an internationalist business community that already sensed the benefits inherent in the growth of a new world economy, and anti-Communist but progressive liberals. The new postwar imperialism appealed to both expansionist nationalists and liberal internationalists, particularly as Americans felt that this new hegemonic role could be assumed with little or no assistance from outside.

The hegemonic period was short-lived. A new page was turned in 1973 as the United States withdrew its troops from Vietnam, the oil-producing countries of the Third World imposed a dramatic shift in the terms of trade, and the Bretton Woods monetary regime collapsed and with it the "dollar standard" that had governed monetary affairs since 1945. Since that time there has been growing unwillingness among Americans to continue to shoulder the burdens of world leadership. Right-wing nationalists retreat to the vision of a "fortress America," and left-wing protectionists advocate cutting the United States off from the world economy. Victory in the Gulf silenced these voices temporarily. But only the moderate center, currently represented by the Bush administration, continues anxiously to press ahead with a vision of a United States very much involved in the world.

Despite this growing reluctance foreign observers of international politics—and those I have read include French, British, Arab, Chinese, and Russian writers—assert quite frankly that a smashing victory in the Gulf War has made the United States the world's supreme power once again. Arab writers extol the virtues of the New World Order, and even the Chinese, ever cautious and hostile to globalism, recognize that there is something special about the U.S. role in world politics. How will the United States respond to the responsibilities of world leadership that it now seems to assume by default at a time when the consensus that made hegemony possible a half century earlier shows signs of having disintegrated?

The world-spanning imperium that the United States created after World War II was ideologically an amalgam of older nationalist and internationalist currents. Politically it grew out of the grand alliance between government, business, and labor that led the United States to unprecedented global victory during World War II. Nationalists supported the idea of imperium because they wanted the United States to be strong, to lead, to excel. Nationalism in the United States is still informed ideologically by the notion of manifest destiny that presided over American expansionism throughout the nineteenth century. That ideology resurfaced during World War II and a decade later was a driving force behind the notion that the United States was the leader of the Free World.

Internationalism as an ideology also has deep roots in American history. It can be traced back to the Federalists, many of whom wanted to retain trade and cultural links with Great Britain. When British capital financed much of America's industrialization in the nineteenth and twentieth centuries, much of the Eastern elite came to identify strongly with Great Britain and (after 1904) its ally, France.[23] Woodrow Wilson, a Princeton professor, shared that identification. As president, that identification inclined him to lead the United States into war on the side of the British and French in 1917. Similarly, the aristocratic Franklin Roosevelt, of old Hudson River Dutch stock, shared that identification, and showed even less patience with American isolationism than did Wilson.

Today the presidency is occupied by yet another representative of the old East Coast establishment who once again is trying to lead the United States into a New World Order. He is supported by America's business elite, which has arguably become the strongest proponent of the New World Order. His efforts, however, are encountering a new nationalist xenophobia, fueled by the continued growth of Japan's economic might (one reads magazine articles that speculate openly about a possible war with Japan) and the emergence of China as a new colossus. As the presidential campaign of 1992 began, Republican business-led internationalists were facing, to their right, a nationalist, isolationist revolt within the party's ranks and, to their left, a Democratic party that has become increasingly protectionist and particularly hostile to the new Asian economic powers. The nationalists of the right want to enhance American military might and technological superiority. The nationalists of the left want the U.S. economy to become once again the preeminent economy of the world.

The golden age of American preeminence seemed once again to be at hand as the United States reclaimed the title of the world's "solo superpower." But Bush poured cold water on their enthusiasm when he called a halt to the ground war. He and his advisors, especially Secretary of State James Baker, chose to pursue the New World Order, conceived as a partnership of the Northern industrialized powers, a League of the North. This New World Order is not to be an imperium in which the United States, according to the nationalist expansionist vision, acts unilaterally as hegemon to preserve what it sees as the interests of the Free World. The internationalists will be satisfied if the United States is merely recognized as the first among equals, or primus inter pares. The nationalists, however, insist that the United States clearly remain primus. Although they hardly advocate a *novum imperium americanum*, given their protectionist proclivities, they do want the United States to retain military, technological, and moral leadership in the world—to be in effect, as the Romans said, imperator, a status that becomes the United States as the victor in war.[24]

This tension between two ideological currents, nationalism and internationalism, has cropped up before in American political discourse. Sometimes the gap between the two was unbridgeable, as after World War I, but sometimes the two strains were brought together to inform a coherent mission for U.S. foreign policy. Universalism, as an ideological vision, has historically succeeded in bringing nationalists and internationalists together. The universalist advocates the construction of "One World," a term coined by Wendell Wilkie during the 1940 presidential campaign in the hope of bringing together the Republican nationalist and isolationist wing of the West and Midwest with the internationalist wing of the elite East Coast establishment. The vision is not without appeal and efficacity. Its roots penetrate deeply into Protestant religious traditions. Universalism was the way of salvation for a fractured, devastated, poor, suffering, and mortally endangered globe. Within this vision the United States was the savior, blessed by God with such astounding wealth and intelligence.

The vision of a universalist world order goes back to Woodrow Wilson and Franklin D. Roosevelt. Both the League of Nations and the United Nations were intended by their most fervent advocates to supply a kind of provisional world government. That is why the more fervent among the nationalists lashed out at both in great fury, dismissing the universalist vision that informed both efforts as nothing more than a variant on the elite and effete internationalism that sought to sell out the United States to the British, the Masons, the Jews, and/or the Communists. Populists of the left added Big International Capital to the list of potential buyers. Nationalist opposition overcame Wilson's efforts and caused them—and him—to collapse. Roosevelt, however, was able to lure a large part of the nationalists' audience to his own universalist vision of America's destiny. Following World War II universalism, as an ideology, was able to yoke the nationalist ox to the internationalist cart.

How will this tension between nationalism and internationalism, which is so apparent in the aftermath of the Gulf War, play itself out? The situation is complex. George Bush has sought to satisfy the business internationalists by vigorously pursuing free trade policies and working closely with the G-7 to provide a kind of informal governance of the world economy. Yet at the same time his successful gambit in the Gulf appealed to widespread nationalist sentiment in the United States. But universalism has not been able in the 1990s to achieve the sort of melding of nationalist and internationalist aspirations that characterized the Roosevelt era. Nationalists remain critical and suspicious of internationalists. Nationalists contend that U.S. excessive internationalism is the cause of its decline. Technology, industry, education, morality, motivation, a tradition of excellence, cleanliness, order—all are threatened because America's rich and powerful have been engaged in too many foreign adventures. Nationalists of the left abhor multinational business, while nationalists of the right think that American business is being expropriated by foreigners. Internationalists, conversely, view such nationalism as short-sighted and ultimately very dangerous. They argue that Americans live as well as they do because in the end the United States profits from cheap imports, foreign investment, and especially, from the arrival of new immigrants. In an inescapably interdependent world, internationalists argue, isolationism and protectionism will lead the United States to suffer the fate of all nations that went the import-substitution route. The Soviet Union, which implemented the most ambitious import substitution program in history, failed to the point of extinction.

It is not evident that the internationalists can win this battle without the help of some universalist synthesis. The internationalists have no popular base—the nationalists do. It is not inconceivable that a candidate running on a strong nationalist platform could win the presidency and try to pry the U.S. economy out of its interdependence with the rest of the world economy, wreaking lasting havoc in the international economy in the process. But nationalism does not need to win the presidency to lure policy away from its internationalist course. As the Ollie North fiasco showed, nationalist patriotism, even without the White House, can threaten American capacity to assume international responsibilities simply by weakening the presidency, the principal instrument of internationalism in foreign policy.

Universalism is still a force in American political life. In the 1990s it is characterized by concern over human rights, environmental degradation, and nondemocratic regimes. Universalism remains strong in Congress and is supported by powerful advocacy groups in Washington, throughout the country, and abroad. The advocates of universalism want the United States to act uniformly in support of certain key values throughout the world. And many of the advocates, as Edward P. Alden and I have pointed out, strongly favor unilateral American intervention in the internal affairs of other nations in order that they be implemented. Unlike internationalists, universalists are not content just to seek a working and pragmatic partnership with other nations. On the contrary, universalists, like nationalists, support unilateral American action but on the condition that it promote their values. Unlike the nationalists, on the other hand, they want the United States to act on a global, planetary scale. Their vision is not limited by the boundaries of a Free World or by those of an industrialized American sphere of influence located on the Pacific Rim. As George Bush calls for a New World Order, universalists answer "present" but call for amendments. They want more than an international order based on pragmatism and good business sense. They want an order in which democracy triumphs, in which modern consumerism is severely restrained, and in which the preservation and conservation of nature is the highest priority.

Is this universalist ideology—so deeply rooted in America's unique political culture—on the march again, as it has so often been in the past? Or is history finally taking command of the United States as it has of so many other nations and civilizations? Will the decline of the traditional ideologies of left and right increase the audience of universalism, America's unique contribution to the ideological panoply?

CONCLUSION: THE GRAYING OF AMERICA

When nations, like people, get older, time matters. Less of a future is left, the present becomes too complex, and more and more of the past looms up in their consciousness. Nations change just as people change. The way nations change in time is affected by their perceptions of time itself, as it manifests itself in its three dimensions—present, past, and future. Change is accomplished by action in the present. But change is also affected by the way actors view the future, by the dreams, visions, and hopes of a tomorrow that is somehow better than today. And it is affected by perceptions of the past, that is, by the legacy of memories that never die or that come to life again.

People—and philosophers—differ over which of these three dimensions is the most determinant. The Christian tradition that has been so influential in the West puts the future in command. It is a tradition of conversion and eschatological vision. Christian eschatology is the spiritual source of all modern future-directed Western ideologies. The ideological drive toward an imagined future assumed dominance at the time of the American and French revolutions, inspired as they were by ideas of political reform and perfection propounded and debated during the eighteenth-century Enlightenment. But the philosophers of the Enlightenment were succeeded by the Romantics, who discovered the heavy hand of the past on humankind's efforts to construct an ideal future. The Romantics denied the freedom of the will, the power to convert, to make a direction-changing choice at any period in one's life, which was such a fundamental part of the Christian tradition.[25] Simultaneously, the liberal creed was evolving out of the writings of John Locke in the seventeenth century, Adam Smith in the eighteenth century, and the Utilitarians in the nineteenth century. Liberalism rejected the notion that people and nations should be moved by either the past or the future. We should live in the present, liberals taught, as rational, calculating individuals responding to the motivations of an honest self-interest. If we do so, the consequence will be the attainment of the greatest good for the greatest number.

Present, future, and, now more than ever, past struggle with one another to guide political action in the United States. The late historian David Potter wrote that the accumulation of wealth in the present was the primary preoccupation of Americans, and it was achieved through guile, shrewdness, and sophisticated robbery. In populist cartoons of the early twentieth century plutocrats were depicted as obese, cigar-chewing, fabulously attired men who wore a permanent smirk of self-confidence. Opposing them were the enraged poor and the exploited who defied the rich with clenched fists. Rage came easily. Abolitionists, Populists, and Prohibitionists were enraged. So, too, were the various civil rights, antiwar, and liberation movements that arose in the 1960s. The rage of blacks, students, women, and others was in the tradition of Christian rage. Rage arose from a deep sense that humans must battle against the wicked City of Man and be guided by the vision of a future that was the only reality that counted. The city of the future was a far more wondrous reality than the baubles and bubbles of America's famed consumer affluence.

Using terms from my other writings, especially *The Logic of World Power*, I refer to political actions guided by the present as belonging to the "realm of interests." Actions guided by a vision of a future that actors seek to create belong to the "realm of ideology." But also belonging to the realm of ideology are the actions of those who want to use their rich memories of a particular past to shape the future of their people. The advocates of the past grapple with the advocates of the future within the arena of ideology, as Fascists and Communists did during the 1920s and 1930s.

Of the three temporal referents, the past has not had nearly the power to shape ideals and action in the United States that it has had in other countries. Although Ronald Reagan could appeal to a mythological golden age—the 1950s—history has not typically generated past-linked political ideals in the United States. American political life has tended to revolve around the debate between those who argue present-linked interests and those who offer future-linked ideals. Potter focused on the search for wealth, the indulgence in a marvelous present, as a guiding vector of America's history. Another historian, Frederick Jackson Turner, focused on the frontier, the city beyond the hill that always beckoned Americans to move onward toward some future happiness. The United States alone of all major nations was not enslaved to history. The United States is a country that for 200 years denied history. It did so by substituting interest and a future-oriented ideological vision in its place. Ideology informed policy with ideas whose vectors led into the future rather than with ideas that were only memories of the past. In the words of Goethe, America had no ancient castles to bemoan.[26]

Just as present and future have shared dominance over domestic political discourse, they have also guided U.S. involvement in world affairs. Pragmatic, present-oriented internationalists have on occasion crossed swords but on other occasions entered into alliance with their ideological future-oriented rivals-cum-partners, who themselves have appeared in two distinct guises, one nationalist and the other universalist. As this ménage à trois continues to evolve in the 1990s, one is struck by the predominance of the pragmatic concern with the present—especially as it manifests itself in economic and social issues. Average Americans have too many here-and-now problems to be concerned about a future over which they feel little control. Ironically, the strongest future-oriented ideological thrust is coming from the presidency, as it tries to fashion its vision of the New World Order.

The novelty of the present era is the discovery of the past. The past has come to weigh heavily in the isolationist nationalism of both the right and the left. Right-wing nationalists display a thinly veiled nostalgia for American, or more broadly, for white, supremacy (the two are often equated in their minds). The isolationist nationalism of the left yearns for the 1930s and 1940s, when unions were combative, when government was strong, and when the left was waging the good fight against what it perceived to be the goon squads of the fascist right on the payroll of monopoly capitalism. It is this new, backward-looking, past-oriented nationalism on both the right and the left—very different from the more vigorous and youthful nationalism that pressed us on to the Pacific—that is mounting attacks on Bush's New World Order ideology—again unlike the nationalism that found common ground with the universalism of Franklin D. Roosevelt. The vision of a New World Order is supported primarily by the business class that, in its present-linked pragmatism, has realized that its own survival depends entirely on the world economy, in which it and the American government, for all their weaknesses, still play a powerful role.

In recent years a Spenglerian mood has come over many American intellectuals, a mood of decline, of fin de siècle, of "the end of history," that the victory in the Gulf has not erased. Visions of a future that is better than either the present or the past are reflected chiefly in the aspirations of those classes and peoples who feel little stake in either. For this reason, aspirations of future betterment proliferate in many parts of the world, though in new guises. Socialism, which took on a religious coloration in its Communist manifestation, was posited on the promise of a better future. As such, it entered into a bitter combat with present-oriented capitalism, and it lost. But two kinds of vision, religious and nationalist, are now arising out of the ashes of the grand vision of socialism. Religion always looks to the future, to a higher plane, a better world, a transcendence. Nationalism is, in most countries of the world, fed by memories of the past that often become richer the more remote that past happens to be. In many parts of the world popular religious and nationalist visions energize the political class. The stuff that written history is made of—the politics of movements, reform, revolution, war, momentous change—fills the newspapers.

In American newspapers, however, more and more of the gripping news is foreign. Domestic coverage shrinks, and the columns are enlivened only by speculation over coming elections or by a rare journalistic windfall such as the Gulf War. Our journalistic doldrums reflect the Spenglerian mood that has taken hold of much of the American intelligentsia. Except for an elite universalism the American political class is unmoved by ideology. It dislikes the religious sentiment that is rapidly spreading among "the masses," as many used to say, and is horrified by the appearance of popular right-wing nationalism.

The search for wealth and the good life in the here and now of the present has always been a powerful motivation in American history. Chances are that in the years ahead a present-oriented pragmatism motivated by real interests will continue to dominate the American political class. But is it sufficient to endow our foreign policy with the energy and vision required to build, to manage, or even to participate in a New World Order?

It may be that the old world order is not as rickety as its critics maintain. It bears a good deal of resemblance to the old Roman Empire of the first century A.D., when the city of Rome and all of Italy were showing signs of real decay but the empire as a whole was still flourishing as a great Mediterranean commercial and cultural bloc. Pragmatism in this case may be all that is required. Conversely, the analogy with ancient Rome reminds us that some new future-oriented vision, a religious vision, may well up from the grass-roots and link up with some segment of the political class, synthesize the visions of the nationalist and the internationalist and endow the political class with a new energy and a new enthusiasm capable of conferring success on efforts to create an authentic New World Order through the implementation of fundamental political reforms. The persistence of ideology, even in its current elitist, universalist form, seems to indicate that a hunger for a more future-oriented vision continues to exist within the political class. Alternatively, that hunger may with equal probability give rise to some religious or nationalist vision that would challenge the pragmatism of the internationalist class and threaten its grip on power. Such an eventuality would almost certainly spell the end of the New World Order.

NOTES

CHAPTER 2

1. A revised version of this chapter was published as "Trilateralism and the New World Order," *World Policy Journal*, Spring 1991.

2. Richard Gardner, "The Return of Internationalism," *Washington Quarterly* 13/3 (Summer 1990): 23–39.

3. Neal Ascherson (p. 63) and George Steiner (pp. 129–130) in "New Europe," *Granta* 30 (Winter 1990).

4. Rosenthal's essays on Germany need no documentation; for his alarmist distrust of contemporary Japan, see "MacArthur Was Right," *New York Times*, October 19, 1990.

5. Quoted in the *New York Times*, January 25, 1991.

6. This point is emphasized by Mary Kaldor, who argues that people's movements in Western and Eastern Europe were essential in demolishing the Iron Curtain and ending the Cold War. See "After the Cold War," *New Left Review*, no. 180 (March-April 1990): 25–40.

7. Fred Halliday in "The Ends of the Cold War" (*New Left Review* 180 [March-April 1990], 10) both stress the Allies' overweening concern with Bolshevism at Versailles. I agree but also argue that the problem of Bolshevism was made utterly urgent because of Stalin's industrialization successes and the vast increase in the reach of Soviet power during and after World War II.

8. Karl Polanyi, *The Great Transformation* (New York: Beacon Press, 1944), 26–27.

9. Ibid., 3.

10. Ibid., 14–15.

11. Ibid., 22, 212.

12. Ibid., 247.

13. Polanyi wrote that "socialism in one country was brought about by the incapacity of market economy to provide a link between all countries; what appeared as Russian autarchy was merely the passing of capitalist internationalism." (Ibid., 248.)

14. See, in particular, Polanyi's last chapter, "Freedom in a Complex Society," ibid., which ends with moving passages on "the three constitutive facts in the consciousness of Western man: knowledge of death, knowledge of freedom, knowledge of society," followed by the oddly Nietzschean conclusion that "life springs from ultimate resignation." The other text—also well worth reading today—is E. H. Carr, *The 20 Years' Crisis, 1919–1939* (London: Macmillan, 1939).

15. Central Intelligence Agency, *Fact Book, 1990*, CIA, Washington, D.C.

16. Peter J. Katzenstein, *Policy and Politics in West Germany: The Growth of a Semisovereign State* (Philadelphia: Temple University Press, 1987), 9–10, 15–23, 371–385.

17. Polanyi, *Great Transformation*, 133.

18. Perry Anderson, "Modernity and Revolution," *New Left Review*, no. 144 (March-April 1984): 96–113.

19. Kaldor, "After the Cold War," 31–32.

20. The *Far Eastern Economic Review* (July 21, 1990) has estimated this Pacific community of consumers also at around 330 million, and that number does not include the 150 to 200 million consumers capable of consumer-durable purchases in coastal and urban China.

21. Carr, *20 Years' Crisis*, 233.

22. See C. Fred Bergsten, Georges Berthoin, and Kinhide Mushakoji, *The Reform of International Institutions*, Triangle Paper no. 11 (Washington, D.C.: Trilateral Commission, 1976); Richard Ullman, "Trilateralism: 'Partnership' for What?" *Foreign Affairs* 55/1 (October 1976); Holly Sklar, ed., *Trilateralism* (Boston: South End Press, 1980); and my critique in "Chinatown: Foreign Policy and Elite Transition," in Thomas Ferguson and Joel Rogers, eds., *The Hidden Election* (New York: Pantheon Books, 1982).

23. Zbigniew Brzezinski, *The Fragile Blossom: Crisis and Change in Japan* (New York: Harper and Row, 1972).

24. Zbigniew Brzezinski, "America's New Geostrategy," *Foreign Affairs* 66/4 (Spring 1988): 680–699.

25. Quoted in Carr, *20 Years' Crisis*, 233.

26. Ibid., 696–697.

27. See Akira Iriye, *Across the Pacific: An Inner History of American-East Asian Relations* (Cambridge: Harvard University Press, 1967), his most brilliant and original book; also *Pacific Estrangement: Japanese and American Expansion, 1897–1911* (Cambridge: Harvard University Press, 1972); *After Imperialism* (Cambridge: Harvard University Press, 1965); and the deeply revisionist *Power and Culture: The Japanese-American War, 1941–45* (Cambridge: Harvard University Press, 1981).

28. Iriye, *Pacific Estrangement*, viii, 18–19, 26–27, 35–36.

29. Ibid., 3–4, 15, 20, 25–27.

30. Iriye, *Power and Culture*, 1–2.

31. William Appleman Williams, *Tragedy of American Diplomacy* (New York: Delta Books, 1961).

32. Michael Hunt, *The Making of a Special Relationship* (New York: Columbia University Press, 1983), 206–210.

33. See Carl P. Parrini, *Heir to Empire: The United States Economic Diplomacy, 1916–1923* (Pittsburgh: University of Pittsburgh Press, 1969).

34. Iriye, *Power and Culture*, 15.

35. Ibid., 15, 25–27, 65, 81, 83, 97, 148–149.

36. Senator Frank Church's speech of April 22, 1963, was probably the opening curtain in this long-running drama. See Makato Momoi, "Basic Trends in Japanese Security Policies," in Robert Scalapino, ed., *The Foreign Policy of Modern Japan* (Berkeley: University of California Press, 1977), 353.

37. *Far Eastern Economic Review,* July 21, 1990, and August 30, 1990.

38. *Far Eastern Economic Review,* August 9, 1990.

39. John Lewis Gaddis, *The Long Peace: Inquiries into the History of the Cold War* (New York: Oxford University Press, 1987).

40. See Bruce Cumings, *The Origins of the Korean War,* vol. 2, *The Roaring of the Cataract, 1947–1950* (Princeton: Princeton University Press, 1990), chap. 2; also "Power and Plenty in Northeast Asia," *World Policy Journal* (Winter 1987–1988): 79–106.

41. Bergsten, Berthoin, and Mushakoji, *Reform of International Institutions.* See also Trilateral Commission, "The Crisis of International Cooperation" (New York, 1973).

42. This point is made strongly by Hans Magnus Enzensberger, in "New Europe," *Granta* 30 (Winter 1990): 140–142.

43. See Robin Luckham, "American Militarism and the Third World: The End of the Cold War?" Working Paper no. 94, Peace Research Center, Australian National University, Canberra, October 1990, 2.

44. Thomas Ferguson, "The Economic Incentives for War," *Nation,* January 28, 1991.

45. Carr, *20 Years' Crisis,* 237.

CHAPTER 3

A shorter version of this chapter was published as "Things to Come: The Shape of the New World Order," *National Interest,* Summer 1991.

1. Thomas J. McCormick, *America's Half-Century: United States Foreign Policy in the Cold War* (Baltimore: Johns Hopkins University Press, 1990).

2. John J. Mearsheimer, *Conventional Deterrence* (Ithaca: Cornell University Press, 1983).

3. David S. Painter, *Oil and the American Century: The Political Economy of U.S. Foreign Oil Policy, 1941–1954* (Baltimore: Johns Hopkins University Press, 1986).

4. Charles P. Kindleberger, *The World in Depression, 1929–1939* (Berkeley: University of California Press, 1973).

5. Hugh Seton-Watson, *The East-European Revolution* (New York: Praeger, 1964); James R. Kurth, "Economic Change and State Development," in Jan F. Triska, ed., *Dominant Powers and Subodinate States: The United States in Latin America and the Soviet Union in Eastern Europe* (Durham: Duke University Press, 1988), 85–101.

6. Francis Fukuyama, "The End of History?" *National Interest* 16 (Summer 1989): 3–18.

7. Paul Kennedy, *The Rise and Fall of the Great Powers: Economic Change and Military Conflict from 1500 to 2000* (New York: Random House, 1987).

8. Stephen R. Graubard, ed., *Eastern Europe . . . Central Europe . . . Europe* (Boulder: Westview Press, 1991).

9. Fukuyama, "The End of History?"

10. Eric O. Hanson, *The Catholic Church in World Politics* (Princeton: Princeton University Press, 1987).

11. Pope John Paul II, *Centesimus annus.*

12. James R. Kurth, "The Pacific Basin Versus the Atlantic Alliance: Two Paradigms of International Relations," *Annals of the American Academy of Political and Social Science* 505 (September 1989): 34–45.

13. Richard Rosecrance, *The Rise of the Trading State: Commerce and Conquest in the Modern World* (New York: Basic Books, 1986).

14. The close connection between industrial society and the nation-state is argued by Ernest Gellner, *Nations and Nationalism* (Ithaca: Cornell University Press, 1983).

CHAPTER 4

I would like to thank James Goldgeier, Stanley Hoffmann, David Laitin, John Mearsheimer, Thomas Risse-Kappen, John Stephens, Sidney Tarrow, Hellmut Wollmann, and Meredith Woo-Cumings for their criticisms of earlier drafts of this chapter. Research and writing were supported by a grant of the German Marshall Fund of the United States (#3-53597).

1. A shorter version of this chapter was published in 1991 under the title "Die Fesselung der deutschen Macht im internationalen System: Der Einigungsprozess 1898–90," in Bernhard Blanke and Hellmut Wollman, eds., *Die alte Bundesrepublik: Kontinuität und Wandel*, 68–80, special issue of *Leviathan* 12/1991 (Opladen: Westdeutscher Verlag, 1991).

2. John J. Mearsheimer, "Why We Will Soon Miss the Cold War," *Atlantic* (August 1990): 35–50; other works by Mearsheimer are: "Back to the Future: Instability in Europe After the Cold War," *International Security* 15/1 (Summer 1990): 5–56; "Correspondence. Back to the Future, Part II: International Relations Theory and Post–Cold War Europe," *International Security* 15/2 (Fall 1990): 194–199; "Correspondence. Back to the Future, Part III: Realism and the Realities of European Security," *International Security* 15/3 (Winter 1990–1991): 219–222.

3. Mearsheimer, "Why We Will Miss the Cold War," 46.

4. Friedrich Meinecke, *The German Catastrophe: Reflections and Recollections* (Boston: Beacon, 1963).

5. Mearsheimer, "Back to the Future," 38–39.

6. Stephen Van Evera, "Primed for Peace: Europe After the Cold War," *International Security* 15/3 (1990–1991): 7–57; Stanley Hoffmann, "Correspondence. Back to the Future, Part II: International Relations Theory and Post–Cold War Europe," *International Security* 15/2 (Fall 1990): 191–192; Robert Keohane, "Correspondence. Back to the Future, Part II: International Relations Theory and Post–Cold War Europe," *International Security* 15/2 (Fall 1990): 192–194; Thomas Risse-Kappen, "Correspondence. Back to the Future, Part III: Realism and the Realities of European Security," *International Security* 15/3 (Winter 1990–1991): 218–219; Bruce Russett, "Correspondence. Back to the Future, Part III: Realism and the Realities of European Security," *International Security* 15/3 (Winter 1990–1991): 216–218; James Goldgeier and Micheal McFaul, "A Tale of Two Worlds: Core and Periphery in the Post–Cold War Era," *International Organization* 46/2 (Spring 1990): 469–493.

7. Mearsheimer, "Correspondence. Back to the Future, Part II," 194.

8. Van Evera, "Primed for Peace," James Sperling, "German Security Policy and the Future European Security Order," in Michael Huelshoff, Simon Reich and Andrei Markovits, eds., *The New Germany in the New Europe* (Ann Arbor: University of Michigan Press, 1991); Jefferey Anderson and John Goodman, "Mars or Minerva? A United Germany in a Post-Cold War Europe," Working Paper no. 91-8, Center for International Affairs, Harvard University, Cambridge, Mass., 1991.

9. Stephen Van Evera, "Managing the Eastern Crisis: Preventing War in the Former Soviet Empire," *DACS Working Papers* (January 6, 1992), Center for International Studies, Massachusetts Institute of Technology, Cambridge, Mass.

10. Mearsheimer, "Correspondence. Back to the Future, Part II," 195; and Mearsheimer, 222.

11. Mearsheimer, "Why We Will Miss the Cold War," 44.

12. Kenneth Waltz, paper presented at the Conference on The Transformation of the International System and International Relations Theory, Cornell University, Ithaca, N.Y., October 18–19, 1991.

13. Mearsheimer, "Correspondence. Back to the Future, Part III," 222; and Mearsheimer, "Correspondence. Back to the Future, Part II," 25.

14. David Calleo, *The German Problem Reconsidered: Germany and the World Order, 1870 to the Present* (New York: Cambridge University Press, 1978).

15. Peter J. Katzenstein, "Problem or Model? West Germany in the 1980s," *World Politics* 32/4 (July 1980): 577–598.

16. Dominic Lawson, "Saying the Unsayable About the Germans," *Spectator* (London), July 14, 1990: 8–10.

17. Robert Melcher and Roman Rollnick, "Axis Urged to Counter Bonn," *European* (July 27–29, 1990).

18. Leopold Bellak, "Why I Fear the Germans," *New York Times,* April 25, 1990, A29.

19. Sidney Verba, "Germany: The Remaking of Political Culture," in Lucian W. Pye and Sidney Verba, eds., *Political Culture and Political Development* (Princeton: Princeton University Press, 1965), 130–170; David P. Conradt, "Changing German Political Culture," in Gabriel A. Almond and Sidney Verba, eds., *The Civic Culture Revisited* (Boston: Little, Brown, 1980), 212–272; Kendell L. Baker, Russell J. Dalton, and Kai Hildebrandt, *Germany Transformed: Political Culture and the New Politics* (Cambridge: Harvard University Press, 1981).

20. Alan Dundes, *Life is Like a Chicken Coop Ladder: A Portrait of German Culture Through Folklore* (New York: Columbia University Press, 1984).

21. *Historikerstreit: Die Dokumentation der Kontroverse um die Einzigartigkeit der nationalsozialistischen Judenvernichtung* (Munich: Piper); Charles S. Maier, *The Unmasterable Past: History, Holocaust, and German National Identity* (Cambridge: Harvard University Press, 1988); Fritz Stern, *Dreams and Delusions: The Drama of German History* (New York: Knopf, 1987), 243–273.

22. Peter J. Katzenstein, *Policy and Politics in West Germany: The Growth of a Semisovereign State* (Philadelphia: Temple University Press, 1987), 5–15.

23. Peter J. Katzenstein, ed. *Industry and Politics in West Germany: Toward the Third Republic* (Ithaca: Cornell University Press, 1989); Katzenstein, *Policy and Politics.*

24. John Ardagh, *Germany and the Germans: An Anatomy of Society Today* (New York: Harper and Row, 1989); Klaus von Beyme and Manfred Schmidt, eds., *Politik in der Bundesrepublik Deutschland* (Opladen: Westdeutscher Verlag, 1990); Simon Bulmer and William Paterson, *The Federal Republic of Germany and the European Community* (London: Allen and Unwin, 1987); Gordon A. Craig, "A New, New Reich?" *New York Review of Books* 36/21–22 (January 18, 1990): 28–33; Anne-Marie Le Gloannec, *La Nation Orpheline: Les Allemagnes en Europe* (Paris: Calmann-Levy, 1989); David Marsh, *The Germans: A People at the Crossroads* (New York: St. Martin's, 1989); Peter Merkl, ed., *The Federal Republic of Germany at Forty* (New York: New York University Press, 1989); Gordon Smith, William E. Paterson, and Peter Merkl, eds., *Developments in West German Politics* (Durham: Duke University Press, 1989); Henry Ashby Turner, Jr., *The Two Germanies since 1945* (New Haven: Yale University Press, 1987); Katzenstein, *Policy and Politics* and *Industry and Politics*.

25. Peter J. Katzenstein, *Corporatism and Change: Austria, Switzerland, and the Politics of Industry* (Ithaca: Cornell University Press, 1984); Peter J. Katzenstein, *Small States in World Markets: Industrial Policy in Europe* (Ithaca: Cornell University Press, 1985).

26. Wolfram Hanrieder, *West German Foreign Policy, 1949–1963: International Pressure and Domestic Response* (Stanford: Stanford University Press, 1967); Ulrich Scheuner, ed., *Außenpolitische Perspektiven des westdeutschen Staates: Band 1—Das Ende des Provisoriums* (Munich: R. Oldenbourg, 1971); Ulrich Scheuner, ed. *Außenpolitische Perspektiven des westdeutschen Staates: Band 2—Das Vordringen neuer Kräfte* (Munich: R. Oldenbourg, 1972); Richard Löwenthal, ed., *AuBenpolitische Perspektiven des westdeutschen Staates: Band 3—Der Zwang zur Partnerschaft* (Munich: R. Oldenbourg, 1972).

27. Wolfram Hanrieder, *Germany, America, Europe: Forty Years of German Foreign Policy* (New Haven: Yale University Press, 1989); Edwina S. Campbell, *Germany's Past and Europe's Future* (Washington, D.C.: Pergamon-Brassey's, 1989); Stephen F. Szabo, *The Changing Politics of German Security* (New York: St. Martin's, 1990); F. Stephen Larrabee, ed., *The Two German States and European Security* (New York: Institute for East-West Security Studies, 1989).

28. Michael Geyer, *Deutsche Rüstungspolitik 1860–1980* (Frankfurt: Suhrkamp, 1984).

29. Catherine McArdle Kelleher, "The Defense Policy of the Federal Republic of Germany," in Douglas J. Murray and Paul R. Viottie, eds., *The Defense Policies of Nations: A Comparative Study* (Baltimore: Johns Hopkins University Press, 1982), 283.

30. Helga Haftendorn, "West Germany and the Management of Security Relations: Security Policy under Conditions of International Interdependence," in Ekkehart Krippendorff and Volker Rittberger, eds., *The Foreign Policy of West Germany: Formation and Contents* (Beverly Hills: Sage, 1980), 7–32; Helga Haftendorn, Wolf-Dieter Karl, Joachim Krause, and Lothar Wilker, eds., *Verwaltete Außenpolitik: Sicherheits- und entspannungspolitische Entscheidungsprozesse* (Cologne: Verlag Wissenschaft and Politik, 1978).

31. Walter Clemens, *Reluctant Realists: The Christian Democrats and West German Ostpolitik* (Durham: Duke University Press, 1989); Edwina Moreton, ed., *Germany Between East and West* (Cambridge: Cambridge University Press, 1987).

32. Luc Crollen, "NATO and Arms Control," in Lawrence S. Kaplan and Robert W. Clawson, eds., *NATO After Thirty Years* (Wilmington, Del.: Scholarly Resources, 1981), 215–236; Jürgen Schwarz, *Structural Development of the North Atlantic Treaty Organization* (Munich: Hochschule der Bundeswehr, 1982).

33. A. W. DePorte, *Europe Between the Superpowers: The Enduring Balance* (New Haven: Yale University Press, 1979), 183.

34. Steve Weber, "Does NATO Have a Future?" University of California, Berkeley, 1991; Harald Müller, "Institutional Theory of International Relations and the End of the East-West Conflict," paper prepared for the joint PSP/PRIF Conference, Cornell University, Ithaca, September 1991.

35. Simon Bulmer and William Paterson, "West Germany's Role in Europe: 'Man-Mountain' or 'Semi-Gulliver,'" *Journal of Common Market Studies* 28/2 (December 1989): 95–117; Hans-Peter Schwarz, *Die gezähmten Deutschen: Von der Machtbesessenheit zur Machtvergessenheit* (Stuttgart: Deutsche Verlags-Anstalt, 1985); Simon Bulmer, ed., *The Changing Agenda of West German Public Policy* (Brookfield, Vt.: Gower, 1989).

36. Stanley Hoffman, "European Politics and Security 1990," Harvard University, Cambridge, Mass., 1990, 5–6.

37. Timothy Garton Ash, *The Uses of Adversity: Essays on the Fate of Central Europe* (New York: Random House, Vintage Books, 1990); Timothy Garton Ash, "The German Revolution," *New York Review of Books* 36/20 (December 21, 1989): 14–19; Gary Geipel, ed., *The Future of Germany* (Indianapolis: Hudson Institute, 1990); "German Unification: Power, Process, and Problems," *German Politics and Society* 22 (Spring 1991); "Germany: From Plural to Singular," *German Politics and Society* 20 (Summer 1990); Karl Kaiser, "Germany's Unification," *Foreign Affairs* 70/1 (1991): 179–205; Leslie Lipschitz and Donough McConald, eds., *German Unification: Economic Issues* (Washington: International Monetary Fund, 1990); Elizabeth Pond, *After the Wall: American Policy toward Germany* (New York: Priority Press, 1990); Elizabeth Pond, "A Wall Destroyed: The Dynamics of German Unification in the GDR," *International Security* 15/2 (Fall 1990): 35–66; Carl-Christoph Schweitzer and Detlev Karsten, *The Federal Republic of Germany and EC Membership Evaluated* (New York: St. Martin's, 1990).

38. Stephen Kinzer, "Germany Will Mediate Japan-Russia Island Rift," *New York Times,* March 1, 1992, A14.

39. Hans-Peter Schwarz, *Die Gezähmten Deutschen.*

CHAPTER 5

1. Eastern France also benefitted from this traffic. The trade fairs of Champagne were one of the major commercial events of the Middle Ages. But the extension of French royal control to the Rhine nipped the commercial development of eastern France in the bud.

2. Stein Rokkan, "Dimensions of State Formation and Nation-Building: A Possible Paradigm for Research on Variations Within Europe," in Charles Tilly, ed., *The Formation of National States in Western Europe* (Princeton: Princeton University Press, 1975). Passages quoted on pp. 576, 577, and 589.

3. The iron ore of Lorraine, however, was of low quality and could not be economically exploited until new techniques were developed following World War I.

4. Maurice Niveau, *Histoire des faits économiques contemporains* (Paris: Presses universitaires de France, 1970), 92–93.

5. Jacques Valette, *Vie économique et sociale des grands pays de l'Europe occidentale et des États-Unis: Début du XXᵉ Siècle—1939* (Paris: SEDES, 1976), 41–44.

6. Ibid., *Vie économique*, 5.

7. Great Britain's foreign trade grew by 34 percent and that of the United States by 80 percent.

8. Henry Blumenthal, *Illusion and Reality in Franco-American Diplomacy, 1914–1918* (Baton Rouge: Louisiana State University Press, 1986), 74–78.

9. Ibid., 83–86.

10. Ibid., 78.

11. Wilson agreed to this compromise in exchange for French recognition of the Monroe Doctrine.

12. French disregard for the interests of its allies was reinforced when in February 1922 the Washington Arms Limitation Conference assigned to France a naval capacity that was inferior not only to that of the United States and Great Britain (though France's empire was no less extensive than Britain's) but to that of Japan, as well, and equal to that of Italy. From this period date the suspicions of "Anglo-Saxon perfidy" that so marked the post–World War II era and that we tend too quickly to assign to the sole psychology of General de Gaulle.

13. A. W. DePorte, *Europe Between the Superpowers: The Enduring Balance* (New Haven: Yale University Press, 1979), 145–146.

14. Alan Milward, *The Reconstruction of Western Europe: 1945–51* (Berkeley: University of California Press, 1984), 137.

15. Stephen A. Schuker, *The End of French Predominance in Europe* (Chapel Hill: University of North Carolina Press, 1976), 222–229.

16. Blumenthal, *Illusion and Reality*, 120.

17. It was agreed, however, that a referendum would ultimately determine whether the region would revert to Germany or remain independent.

18. See Milward, *Reconstruction*, 54, 75, 142. See also Robert A. Pollard, *Economic Security and the Origins of the Cold War, 1945–1950* (New York: Columbia University Press, 1985), 140–144. The United States also committed American troops to a prolonged occupation of Germany, thus addressing French security concerns.

19. Britain was concerned about U.S. intentions regarding the empire and the sterling zone.

20. Milward, *Reconstruction*, 392.

21. Ibid., 475.

22. Jean-Pierre Rioux, *The Fourth Republic, 1944–1958* (Cambridge: Cambridge University Press, 1987), 144.

23. Alfred Grosser, *Affaires Extérieures: La politique de la France* (Paris: Flammarion, 1984), 86.

24. Ibid., 89.

25. The Soviet sector remained occupied, and the Soviet Union was not about to give recognition to the Federal Republic. The state of Prussia was officially abolished at the Moscow conference of the Allied foreign ministers in 1947.

26. This strategic preference may also explain its remarkable tilt toward the tenets of economic liberalism in its domestic economic policy, an orientation in stark contrast with past policies and one, moreover, that would pay dividends in the 1970s and 1980s. See Wolfram Hanrieder, *Germany, America, Europe: Forty Years of German Foreign Policy* (New Haven: Yale University Press, 1989), chap. 8.

27. Grosser, *Affaires Extérieures*, 123.

28. Michael M. Harrison, *The Reluctant Ally: France and Atlantic Security* (Baltimore: Johns Hopkins University Press, 1981), 44.

29. De Gaulle had been one of the principal adversaries of the EDC and opposed any abandonment of French national sovereignty to a supranational organization.

30. The treaty also created the highly successful Franco-German Youth Office, a truly supranational agency for the promotion of student exchange and understanding.

31. Grosser, *Affaires Extérieures*, 185.

32. A. W. DePorte, "The Fifth Republic in Europe," in William Andrews and Stanley Hoffmann, eds., *The Fifth Republic at Twenty* (Albany: SUNY Press, 1981), 406.

33. Blumenthal, *Illusion and Reality*, 118.

34. Ibid., 119.

35. Ibid., 130–131.

36. Ibid., 135.

37. Pierre Renouvin, *Les crises du XXe Siècle*, vol. 1, *De 1914 à 1929* (Paris: Hachette, 1969), 259.

38. Blumenthal, *Illusion and Reality*, 158.

39. Ibid., 164–165.

40. Shortly after Thoiry the French began to explore a negotiated solution to the debt problem, an obstruction to closer relations with the United States. In April 1926 the Mellon-Bérenger agreements seemed to settle this dispute, though France did not ratify the agreement for another three years.

41. Blumenthal, *Illusion and Reality*, 140. Blumenthal argues that this was a theme in a long-range plan to halt and diminish Anglo-Saxon penetration in Europe.

42. Advocates of French internationalism advanced a variety of sometimes incompatible arguments and proposals, however. Aristide Briand dreamed of a United States of Europe that would allow France both to appeal to the United States to contain German supremacy while counterbalancing U.S. influence in Europe. Publicist and diplomat Wladimir d'Ormesson argued that the United States now occupied the position of leadership in international affairs that had once been Great Britain's and, like Briand, argued in favor of developing European institutions that could benefit from American leadership and exercise some control over it. Pierre Étienne Flandin spoke tirelessly of the need to promote better Franco-American relations and complained that the United States was not showing the leadership that the turn of world affairs had thrust on it and therefore looked to closer Franco-British cooperation to counterbalance American influence in Europe. French preoccupation with the development of firmer tripartite ties with the British and the Americans was still apparent in the early 1930s, as financial crisis began to swamp the world economy. Foreign Minister Joseph Paul-Boncour instructed

Paul Claudel, ambassador to the United States, to encourage the United States to implement the Lausanne accords, to undertake a cooperative effort to stabilize currencies, to return to the gold standard, to create an international monetary fund to regularize international monetary affairs, to promote trade liberalization, and to restore business confidence through the voluntary cooperation of France, Great Britain, and the United States. It should not be lost from sight, however, that much unilateralism continued to characterize the foreign policies of France as well as those of Great Britain and the United States during this period.

43. This situation is analyzed in Michael Loriaux, *France After Hegemony: International Change and Financial Reform* (Ithaca: Cornell University Press, 1991).

44. What nevertheless distinguishes contemporary French internationalism from the interwar variety is the persistent effort to diminish U.S. influence in Europe. France's attitude can be explained by the perception that the U.S. role in Europe today is bound to diminish and that arrangements that try to preserve a role for the United States have the effect of diluting rather than strengthening international constraints on German policy.

45. At least as a long-term consideration. Observers have explained Germany's interest in "deepening" and "widening" the Community by its desire to win international acceptance and support for the recent reunification.

46. See Chapter 4 in this volume, by Peter Katzenstein, as well as his *Small States in World Markets: Industrial Policy in Europe* (Ithaca: Cornell University Press, 1985) and *Corporatism and Change: Austria, Switzerland, and the Politics of Industry* (Ithaca: Cornell University Press, 1984).

CHAPTER 6

I would like to thank Walter Pintner, Thomas Risse-Kappen, Peter Hayes, Peter Katzenstein, and the participants in both the Peace Studies Seminar and the Seminar on Transitions from State Socialism at Cornell for their useful (and sometimes frustrating!) comments on this chapter. I would also like to thank John Bushnell and Michael Marrese for the ideas they circulated in the joint course we taught at Northwestern University on the reforms of Gorbachev and Alexander II.

1. Throughout this paper, I will use the term *Russia* to refer to both Russia as it was defined in the nineteenth century and the Soviet Union as it was defined from the 1920s until 1991. Given that the entity in question is "neither of the above," there is no good term to use for this system. However, given events in 1991, it is less problematic than before to use the term *Russia* to denote the country.

2. There is no consensus on how to define "major reforms." For some (see especially Michel Oksenberg and Bruce Dickson, "The Origins, Process, and Outcome of Great Political Reform: A Framework of Analysis," in Dankwart Rustow and Kenneth Paul Erickson, eds., *Comparative Political Dynamics: Global Research Perspectives* [New York: Harper Collins, 1991], 104–135) major reforms are those changes in politics and policy that fall in between revolutionary and incremental change. However, this seems to me to be too loose a definition. I would argue that major reforms are changes introduced by the political leadership—that is, from above—that alter the structure of political power through reforms in institutions,

procedures and political participation, the structure of the economy, and finally, the relationship of the state to the international system. This definition would leave us with very few cases of major reforms—Atatürk's Turkey, the Meiji Restoration in Japan, perhaps the T'ung Chih Restoration in China and, significantly, not just the cases of Gorbachev and Alexander II but also arguably the reforms introduced by Peter I and Catherine in Russia and Stalin and Khrushchev in the Soviet Union.

3. See, for example, Samuel Huntington, *Political Order in Changing Societies* (New Haven: Yale University Press, 1968; Oksenberg and Dickson, 1989; Ellen Kay Trimberger, "A Theory of Elite Revolutions," in Jack Goldstone, ed., *Revolution* (New York: Harper and Row, 1978), 159–172.

4. Trimberger, "Theory of Elite Revolutions," 1978.

5. See especially Gabriel Almond and Robert J. Mundt, "Crises, Choice and Change: Some Tentative Conclusions," in Gabriel Almond, Robert J. Mundt, and Scott C. Flanagan, eds., *Crisis, Choice, and Change: Historical Studies of Political Development* (Boston: Little, Brown, 1973), 619–650.

6. See Val Bunce, *Do New Leaders Make a Difference? Executive Succession and Public Policy Under Capitalism and Socialism* (Princeton: Princeton University Press, 1981).

7. See especially William Rosenberg, "Conclusion: On the Problem of Reform in Russia and the Soviet Union," in Robert O. Crummey, ed., *Reform in Russia and the USSR* (Champaign: University of Illinois Press, 1989), 277–289; and other chapters in Crummey, 1989.

8. On the state socialist case, see Bunce, *Do New Leaders Make a Difference?*

9. There were, of course, two general secretaries in between Brezhnev and Gorbachev. However, the brevity of their rule (a mere two-and-one-half years total) makes it reasonable to treat Brezhnev as Gorbachev's predecessor.

10. See especially E. J. Hobsbawm, *Industry and Empire* (New York: Penguin, 1968), on British decline.

11. The latter being, of course, much less of a regime; see Robert Jervis, "Security Regimes," *International Organization* 36 (Spring 1982): 357–378.

12. See, for instance, W. Bruce Lincoln, *Nicolas I: Emperor and Autocrat of All the Russias* (Champaign: University of Illinois Press, 1989); Walter Pintner, "Reformability in the Age of Reform and Counterreform, 1855–1894," in Crummey, *Reform in Russia,* 86–99; Anatole Leroy-Beaulieu, *The Empire of the Csars and the Russians* (New York: G. P. Putnam's Sons, 1898); William McNeill, *The Pursuit of Power* (Chicago: University of Chicago Press, 1982), 221–224; Matthew Evangelista, "Economic Reform and Military Technology in Soviet Security Policy," *Harriman Institute Forum* 2 (January 1989): 1–8; Mikhail Gorbachev, "Doklad General'nogo Ts.K. KPSS M.S. Gorbacheva," *Pravda,* April 26, 1989.

13. Also see Victor Nee, "Sleeping with the Enemy: Why Communists Love the Market," Cornell University, Ithaca, N.Y., December 1991, on the economic failures of state socialism.

14. See, for instance, Valerie Bunce, "The Empire Strikes Back: The Evolution of the Eastern Bloc from a Soviet Asset to a Soviet Liability," *International Organization* 39 (Winter 1985): 1–46; Gerhard Wettig, *Changes in Soviet Policy Towards the West* (London: Pinter, 1991); Jerry Hough, *Russia and the West: Gorbachev and the Politics*

of Reform (New York: Simon and Schuster, 1988); Evangelista, *Economic Reform;* Nee, *Sleeping with the Enemy;* Timothy Colton, "Gorbachev and the Politics of System Renewal," in Robert O. Crummey, 207–242; and *The Dilemma of Reform in the Soviet Union* (New York: Council on Foreign Relations, 1986); Oleg Bogomolov, "Meniaiushchiitsiia oblik sotsializma," *Kommunist* 11 (July 1989): 33–42; Gorbachev, "Doklad General'nogo Ts.K. KPSS M.S. Gorbacheva"; Mikhail Gorbachev, "K polnovlastiiu sovetov iz sozdaniiu sotsialisticheskogo pravovogo gosudarstva," *Pravda,* November 30, 1988, 1–3; and Mikhail Gorbachev, "Korrenoi vopros perestroiki: beseda s akademikom T. Zaslavskoi," *Izvestiia,* June 4, 1988, 3.

15. See Hugh Seton-Watson, *The Russian Empire, 1801–1917* (New York: Oxford University Press, 1967).

16. See especially Robert C. Binkley, *Realism and Nationalism, 1852–1871* (New York: Harper and Row, 1935), 124–145; Richard Rosecrance, *Action and Reaction in World Politics* (Boston: Little, Brown, 1963), 103–124.

17. See especially McNeill, *Pursuit of Power,* 221–226, on the costs by the 1850s of relying on traditional methods of supplying troops.

18. See especially Richard S. Wortman, *The Development of a Russian Legal Consciousness* (Chicago: University of Chicago, 1976); George Yaney, "Law, Society and the Domestic Regime in Russia in Historical Perspective," *American Political Science Review* 59 (1965): 379–390; Leroy-Beaulieu, *Empire of the Csars,* 58–68.

19. See, for instance, Olga Crisp, *Studies in the Russian Economy Before 1914* (London: University of London, 1976).

20. See, for instance, McNeill, *Pursuit of Power;* Alexander Gerschenkron, "Agrarian Politics and Industrialization, Russia 1861–1917," in H. J. Habakkuk and N. Postan, eds., *The Cambridge Economic History of Europe,* vol. 6 (Cambridge: Cambridge University Press, 1966), 706–799.

21. Crisp, *Studies in the Russian Economy,* 7.

22. See S. Frederick Starr, *Decentralization and Self-Government in Russia, 1830–1870* (Princeton: Princeton University Press, 1972), 185–240.

23. Quoted in Paul Kennedy, *The Rise and Fall of the Great Powers: Economic Change and Military Conflict from 1500 to 2000* (New York: Random House, 1987), 177.

24. Donald Schwartz, "Autocracy in Nineteenth-Century Russia," in Metin Heper, ed., *The State and Public Bureaucracies: A Comparative Perspective* (Westport, Conn.: Greenwood Press, 1988), 109–130.

25. See, for instance, for the case of Alexander II, Alfred J. Reiber, "Alexander II: A Revisionist View," *Journal of Modern History* 43 (March 1966): 42–58; Vladimir Shlapentokh, "Aleksandr i Mikhail Gorbachev," *Vremia i mi* 97 (1987): 104–123; Gavriil Popov, "Fasad i kukhia velikoi reformy," *EKO* (1987): 145–175; Martin McCauley and Peter Waldron, *The Emergence of the Modern Russian State, 1855–1881* (New York: Barnes and Noble, 1988); Daniel T. Orlovsky, *The Limits of Reform: The Ministry of International Affairs in Imperial Russia, 1802–1881* (Cambridge: Harvard University Press, 1981); W. Bruce Lincoln, *The Great Reforms: Autocracy, Bureaucracy, and the Politics of Change in Imperial Russia* (DeKalb: Northern Illinois University Press, 1990).

26. See Alexander Yanov, *The Origins of Autocracy: Ivan the Terrible in Russian History* (Berkeley: University of California Press, 1981); Yanov, "The Drama of the Time of Troubles," *Canadian/American Slavic Studies* 12 (1978): 1–59; B. H. Sumner, "Peter's Accomplishments and Their Historical Significance," in Marc Raeff, ed., *Peter the Great Changes Russia* (Lexington, Mass.: D. C. Heath, 1972), 188–194.

27. W. Bruce Lincoln, *In the Vanguard of Reform: Russia's Enlightened Bureaucrats, 1825–1861* (DeKalb: Northern Illinois University Press, 1982).

28. Yanov, "The Drama of the Time of Troubles."

29. For analyses of these two reforms, see, for instance, Daniel Field, *The End of Serfdom: Nobility and Bureaucracy in Russia, 1855–1861* (Cambridge: Harvard University Press, 1976); Lincoln, *Nicholas I;* Lilia Shevtsova, "Politika i ideologiia: ot monologa vlasti k obshchestvennomu dialogi," in Oleg Bogomolov, ed., *Perestroika: glasnost', demokratiia, sotsializm* (Moscow: Progress, 1989); George Breslauer, "Evaluating Gorbachev as a Leader," *Soviet Economy* 5 (October-December 1990): 299–319; Archie Brown, "Reconstructing the Soviet Political System," in Abraham Brumburg, ed., *Chronicle of a Revolution: A Western-Soviet Inquiry into Perestroika* (New York: Pantheon, 1990), 31–49; Valerie Bunce, "The Soviet Union Under Gorbachev: Ending Stalinism and Ending the Cold War," *International Journal* 46 (Spring 1991): 220–241; and Valerie Bunce, "Soviet Decline as a Regional Hegemon: Gorbachev and Eastern Europe," *Eastern European Politics and Societies* (Spring 1989): 235–267; Joel Moses, "Democratic Reform in the Gorbachev Era: Dimensions of Reform in the Soviet Union," *Russian Review* 48 (1989): 235–269; Iu Feofanov, "Demokratiia i pravoi," *Izvestiia,* July 10, 1988; Gail Lapidus, "The Impact of Perestroika on the National Question," unpublished manuscript, University of California at Berkeley, 1990.

30. Theodore H. Von Laue, *Why Lenin? Why Stalin?* (New York: J. B. Lippincott, 1963), 11; also see Lincoln, *Great Reforms;* Oleg Bogomolov, ed., *Perestroika: glasnost', demokratiia, sotsializm. Sotsializm: mezhdu proshlym i budushchim* (Moscow: Progress, 1989).

31. See Oksenberg and Dickson, *Origins, Process, and Outcome.*

32. On the Gorbachev case see Jerry Hough, "Gorbachev's Endgame," *World Policy Journal* (Fall 1990): 639–672.

33. Ibid.

34. See, for instance, Stephen White, "Democratization in the USSR," *Soviet Studies* 42 (January 1990): 3–25, and *Gorbachev in Power* (Cambridge: Cambridge University Press, 1990); Bunce, "Soviet Union Under Gorbachev"; Breslauer, "Evaluating Gorbachev"; Hough, "Gorbachev's Endgame"; Moses, "Democratic Reform."

35. See especially V. Zakharova, "Samoderzhavie i reformi 60-kh godov XIX veka v rossii," paper presented at the Conference on the Great Reforms at the University of Pennsylvania, Philadelphia, May 15, 1989; Shlapentokh, "Aleksandr i Mikhail Gorbachev."

36. The main differences are as follows. First, although the Alexandrine reforms involved some changes in Russian foreign policy (for instance, the alliance with Prussia, a reduction in Russian expansionism and a withdrawal—until the Balkan

Wars—of Russian active engagement in European military affairs), these reforms did not in any way involve a "rethinking" of the Russian role in the international system. By contrast, "new thinking" under Gorbachev was revolutionary in its reconception of the Soviet role in international politics and the roles and interests of states, more generally, in the international system. Second, Gorbachev's reforms went much further with respect to liberalization of politics. Finally, as is obvious, the impact of the Gorbachev reforms was far greater, given the breakup of the Soviet empire and the collapse of the Soviet state.

37. Quoted in Lincoln, *Great Reforms*, 53.

38. See especially Michael E. Urban, *More Power to the Soviets: The Democratic Revolution in the USSR* (Brookfield, Vt.: Gower, 1991).

39. See especially Hough, "Gorbachev's Endgame," and Rieber, "Alexander II."

40. See Wortman, *Russian Legal Consciousness*; and Feofanov, "Demokratiia i pravoi."

41. Quoted in Lincoln, *Great Reforms*, 13.

42. Michael Marrese, "Memorandum," report on December 1990, visit to the Soviet Union sponsored by the Centre for Cooperation with European Economies in Transition, January 11, 1991.

43. See Orlovsky, *Limits of Reform*, 132–135; Peter Gatrell, "Continuity and Discontinuity in Russian Economic Development." Paper presented at the Conference on the Great Reforms, University of Pennsylvania, May 13, 1989.

44. Hough, *Russia and the West*.

45. On the issue of nationalism, see, for instance, Ronald Suny, "Nationalist and Ethnic Unrest in the Soviet Union," *World Policy Journal* 3 (Summer 1989): 504–528; and Lapidus, "Impact of Perestroika."

46. See, for instance, John J. Mearsheimer, "Back to the Future: Instability in Europe After the Cold War," *International Security* 15 (Summer 1990): 5–56; Jack Snyder, "Averting Anarchy in the New Europe," *International Security* 14 (Spring 1990): 5–41; Stephen Van Evera, "Primed for Peace: Europe After the Cold War," *International Security* 15 (Winter 1990-1991): 7–57.

47. Yanov, "The Drama of the Time of Troubles."

48. See Rosecrance, *Action and Reaction*; Ludwig Dehio, *The Precarious Balance: Four Centuries of the European Power Struggle* (New York: Alfred A. Knopf, 1962); Binkley, *Realism and Nationalism*.

49. As implied in, for instance, John Lewis Gaddis, "The Long Peace: Elements of Stability in the Postwar International Order," *International Security* 10 (Spring 1986): 99–142; Van Evera, "Primed for Peace"; also see Thomas Risse-Kappen, "The End of the Cold War and Theories of Change in International Relations," paper prepared for the Conference on The Transformation of the International System and International Relations Theory, Cornell University, Ithaca, N.Y., October 18–19; and Friedrich Kratochwil, "The Embarrassment of Change: Structural Realism as the Science of *Realpolitik* without Politics," paper prepared for the Conference on The Transformation of the International System and International Relations Theory, Cornell University, Ithaca, N.Y., October 18–19, 1991 for critical views of this literature and, more generally, the literature on international relations.

50. See especially Perry Anderson, *Lineages of the Absolutist State* (London: NLB, 1974).

51. Yaney, "Law, Society and the Domestic Regime."

52. Also see Schwartz, "Autocracy in Nineteenth Century Russia."

53. See Michael Mann, "The Autonomous Power of the State: Its Origins, Mechanisms and Results," in John A. Hall, ed., *State in History* (Cambridge, Mass.: Basil Blackwell, 1986), 109–136 for this distinction and its relationship to state autonomy.

54. See McCauley and Waldron, *Emergence of the Modern Russian State, 7.*

55. See McNeill, *The Pursuit of Power.*

56. Quoted in Dmytryshyn, *Modernization of Russian Under Peter I and Catherine II* (New York: John Wiley, 1974), 65.

CHAPTER 7

A revised version of this chapter was published as "East Asia's America Problem," *World Policy Journal,* Summer 1991.

1. Franz Schurmann, *The Logic of World Power* (New York: Pantheon, 1974).

2. *Newsweek,* May 27, 1991, p. 35; *New York Times,* May 20, 1991.

3. Edward Said, *Orientalism* (New York: Random House, 1978).

4. Allan Bloom, *The Closing of the American Mind* (New York: Simon and Schuster, 1988), 34.

5. *New York Times,* April 4, 1991.

6. Karel van Wolferen, *The Enigma of Japanese Power: People and Politics in a Stateless Nation* (New York: Alfred A. Knopf, 1989), 8, 10, 20, 23.

7. Karel van Wolferen, "The Japan Problem Revisited," *Foreign Affairs* (Fall 1990): 42–55.

8. Ian Buruma, "Jingo Olympics," *New York Review of Books,* November 10, 1988.

9. Ian Buruma, "The Pax Axis," *New York Review of Books,* May 22, 1991.

10. George Friedman and Meredith Lebard, *The Coming War With Japan* (New York: St. Martin's Press, 1991). Readers who want a sincere and thoughtful appraisal of racism in the last war with Japan ought to read John W. Dower's *War Without Mercy: Race and Power in the Pacific War* (New York: Pantheon Books, 1986).

11. Akio Morita and Shintaro Ishihara, *The Japan That Can Say No* (bootleg edition, 1990).

12. Alexander Woodside, paper presented at the Conference on the Asia-Pacific, Duke University, Durham, N.C., March 22–24, 1991. See John Naisbitt and Patricia Aburdene, *Megatrends 2000* (New York: Avon Books, 1990); and Alvin Toffler, *Third Wave* (New York: Morrow, 1990).

13. Kent Calder and Roy Hofheinz, *The East Asia Edge* (New York: Basic Books, 1983); Michio Morishima, *Why Japan Has Succeeded: Western Technology and the Japanese Ethos* (New York: Cambridge University Press, 1982); Lucien Pye, *Asian Power and Politics: The Cultural Dimension of Authority* (Cambridge, Mass.: Belknap Press, 1982).

14. Masao Miyoshi at the Conference on the Asia-Pacific, Duke University, Durham, N.C., March 22–24, 1991.

15. The reference is to Karl Marx's *The 18th Brumaire of Louis Bonaparte* (New York: International Publisher, 1981).

16. T. J. Pempel, "The Developmental Regime in a Changing World Economy," paper presented at the Annual Meeting of the American Political Science Association, San Francisco, August 31, 1990.

17. Albert O. Hirschman, *National Power and the Structure of Foreign Trade* (Berkeley: University of California Press, 1945).

18. Sylvia Maxfield and James Nolt, "Protectionism and the Internationalization of Capital: U.S. Sponsorship of Import Substitution Industrialization in the Philippines, Turkey, and Argentina," *International Studies Quarterly* 34/1 (March 1990).

19. Jung-en Woo, *Race to the Swift: State and Finance in Korean Industrialization* (New York: Columbia University Press, 1991): 56.

20. John Dower, *Empire and Aftermath: Yoshida Shigeru and the Japanese Experience, 1878–1954* (Cambridge: Harvard University Press, 1979), 316.

21. For discussion of Japanese and Korean industrial structures, see Peter A. Petri, "Korea's Export Niche: Origins and Prospects," *World Development*, January 1988, 47–68.

22. David Calleo, *The Imperious Economy* (Cambridge: Harvard University Press, 1982), 66.

23. Jung-en Woo, *Race to the Swift*, chap. 7.

24. *Fortune*, May 6, 1991.

25. Akira Iriye, *Power and Culture: The Japanese-American War, 1941–1945* (Cambridge: Harvard University Press, 1981), chap. 2.

26. Bruce Cumings, "The Origins and Development of the Northeast Asian Political Economy: Industrial Sectors, Product Cycles and Political Consequences," *International Organization* (Winter 1984): 1–40.

27. *Wall Street Journal*, December 13, 1990.

28. *Far Eastern Economic Review*, December 13, 1990, 28.

CHAPTER 8

1. Elected presidents replaced authoritarian rulers in Argentina (1983), Bolivia (1982), Brazil (1985, indirect election), Chile (1990), Ecuador (1979), Guatemala (1986), Honduras (1982), Paraguay (1989), Peru (1980), and Uruguay (1986). Revolutionary or provisional regimes took power in El Salvador (1979), Haiti (1986), and Nicaragua (1979). In 1984 Panama held its first presidential elections since 1968.

2. The notable cases of party alternation in subsequent electoral contests were Argentina (1989), Bolivia (1985), Brazil (1990), Ecuador (1988), Guatemala (1990), Honduras (1986), Nicaragua (1990), Peru (1985), Uruguay (1990). In addition, a coalition of opposition parties was installed in Panama in 1989 by the U.S. military intervention.

3. The case of Hungary, with its greater tolerance of dissent—and freedom of travel abroad—constituted a partial exception to this rule. The initial reaction of Polish authorities to Solidarity was another.

4. This was clearly the case in Argentina, Brazil, Chile, Ecuador, Guatemala and, arguably, Honduras. In Bolivia, Peru, and Uruguay the new democratic regimes were similar in political coloration to those ousted by the military.

5. In the larger countries modern light manufacturing first developed in the wake of export booms at the end of the nineteenth century. See, for example, Stephen Haber, *Industry and Underdevelopment: The Industrialization of Mexico, 1890–1940* (Stanford: Stanford University Press, 1989). For the impact of the Great Depression, see the essays in Rosemary Thorp, ed., *Latin America in the 1930s: The Role of the Periphery in the World Crisis* (New York: St. Martin's Press, 1984).

6. On the postwar shift in foreign investment, see United Nations, Economic Commission for Latin America, *External Financing in Latin America* (New York: United Nations, 1963), chap. 1.

7. James Nolt and Sylvia Maxfield, "Protectionism and the Internationalization of Capital: U.S. Sponsorship of Import Substitution Industrialization in the Philippines, Turkey, and Argentina," *International Studies Quarterly* 34/1 (March 1990): 49–81.

8. See the essays in Gary Gereffi and Donald L. Wyman, eds., *Manufacturing Miracles: Paths of Industrialization in Latin America and East Asia* (Princeton: Princeton University Press, 1990).

9. See Gary Gereffi, "Paths of Industrialization: An Overview," in Gereffi and Wyman, *Manufacturing Miracles,* 14–16; see also Fernando Fajnzylber, *Unavoidable Industrial Restructuring in Latin America* (Durham: Duke University Press, 1990), chap. 6.

10. The antistatist rhetoric of U.S. politicians and diplomats glossed over a striking double standard. The United States did not object when governments considered friendly to U.S. security and general economic aims employed statist measures, including nationalization. In other cases, quite moderate measures provoked U.S. condemnation. This point has been emphasized repeatedly in analysis of the contrasting U.S. response to the Bolivian revolution of 1952 (which received U.S. aid) and Guatemalan democracy (which the United States liquidated in 1954). See Cole Blasier, *The Hovering Giant: U.S. Response to Revolutionary Change in Latin America* (Pittsburgh: University of Pittsburgh Press, 1976), especially chap. 7.

11. Adam Przeworski, "The 'East' Becomes the 'South'? The 'Autumn of the People' and the Future of Eastern Europe" ("Remarks" presented at the Annual Meeting of the American Political Science Association, San Francisco, August 1990). For a more extended discussion of these issues, see his *Democracy and the Market: Political and Economic Reforms in Eastern Europe and Latin America* (Cambridge: Cambridge University Press, 1991).

12. Przeworski, *Democracy and the Market,* 13.

13. See Richard J. Evans, "Revolution and Reunification in Germany, 1989–90: Nationalism, Identity, and the Burdens of History," paper presented at the Dean's Symposium of the Division of Social Sciences, University of Chicago, February 22, 1991.

14. The issues of labor discipline in some of the East European countries could subvert the thrust of this comparison. The East's relatively well educated and skilled workers are not accustomed to the intensity of labor demanded by capitalist

enterprise. Nor are their specific skills necessarily suitable to the needs of the new order. On both counts East Germans will do better than Poles, for example. In Latin America, the labor force has largely accommodated to greater intensity of productive effort but has also developed a notable capacity for collective self-organization in unions and political parties. Abstracting from national variations, which are considerable, the balance still seems to favor Eastern Europe.

15. Notably in Colombia, Peru, El Salvador, and Nicaragua.

16. Salinas's discovery led him to reverse his earlier opposition to a North American free trade zone and push Mexican-United States economic integration in order to make Mexico more competitive in a world where capital is becoming relatively more scarce. "A new study by Morgan Stanley & Company," reported the *New York Times* recently, "said the total demand for capital by Eastern Europe, Latin America, and the Middle East would exceed the Western world's supply by more than $200 billion in the next few years." See *New York Times*, March 26, 1991, 1ff.

17. See Peter H. Smith, "Japan, Latin America, and the New International Order," paper presented at the conference on the Third World and the Cold War at the University of Chicago, Chicago, Ill., October 1990.

18. Ambassador Guido di Tella, in a speech to the Chicago Committee of the Chicago Council on Foreign Relations, February 1990.

19. See Delal Baer, "North American Free Trade," *Foreign Affairs* 70/4 (Fall 1991): 132–149.

20. Larry Sjaastad, paper presented at the conference on Mexico and the United States: Threshold of a Trade Revolution at the University of Chicago, April 1990.

21. Peter H. Smith, "Japan, Latin America, and the New International Order," 28ff; and Howard J. Wiarda, "Europe's Ambiguous Relations with Latin America: Blowing Hot and Cold in the Western Hemisphere," *Washington Quarterly* 13/2 (Spring 1990): 153–167.

22. This seems to be the message implicit in the otherwise tepid recommendations of the Trilateral Commission Report on *Latin America at the Crossroads: The Challenge to the Trilateral Countries*, prepared by George W. Landau, Julio Feo, and Akio Hosono (New York: Trilateral Commission, 1990).

23. Jorge Castañeda, "Latin America and the End of the Cold War," *World Policy Journal* 4 (1987): 1–40.

24. The full text of the Secretary's submission was reprinted in the *New York Times*, January 13, 1927, 2.

CHAPTER 9

1. Frequently I will refer to the "political class." Gaetano Mosca's term "political class" is useful because it indicates a class of people with feet in society but arms in the state. As a term it implies a kind of autonomy of the state that the nineteenth century term "ruling class" did not. A ruling class, however, is solidly imbedded in the productive and proprietary base of society and therefore, according to Marxist theory, is able to rule. The state, "the executive committee of the ruling class," becomes the dependent variable in the equation of state and society (or more

strictly, a mode of production). In another paper I have coined the term "political tribe" to indicate a politically significant class linked solely to the state, the opposite of a ruling class.

2. See, for example, Seymour Martin Lipset, *The First New Nation* (New York: Basic Books, 1963), which removes the United States from its particularist context and places it in a more global, cosmopolitan context.

3. I develop these subjects in more detail in my book, *The Grand Design: The Foreign Politics of Richard Nixon* (Berkeley: Institute of International Studies, University of California, 1987).

4. Since this chapter was written, the Soviet Union has ceased to exist. As of 1992 it appears to be the strong desire of the other four nations that the linkage continue with the new Russia.

5. This chapter reflects thinking from earlier works and many commentaries on the Gulf War I wrote for *Pacific News Service* that appeared in various American newspapers. It also has been shaped by various plunges I have made into Bruce Cumings's *The Roaring of the Cataract* (Princeton: Princeton University Press, 1991). Cumings's comment that his interpretations do "not begin to fit the labels and symbols with which Americans think about their politics" (p. 80) of course applies to my own interpretations, about which he comments so generously.

6. The inhabitants of the oil-producing territories along the Gulf are mainly Shi'i, not Sunni, the dominant faith of Saudi Arabia. And Shi'i form a small majority of Iraq's population.

7. Saddam Hussein was elevated to supreme power in Iraq in July 1979.

8. McFarlane is the one who made the fateful secret trip to Teheran, on the surface similar to the one Kissinger made to Beijing in 1971 but with opposite results.

9. Franz Schurmann, *The Logic of World Power* (New York: Pantheon, 1974).

10. Many social democrats had already transformed themselves into Reagan-era "neoconservatives," however, and were thus able to remain in the chorus that was denouncing the State Department's tilt toward Iraq.

11. Their miscalculation was in every way comparable to that of the pro-Israeli factions that, in 1982, accepted too literally Prime Minister Menachem Begin's word that Israel's incursion into Lebanon was designed only to bring "peace for Galilee" and did not imagine that Ariel Sharon's forces would roll all the way to Beirut.

12. This was also the case of the pro-Arab factions in the Mitterrand government (those linked to former defense minister Jean-Pierre Chevènement), though there was a strong pro-Israeli faction that wanted to go further and even send military forces to the Gulf to join the coalition.

13. There was another ideological force that was making itself felt, though more strongly in France and Britain than in the United States. This current argued that democratic and secular political systems were the only viable option for the Arab and Muslim Middle East. Both Saddam's murderous secular nationalism and Iran's equally murderous Islamic fundamentalism were unacceptable.

14. At the 1984 Republican national convention some 70 percent of the delegates indicated they were in favor of arms control agreements with the Soviet Union.

15. It recovered some power when Kissinger became secretary of state.

16. Frederick Jackson Turner, in *The Frontier in American History* (Tucson: University of Arizona Press, 1986), attributes the development of American political culture, especially its conceptualization of democratic government, to America's frontier experience.

17. The United States was "central," as I argue in *Foreign Politics of Richard Nixon*. The predominance of the United States was apparent to all when the failed coup in the Soviet Union provoked a massive transfer of capital to the United States. As Erik Izraelewicz of *Le Monde* (August 24, 1991) commented, "the dollar remains the value of refuge for the entire world."

18. Perhaps the encounter between the two aristocratic bodies, Navy and State, was facilitated by their shared distaste for the learned crudities of the national security types with their RAND Corporation airs.

19. The navy had shown interest in expanding the American empire since the days of Admiral Thayer Mahan.

20. I call the nuclear game ideological in *Logic of World Power*. In *Ideology and Organization in Communist China* (Berkeley: University of California Press, 1968), I distinguish between human and technical organization and indicate that ideologies can also be so distinguished. If Communist ideologies aimed at human organization, for the air force the ideologies that counted were those that put scientists, engineers, and military professionals together to win the lethal technology race.

21. The navy, moreover, may have been hoping to get access some day to Iraq's port at Um al-Qasr where Soviet vessels had been reported to be berthing.

22. Other special relationships with Taiwan before the diplomatic recognition of the People's Republic of China and Israel were not mediated through the presidency but through Congress. The United States has a special relationship with Germany that was not mediated through the presidency but arose naturally out of the postwar occupation and Germany's centrality in Europe. What may also have impeded U.S.-German summitry were memories of the holocaust. The United States also has a special relationship with Saudi Arabia, as President Jimmy Carter said on a visit to Riyadh, but that one went from the oil companies through the State Department into the diplomatic fabric.

23. After the signature of entente cordiale in 1904.

24. In republican Rome soldiers hailed a victorious general as "imperator," or leader. Victory conferred honor on the general as well as the moral authority to lead. The "imperial" reign of Augustus, the first Roman emperor, was founded principally on this moral authority rather than on formal institutional power.

25. Ironically, a number of these Romantics, like Chateaubriand, were devout Christians. Their critiques, however, were aimed at the idea of secular progress through revolution, as defended by the rationalist philosophers of the eighteenth century.

26. The only real past-shackled conservatives were found in the South—and their political importance was weakened by the defeat they suffered in the Civil War.

ABOUT THE BOOK
AND EDITORS

How do we interpret the recent changes in world politics, and what trajectories for the future can we project from them? *Past as Prelude* places the events of the last few years in broad historical context, examining how the political, military, and economic arrangements of the past are reflected in current events. Noted political scientists and historians use critical imagination to chart the political economy of the future by tracing historical patterns in Western Europe, Russia, East Asia, Latin America, and the United States. *Past as Prelude* will provide students and scholars with a new perspective on the pressing questions and conflicts that characterize international politics now and in the years to come.

Meredith Woo-Cumings is associate professor of political science at Northwestern University and specializes in comparative political economy and East Asian politics. She is the author, under the name Jung-en Woo, of *Race to the Swift: State and Finance in Korean Industrialization*. **Michael Loriaux** is assistant professor of political science at Northwestern and works on international relations theory and Western Europe. He is the author of *France After Hegemony: International Change and Financial Reform*.

ABOUT THE CONTRIBUTORS

Valerie Bunce, professor of government at Cornell University, specializes in the politics of Russia and Eastern Europe.

John H. Coatsworth, Munroe Gutman Professor of Latin American Affairs at Harvard University, has written extensively on the political economy of industrialization in Mexico.

Bruce Cumings, professor of international and East Asian history at the University of Chicago, has completed a two-volume study of the Korean War. He specializes in contemporary diplomatic history and has written on the politics of culture.

Peter Katzenstein, Walter S. Carpenter, Jr., Professor of International Studies at Cornell University, specializes in international relations and comparative political economy, focusing in particular on Western Europe.

James Kurth, professor of political science at Swarthmore College, specializes in the study of international political economy and security.

Franz Schurmann, professor of political science and history at the University of California, Berkeley, has written extensively on Chinese politics and U.S. foreign policy. He is the founder and director of the Pacific News Service in San Francisco.

INDEX